A DAUGHTER OF THE SAMURAI

ETSU INAGAKI SUGIMOTO

Published by True Sign Publishing House
Address: SY. No. 21/2 & 21/3, Sonnenahalli,
Krishnarajapural, Bengaluru,
Karnataka - 560049 India
E-mail: truesignbooks@gmail.com
Website: www.truesign.in

A Daughter of the Samurai
Author: Etsu Inagaki Sugimoto

ISBN: 978-93-90852-28-4

First Edition: 2021

Madame Etsu Inagaki Sugimoto

WITH RESPECT AND LOVE AND DEEPEST GRATITUDE
I DEDICATE THESE SACRED MEMORIES
TO
MY TWO MOTHERS
WHOSE LIVES AND ENVIRONMENTS WERE FAR APART, YET
WHOSE HEARTS MET IN MINE

Acknowledgment
To
Nancy Virginia Austen

Whose pleasant friendship, energetic spirit, and practical knowledge encouraged me to believe that a little Etsu-bo, with a heart full of love for old Japan, could gather the falling fragments of samurai spirit and weave them into a fragrant chain for the readers of to-day.

Contents

Introduction

THERE are many happy adventures for those who work in the strange world of printers' ink; and in some lucky moment of inspiration, several years ago, I asked Mrs. Sugimoto to write, for my column in a Philadelphia newspaper, some little memories of her girlhood in Japan. The story of the dog Shiro, whose prosperity in a future life she endangered by giving him her own cushion; her childish sadness about her curly hair; her pensive trouble when she discovered that American women were not really more modest than Japanese—these and a few other charming episodes first found their way into print in that newspaper, and gradually led to this beautiful and thrilling book. It is an honour to be asked by Mrs. Sugimoto to say a word of introduction here. I only wish that I knew how to make it ceremonious enough. For the inner suggestion of her book is surely that life in its highest moments is a kind of ceremony in honour of the unknown gods. "The eyelids of a Samurai," Mrs. Sugimoto tells us, "know not moisture." But the "red barbarians," who have not learned the old stoic art, may be forgiven if they feel occasionally, among her tender paragraphs, that dangerous prickling that great truth conveys.

What a lovely book it is, and how much it has to teach us. I have a secret notion that it will go on for years and years, making friends for itself and for the brave woman who wrote it, and also—this would please her most—friends for Japan. Is it not a perfect book for children to read? I don't know any collection of fairy tales more entrancing. And for parents too: is it not the subtlest kind of treatise on education? For the pure art and humour and simplicity of the narrative: where is there a more charming short story than that of Mr. Toda? A great American writer, who was in many things as far as possible from the old Samurai codes (Walt Whitman), said, "As soon as histories are properly told there is no more need of romances." This book is a history properly told. Some of us may think that Mrs. Sugimoto has been even a little too generous toward the America she adopted. But she came among us as Conrad came among the English; and if the little Etsu-bo, the well-loved tomboy of snowy winters in Echigo, finds beauty in our strange and violent ways, we can only be grateful.

Among her delicate and significant anecdotes, each a gem of artistic thought and feeling, she tells of the Japanese fiancée whose betrothed had a plum-blossom as his family crest, and therefore the young woman must pay particular honour to that flower, and could not even eat plum jelly, which would be disrespectful to the emblem of her future husband. In the same way I feel obscurely that I must not write too much about Mrs. Sugimoto: because I honour her greatly, to write fulsomely here would be disrespectful to her beautiful book. I can only say that this story of a Japanese girlhood and of the brave child who found a seed of liberty stirring in her heart seems to me one of those rare triumphs where two diverse worlds speak openly to one another and both are profited.

One of my pleasantest memories of a time when Mrs. Sugimoto, in her Japanese costume, accompanied as a great lady should be by her daughter and a loved companion, came far downtown in hot weather to visit me in a New York newspaper office. She felt, though surely too generously, that I had tried to be courteous; and this required, on her part, a gesture of appreciation. I have never forgotten it: her gay little figure, charming as a bird or flower in her vivid robe, brightening for a few minutes that busy, noisy place. What the expedition may have cost her, in weariness or alarm or secret distresses, I hesitate to conjecture. Only a brave and great-minded person would have ventured it. That she is brave and great minded and a true daughter of the Samurai no reader will ever doubt. How startled, I suppose, some of her knightly ancestors would be to find her putting her private thoughts on paper for all the world to see. Then indeed the shrines would be pasted up and there would be horrified silence. But it was that old, hard and feudal code that gave her strength to break through paper formalities when she felt it needful. She has given us here a unique picture of the exquisite complexity and beauty of all human life. She is a great teacher, and I would not willingly even tread on her shadow.

CHRISTOPHER MORLEY.

CHAPTER-1

Winters in Echigo

JAPAN is often called by foreign people a land of sunshine and cherry blossoms. This is because tourists generally visit only the eastern and southern parts of the country, where the climate is mild all the year round. On the northwest coast the winters are long, snow often covering the ground from December to March or April.

In the province of Echigo, where was my home, winter usually began with a heavy snow which came down fast and steady until only the thick, round ridge-poles of our thatched roofs could be seen. Then groups of coolies, with straw mats over their shoulders and big woven hats that looked like umbrellas, came and with broad wooden shovels cut tunnels through from one side of the street to the other. The snow was not removed from the middle of the street all winter. It lay in a long pile, towering far above the house-tops. The coolies cut steps, for they were carrying snow at intervals all winter, and we children used to climb up and run along the top. We played many games there, sometimes pretending we were knights rescuing a snow-bound village, or fierce brigands stealing upon it for an attack.

But a still more exciting time for us was before the snow came, when the entire town was making preparations for winter. This always took several weeks, and each day as we went to and from school we would stop to watch the coolies busily wrapping the statues and small shrines along the streets in their winter clothing of straw. The stone lanterns and all the trees and bushes of our gardens were enclosed in straw, and even the outside walls of the temples were protected by sheets of matting fastened on with strips of bamboo, or immense nettings made of straw rope. Every day the streets presented a new appearance, and by the time the big carved lions at the temple steps were covered, we were a city of grotesque straw tents of every shape and size, waiting for the snow that would bury us in for three or four months.

Most large houses had thatched roofs with wide eaves, but the shops on the streets had shingled roofs weighted with stones to prevent avalanches when the snow began to melt in the spring. Above all the sidewalks extended a permanent roof, and during the winter the sidewalks were enclosed by walls of upright boards with an occasional panel of oiled paper, which turned them into long halls, where we could walk all over town in the stormiest weather, entirely protected from wind and snow. These halls were dim, but not dark, for light shines through snow pretty well, and even at the street corners, where we crossed through the snow tunnels, it was light enough for us to read good-sized characters. Many a time, coming home from school, I have read my lessons in the tunnel, pretending that I was one of the ancient sages who studied by snow-light.

Echigo, which means "Behind the Mountains," is so shut off from the rest of Japan by the long Kiso range that during the early feudal days it was considered by the Government only a frozen outpost suitable as a place of exile for offenders too strong in position or influence to be treated as criminals. To this class belonged reformers. In those days Japan had little tolerance for reforms either in politics or religion, and an especially progressive thinker at court or a broad-minded monk was branded as equally obnoxious and sent to some desolate spot where his ambitions would be permanently crushed. Most political offenders that were sent to Echigo either filled the graves of the little cemetery beyond the execution ground or lost themselves in some simple home among the peasants. Our literature holds many a pathetic tale of some rich and titled youth, who, disguised as a pilgrim, wanders through the villages of Echigo, searching for his lost father.

The religious reformers fared better; for they generally spent their lives in working quietly and inoffensively among the people. Some founders of new Buddhist sects exiled for a lifetime, were men of great ability, and gradually their belief spread so widely that Echigo became known all over Japan as the stronghold of reformed Buddhism. From earliest childhood I was familiar with priest tales and was accustomed to seeing pictures of images cut on the rocks or carved figures standing in caves on the mountain-sides—the work of the tireless hands of those ancient monks.

My home was in the old castle town of Nagaoka. Our household consisted of my father and mother, my honored grandmother, my brother, my sister, and myself. Then there was Jiya, my father's head servant, and my nurse, Ishi, besides Kin and Toshi. Several other old servants came and went on occasions. I had married sisters, all in distant homes except the eldest, who lived about half a day's jinrikisha ride from Nagaoka. She came occasionally to visit us, and sometimes I went home with her to spend several days in her big thatched farmhouse, which had been, in ancient days, the fortress of three mountains. Samurai families often married into the farmer class, which was next in rank to the military, and much respected, for "one who owns rice villages holds the life of the nation in his hand."

We lived just on the edge of the town in a huge, rambling house that had been added to from time to time ever since I could remember. As a result, the heavy thatched roof sagged at the gable joinings, the plaster walls had numerous jogs and patches, and the many rooms of various sizes were connected by narrow, crooked halls that twisted about in a most unexpected manner. Surrounding the house, but some distance away, was a high wall of broken boulders, topped with a low, solid fence of wood. The roof of the gateway had tipped-up corners, and patches of moss on the brown thatch. It was supported by immense posts between which swung wooden gates with ornamental iron hinges that reached halfway across the heavy boards. On each side there extended, for a short distance, a plaster wall pierced by a long, narrow window with wooden bars. The gates were always open during the day, but if at night there came knocking and the call "*Tano-mo-o! Tano-mo-o!*" (I ask to enter!) even in the well-known voice of a neighbour, Jiya was so loyal to old-time habit that he invariably ran to peep through one of these windows before opening the gate to the guest.

From the gateway to the house was a walk of large, uneven stones, in the wide cracks of which grew the first foreign flowers that I ever saw—short-stemmed, round-headed little things that Jiya called "giant's buttons." Someone had given him the seed; and as he considered no foreign flower worthy of the dignity of a place in our garden, he cunningly planted them where they would be trod upon by our disrespectful feet. But they were hardy plants and grew as luxuriantly as moss.

That our home was such a makeshift was the result of one of the tragedies of the Restoration. Echigo Province was one of those that had believed in the dual government. To our people, the Mikado was too sacred to be in touch with war, or even annoying civil matters, and so they fought to uphold the shogun power to which, for generations, their ancestors had been loyal. At which time my father was a *karo*, or first counsellor of the daimiate of Nagaoka, a position which he had held since the age of seven, when the sudden death of my grandfather had left it vacant. Because of certain unusual circumstances, my father was the only executive in power, and thus it was that during the wars of the Restoration he had the responsibility and the duties of the office of daimio.

At the bitterest moment that Nagaoka ever knew, Echigo found herself on the defeated side. When my mother learned that her husband's cause was lost and he taken prisoner, she sent her household to a place of safety, and then, to prevent the mansion from falling into the hands of the enemy, she with her own hands set fire to it and from the mountain-side watched it burn to the ground.

After the stormy days of war were past and Father finally was free from the governorship which he had been directed to retain until the central government became stabilized, he gathered together the remains of his family estate, and after sharing with his now "fish-on-land" retainers, he built this temporary home on the site of his former mansion. Then he planted a mulberry grove on a few acres of land near by and prided himself on having levelled his rank to the class of farmer. Men of samurai rank knew nothing about business. It had always been considered a disgrace for them to handle money; so the management of all business affairs was left to faithful but wholly inexperienced Jiya, while Father devoted his life to reading, to memories, and to introducing unwelcome ideas of progressive reform to his less advanced neighbours.

My father, however, held on to one extravagance. The formal once-in-two-years journey to the capital, which, before the Restoration, the law required of men of his position, was now changed to an informal annual trip of which he laughingly called the "window toward growing days." The name was most appropriate; for this yearly visit of my father gave his whole family a distant view of progressing Japan. Besides the wonderful word pictures, he also brought us gifts of strange, unknown things—trinkets for the servants, toys for the children, useful house articles for Mother, and often rare imported things for the much-honoured grandmother.

Jiya always accompanied Father on these trips, and, in his position as business manager, came in contact with tradesmen and heard many tales of the methods of foreigners in dealing with Japanese. The cleverness of the foreign business system was acknowledged by everyone, and although frequently disastrous to the Japanese, it aroused admiration and a desire to imitate. A more honest soul than Jiya never lived, but in his desire to be loyal to the interests of his much-loved master he once got our family name into a tangle of disgrace that took months of time and much money to straighten out. Indeed, I doubt if the matter was ever clearly understood by any of the parties. I know it was a sore puzzle to Jiya as long as he lived. It happened in this way.

Jiya became acquainted with a Japanese man, who, as agent for a foreigner, was buying up cards of silkworm eggs from all the villages around. Such cards were prepared by having painted on them, with a special ink, the name or crest of the owner. Then the cards were placed beneath the butterflies, which lay on them their small, seed-like eggs by the thousands. The cards were finally classified and sold to dealers.

This agent, who was a very wealthy man, told Jiya that if mustard seeds were substituted for the eggs, the cards would sell at a profit that would make his master rich. This, the agent explained, was a foreign business method being adopted now by the merchants of Yokohama. It was known as "the new way of making Japan strong, so the high-nosed barbarian could no longer beat the children of Japan in trade."

As my father's mulberry grove furnished food for many of the silkworms in near-by villages, his name was a good one for the agent to use, and poor Jiya, delighted to be doing business in the clever new way, was of course a willing tool. The man prepared the cards to the value of hundreds of yen—all marked with my father's crest. Probably he pocketed all the money; anyway, the first we knew of the affair was when a very tall, red-faced foreign man, in strange, pipe-like garments, called to see my father. How well I remember that important day! Sister and I, with moistened finger-tips, melted tiny holes in the paper doors, to peep at the wonderful stranger. We knew it was rude and low class, but it was the opportunity of a lifetime.

I have no reason to think that foreign man was in any way to blame; and possibly—possibly—the agent also thought that he was only competing in cleverness with the foreigner. So many things were misunderstood in those strange days. Of course, my father, who had known absolutely nothing of the transaction, paid the price and made good his name, but I doubt if he ever understood what it all meant. This was one of the many pathetic attempts made in those days by simple-minded vassals, whose loyal, blundering hearts were filled with more love than wisdom.

In the long winter evenings I was very fond of slipping away to the servants' hall to watch the work going on there and to hear stories. One evening, when I was about seven years old, I was hurrying along the zigzag porch leading to that part of the house when I heard voices mingling with the thuds of soft snow being thrown from the roof. It was unusual to have the roof cleared after dark, but Jiya was up there arguing with the head coolie and insisting that the work must be done that night.

"At the rate the snow is falling," I heard him say, "it will crush the roof before morning."

One of the coolies muttered something about its being time for temple service, and I noticed the dull tolling of the temple bell. However, Jiya had his way, and the men went on with the work. I was astonished at the daring of the coolie who had ventured to question Jiya's command. To my childish mind, Jiya was a remarkable person who was always right and whose word was law. But with all my respect for his wisdom, I loved him with all my heart; and with reason, for he was never too busy to twist up a straw doll for me, or to tell me a story as I sat on a garden stone watching him work.

The servants' hall was a very large room. One half of the board floor had straw mats scattered here and there. This was the part where the spinning, rice-grinding, and the various occupations of the kitchen went on. The other half, where rough or untidy work was done, was of hard clay. In the middle of the room was the fireplace—a big, clay-lined box sunk in the floor, with a basket of firewood beside it. From a beam high above hung a chain from which swung various implements used in cooking. The smoke passed out through an opening in the centre of the roof, above which was a small extra roof to keep out the rain.

As I entered the big room, the air was filled with the buzz of work mingled with chatter and laughter. In one corner was a maid grinding rice for to-morrow's dumplings; another was making padded scrub-cloths out of an old kimono; two others were tossing from one to the other the shallow basket that shook the dark beans from the white, and a little apart from the others sat Ishi whirling her spinning wheel with a little tapping stick.

There was a rustle of welcome for me, for the servants all liked a visit from "Etsu-bo Sama," as they called me. One hurried to bring me a cushion and another tossed a handful of dried chestnut hulls on the glowing fire. I loved the changing tints of chestnut hull embers, and stopped a moment to watch them.

"Come here, Etsu-bo Sama!" called a soft voice.

It was Ishi. She had moved over on to the mat, leaving her cushion for me. She knew I loved to turn the spinning wheel, so she pushed the cotton ball into my hand, holding her own safely over it. I can yet feel the soft pull of that thread slipping through my fingers as I whirled the big wheel. I am afraid that I spun a very uneven thread, and it was probably fortunate for her work that my attention was soon attracted by Jiya's entrance. He pulled a mat over to the clay side of the room and in a moment was seated with his foot stretched out, holding between his toes one end of the rope he was twisting out of rice-straw.

"Jiya San," called Ishi, "we have an honoured guest."

Jiya looked up quickly, and with a funny, bobby bow above his stretched rope, he smilingly held up a pair of straw shoes dangling from a cord.

"Ah!" I cried, jumping up quickly and running across the clay floor to him, "are they my snow-shoes? Have you finished them?"

"Yes, Etsu-bo Sama," he answered, putting in my hands a pair of small straw boots, "and I have finished them just in time. This is going to be the deepest snow we have had this year. When you go to school to-morrow you can take a short cut, straight over the brooks and fields, for there will be no roads anywhere."

As usual Jiya's prediction was right. Without our snow-boots we girls could not have gone to school at all. Moreover, his persistence with the coolies had saved our roof; for before morning five feet more of snow filled the deep-cut paths and piled on top of the long white mountain in the street.

CHAPTER-2
Curly Hair

ONE day the servants returned from temple service talking excitedly about a fire at Kyoto which had destroyed the great Hongwanji. As this was the prince temple of Shin, the sect most popular among the masses, interest in its rebuilding was widespread, and donations were being sent from every part of the Empire. The Buddhist exiles of ancient time had left their impress upon Echigo to such an extent that it soon excelled all other provinces in eagerness to give, and Nagaoka was the very centre of the enthusiasm.

The first and the fifteenth of each month, being workmen's holidays, were favourite times for collecting; and as our gifts were mostly of our own products, it was interesting to watch the people who thronged the streets on these days. Besides our own townsfolk, each one carrying a basket or bundle, groups kept coming each hour of the day from the mountains and from neighbouring villages. There were men laden with bunches of hemp and coils of rope, or with bundles of bamboo poles, the long ends trailing on the ground as they walked; women from weaving villages weighted down with bolts of silk or cotton; and farmers pulling long carts piled high with bales of "the five grains"—rice, millet, wheat, oats, and beans—with the farmer's wife (frequently with a baby on her back) pushing at the end. All these gifts were taken to a large building put up on purpose for them, and every day the collection grew.

One day Ishi and I were standing just within our big gateway, watching the people go by. I noticed that almost every woman had her head wrapped in the blue-and-white towel that servants wear when dusting or working in the kitchen.

"Why does everybody wear *tenugui* on the streets?" I asked.

"Those women have cut their hair, Etsu-bo Sama," Ishi replied.

"Are they all widows?" I asked in astonishment; for it was the custom for a widow to cut off her hair at the neck and bury half of it with her husband, the other half being kept until her own death.

I thought I had never seen so many widows in my life, but I soon learned that these women had cut off most of their hair that it might be braided into a huge rope to be used in drawing the lumber for the important centre beam of the new temple. Our own servants had cut big bunches from their heads, but, with more moderate enthusiasm than that of the peasant class, they had retained enough to dress it so as to cover their bald crowns. One of the maids, however, in religious fervour, had cut off so much that she had to postpone her marriage for three years; for no girl could marry with short hair. Not a man of those days would be brave enough to risk the ill omen of taking a bride with the cut hair of a widow.

Our family did not belong to the Shin sect of Buddhists, but every woman, of whatever sect, wanted to have a part in the holy cause, so each of us added a few strands. The hair was taken to the building where the donations were kept and braided into long, thick ropes; then, just before the removal to Kyoto, all the gifts were dedicated with an elaborate religious ceremony.

It seemed to my childish mind that almost everybody in the world came to Nagaoka that day. Most certainly the near-by country district and all the neighbouring villages had emptied themselves into the narrow streets through which Ishi took me on our way to the temple. But at last we were stationed in a safe place and I stood holding tight to her hand and looking up wonderingly at the great shrine of gold-and-black lacquer which was placed high on an ox-cart just in front of the temple entrance. The curving doors were wide open, showing the calm-faced Buddha standing with folded hands. Surrounding the base of the shrine, gradually widening and spreading above it, was a delicate framework representing the "five-coloured clouds of Paradise." Many, many lotus blossoms of gold and silver, pink, purple, and orange twisted through the carved clouds and seemed to float in the air. It was wondrously beautiful. The two oxen, loaned by proud farmers for this occasion, were almost covered with strips of bright-coloured silk dangling in long, fluttering streamers from horns and harness.

Suddenly there was a moment's hush. Then with the returning sound of a multitude of voices mingled the beating of gongs and the shrill piping of temple music.

"Look, Etsu-bo Sama!" said Ishi. "The sacred Buddha is starting on the tour of appreciation. It is the first time in many years that the Holy One has come forth from the temple altar. To-day is a great day!"

As the oxen strained and pushed against the big wooden yoke and the shrine with the gilded Buddha began to move, a low murmur of "*Namu Amida Butsu!*" (Hail, Great Buddha!) breathed through the air. With deep reverence I bowed my head, and folding my hands together, I, too, whispered the holy words.

Two long twisted ropes of cloth, purple and white, were fastened to the front of the broad cart and reached far past the oxen to the chanting priests in front. These ropes were held by the eager hands of many men and boys, women and girls, some with babies on their backs, and little children of all ages. I saw a playmate.

"Ishi! Ishi!" I cried, so excited that I almost tore her sleeve. "There is Sadako San holding the rope! Oh, may I walk beside her and hold the rope too? Oh, may I?"

"Hush, little Mistress. You must not forget to be gentle. Yes, I will walk with you. Your little hands shall help the holy Buddha."

And so we walked in the procession—Ishi and I. Never in my life, perhaps, shall I experience an hour more exalted than when we passed through these narrow streets behind the solemn, chanting priests, my hand clasped about the pulling cord of the great swaying, creaking cart, and my heart filled with awe and reverence.

The services of dedication I recall very mistily. The new building was crowded with huge pyramids of donations of every kind. The shrine was carried in and placed before a purple curtain with a big swastika crest on it. There were marching, chanting priests in gorgeous robes with crystal rosaries around their folded hands. There was the fragrance of incense, the sound of soft temple drums, and everywhere low murmurs of "*Namu Amida Butsu!*"

Only one thing in the great room stands clear in my memory. On a platform in front of the altar, with the holy Buddha just above, was the huge coil of jet-black rope—made of the hair of thousands of women. My mind went back to the day when I thought I was seeing so many widows in the street, and to our servants with their scanty hair dressed over bald crowns, and then, with a pang of humiliation, I recalled the day our own offering was sent; for beside the long, glossy straight wisps of my sister's hair lay a shorter strand that curved into ugly mortifying waves.

Even after all these years I feel a bit of pity for the little girl who was myself when I remember how many bitter trials she had to endure because of her wavy hair. Curly hair was not admired in Japan, so although I was younger than my sisters, on hairdressing day, which came three times in ten days, I was placed in the care of the hairdresser as soon as she came into the house. This was unusual, for the eldest should always be attended to first. Immediately after the shampoo, she saturated my hair with almost boiling hot tea mixed with some kind of stiffening oil. Then she pulled the hair back as tight as possible and tied it. Thus I was left while she dressed the hair of my sisters. By that time my whole head was stiff and my eyebrows pulled upward, but my hair was straight for the time being, and could easily be arranged in the two shining loops tied with polished cord, which was the proper style for me. From the time I can remember I was always careful about lying quiet on my little wooden pillow at night, but by the next morning there was sure to be little twists at my neck and a suspicious curve in the loops on top of the head. How I envied the long, straight locks of the court ladies in the roll picture hanging in my room!

One time I rebelled and used return words to my nurse, who was trying to comfort me during one of my "gluing-up" experiences. Kind old Ishi forgave me at once, but my mother overheard and called me to her room. I was a little sullen, I remember, as I bowed and seated myself before her cushion, and she looked at me severely as she spoke.

"Etsu-ko," she said, "do you not know that curly hair is like animal's hair? A samurai's daughter should not be willing to resemble a beast."

I was greatly mortified and never again complained of the discomfort of hot tea and scented oil.

On the day of my "seventh-year" celebration I experienced a humiliation so deep that it still aches me to think of it. This celebration is a very important event in the life of a Japanese girl—as much so as her début party is to an American young lady. All our woman relatives were invited to a great feast, where I, in a beautiful new gown, occupied the place of honour. My hair had been elaborately arranged, but the day was rainy and I suppose some persistent small strands had escaped their stiff prison, for I overheard one of my aunts say, "It's a shameful waste to put a beautiful dress on Etsu. It only attracts attention to her ugly, twisty hair."

How deeply a child can feel! I wanted to shrivel to nothingness inside the gown of which I had been so proud, but I looked straight ahead and did not move. The next moment, when Ishi came in with some rice and looked at me, I saw the pain in her eyes and I knew that she had heard.

That night when she came to undress me she had not removed the little blue-and-white towel that all Japanese servants wear over the hair when at work. I was surprised, for it is not polite to appear before a superior with the head covered, and Ishi was always courteous. I soon found out the truth. She had gone to the temple as soon as the dinner was over, and cutting off her splendid straight hair, had placed it before the shrine, praying the gods to transfer her hair to me. My good Ishi! My heart thanks her yet for her loving sacrifice.

Who shall say that God did not pity the simple soul's ignorant, loving effort to save from humiliation the child she loved? At any rate, her prayer was answered when in later years the hand of fate turned my steps toward a land where my curly hair no longer caused me either sorrow or shame.

CHAPTER-3

Days of Kan

WE DID not have kindergartens when I was a child, but long before the time when I could have been admitted to the new "after-the-sixth-birthday" school, I had acquired a goodly foundation for later study of history and literature. My grandmother was a great reader, and during the shut-in evenings of the long, snowy winters we children spent much time around her fire-box, listening to stories. In this way I became familiar, when very young, with our mythology, with the lives of Japan's greatest historical personages and with the outline stories of many of our best novels. Also I learned much of the old classic dramas from Grandmother's lips. My sister received the usual education for girls, but mine was planned along different lines for the reason that I was supposed to be destined for a priestess. I had been born with the navel cord looped around the neck like a priest's rosary, and it was a common superstition in those days that this was a direct command from Buddha. Both my grandmother and my mother sincerely believed this, and since in a Japanese home the ruling of the house and the children is left to the women, my father silently bowed to the earnest wish of my grandmother to have me educated for a priestess. He, however, selected for my teacher a priest whom he knew—a very scholarly man, who spent little time in teaching me the forms of temple worship, but instructed me most conscientiously in the doctrine of Confucius. This was considered the foundation of all literary culture, and was believed by my father to be the highest moral teaching of the time.

My teacher always came on the days of threes and sevens—that is, the third, seventh, thirteenth, seventeenth, twenty-third, and twenty-seventh. This was in accordance with our moon-calendar custom of dividing days into groups of tens instead of sevens, as is done by the sun calendar. I enjoyed my lessons very much. The stateliness of my teacher's appearance, the ceremony of his manner, and the rigid obedience required of me appealed to my dramatic instinct. Then the surroundings were most impressive to my childish mind. The room was always made ready with especial care the day of my lessons, and when I entered, invariably I saw the same sight. I close my eyes now and all is as clear as if I had seen it but an hour ago.

The room was wide and light and was separated from the garden porch by a row of sliding paper doors crossed with slender bars of wood. The black-bordered straw mats were cream-coloured with time, but immaculate in their dustlessness. Books and desks were there, and in the sacred alcove hung a roll picture of Confucius. Before this was a little teakwood stand from which rose a curling mist of incense. On one side sat my teacher, his flowing gray robes lying in straight, dignified lines about his folded knees, a band of gold brocade across his shoulder, and a crystal rosary round his left wrist. His face was always pale, and his deep, earnest eyes beneath the priestly cap looked like wells of soft velvet. He was the gentlest and the saintliest man I ever saw. Years after, he proved that a holy heart and a progressive mind can climb together, for he was excommunicated from the orthodox temple for advocating a reform doctrine that united the beliefs of Buddhism and Christianity. Whether through accident or design, this broad-minded priest was the teacher chosen for me by my broad-minded though conservative father.

My studies were from books intended only for boys, as it was very unusual for a girl to study Chinese classics. My first lessons were from the "Four Books of Confucius." These are: Daigaku—"Great Learning," which teaches that the wise use of knowledge leads to virtue; Chuyo—"The Unchanging Centre," which treats of the unalterableness of universal law; Rongo and Moshi—which consist of the autobiography, anecdotes, and sayings of Confucius, gathered by his disciples.

I was only six years old, and of course I got not one idea from this heavy reading. My mind was filled with many words in which were hidden grand thoughts, but they meant nothing to me then. Sometimes I would feel curious about a half-caught idea and ask my teacher the meaning. His reply invariably was:

"Meditation will untangle thoughts from words," or "A hundred times reading reveals the meaning." Once he said to me, "You are too young to comprehend the profoundly deep books of Confucius."

This was undoubtedly true, but I loved my lessons. There was a certain rhythmic cadence in the meaningless words that was like music, and I learned readily page after page, until I knew perfectly all the important passages of the four books and could recite them as a child rattles off the senseless jingle of a counting-out game. Yet those busy hours were not wasted. In the years since, the splendid thoughts of the grand old philosopher have gradually dawned upon me; and sometimes when a well-remembered passage has drifted into my mind, the meaning has come flashing like a sudden ray of sunshine.

My priest-teacher taught these books with the same reverence that he taught his religion—that is, with all thought of worldly comfort put away. During my lesson he was obliged, despite the humble wish, to sit on the thick silk cushion the servant brought him, for cushions were our chairs, and the position of instructor was too greatly revered for him to be allowed to sit on a level with his pupil; but throughout my two-hour lesson he never moved the slightest fraction of an inch except with his hands and his lips. And I sat before him on the matting in an equally correct and unchanging position.

Once I moved. It was in the midst of a lesson. For some reason I was restless and swayed my body slightly, allowing my folded knee to slip a trifle from the proper angle. The faintest shade of surprise crossed my instructor's face; then very quietly he closed his book, saying gently but with a stern air:

"Little Miss, it is evident that your mental attitude to-day is not suited for study. You should retire to your room and meditate."

My little heart was almost killed with shame. There was nothing I could do. I humbly bowed to the picture of Confucius and then to my teacher, and backing respectfully from the room, I slowly went to my father to report, as I always did, at the close of my lesson. Father was surprised, as the time was not yet up, and his unconscious remark, "How quickly you have done your work!" was like a death knell. The memory of that moment hurts like a bruise to this very day.

Since absence of bodily comfort while studying was the custom for priests and teachers, of course all lesser people grew to feel that hardship of body meant inspiration of mind. For this reason my studies were purposely arranged so that the hardest lessons and longest hours came during the thirty days of midwinter, which the calendar calls the coldest of the year. The ninth day is considered the most severe, so we were expected to be especially earnest in our study on that day.

I will remember a certain "ninth day" when my sister was about fourteen years old. She was preparing to be married, therefore the task selected for her was sewing. Mine was penmanship. In those days penmanship was considered one of the most important studies for culture. This was not so much for its art—although it is true that practising Japanese penmanship holds the same intense artistic fascination as does the painting of pictures—but it was believed that the highest training in mental control came from patient practice in the complicated brush strokes of character-writing. A careless or perturbed state of mind always betrays itself in the intricate shading of ideographs, for each one requires absolute steadiness and accuracy of touch. Thus, in careful guidance of the hand were we children taught to hold in leash the mind.

With the first gleam of sunrise on this "ninth day," Ishi came to wake me. It was bitterly cold. She helped me dress, then I gathered together the materials for my work, arranging the big sheets of paper in a pile on my desk and carefully wiping every article in my ink-box with a square of silk. Reverence for learning was so strong in Japan at that time that even the tools we used were considered almost sacred. I was supposed to do every-thing for myself on this day, but my kind Ishi hovered around me, helping in every way she could without actually doing the work herself. Finally we went to the porch overlooking the garden. The snow was deep everywhere. I remember how the bamboo grove looked with its feathery tops so snow-laden that they were like wide-spread umbrellas. Once or twice a sharp crack and a great soft fluff of spurting snow against the gray sky told that a trunk had snapped under its too heavy burden. Ishi took me on her back and, pushing her feet into her snow-boots, slowly waded to where I could reach the low branch of a tree, from which I lifted a handful of perfectly pure, untouched snow, just from the sky. This I melted to mix for my penmanship study. I ought to have waded to get the snow myself, but—Ishi did it.

Since the absence of bodily comfort meant inspiration of mind, of course I wrote in a room without a fire. Our architecture is of tropical origin; so the lack of the little brazier of glowing charcoal brought the temperature down to that of outside. Japanese picture-writing is slow and careful work. I froze my fingers that morning without knowing it until I looked back and saw my good nurse softly crying as she watched my purple hand. The training of children, even of my age, was strict in those days, and neither she nor I moved until I had finished my task. Then Ishi wrapped me in a big padded kimono that had been warmed and hurried me into my grandmother's room. There I found a bowl of warm, sweet rice-gruel made by my grandmother's own hands. Tucking my chilled knees beneath the soft, padded quilt that covered the sunken fire-box I drank the gruel, while Ishi rubbed my stiff hand with snow.

Of course, the necessity of this rigid discipline was never questioned by any one, but I think that, because I was a delicate child, it sometimes caused my mother uneasiness. Once I came into the room where she and Father were talking.

"Honorable Husband," she was saying, "I am sometimes so bold as to wonder if Etsu-bo's studies are not a little severe for a not-too-strong child."

My father drew me over to his cushion and rested his hand gently on my shoulder.

"We must not forget, Wife," he replies, "the teaching of a samurai home. The lioness pushes her young over the cliff and watches it climb slowly back from the valley without one sign of pity, though her heart aches for the little creature. So only can it gain strength for its life work."

Because I was having the training and studies of a boy was one of the reasons my family got in the habit of calling me Etsu-bo, the termination *bo* being used for a boy's name, as *ko* is for a girl's. But my lessons were not confined to those for a boy. I also learned all the domestic accomplishments taught my sisters—sewing, weaving, embroidery, cooking, flower-arranging, and the complicated etiquette of ceremonial tea.

Nevertheless my life was not all lessons. I spent many happy hours in play. With the conventional order of old Japan, we children had certain games for each season—the warm, damp days of early spring, the twilight evenings of summer, the crisp, fragrant harvest time, or the clear, cold, snow-shoe days of winter. And I believe I enjoyed every game we ever played—from the simple winter-evening pastime of throwing a threaded needle at a pile of rice-cakes, to see how many each of us could gather on her string, to the exciting memory contests with our various games of poem cards.

We had boisterous games, too, in which a group—all girls, of course—would gather in some large garden or on a quiet street where the houses were hemmed in behind hedges of bamboo and evergreen. Then we would race and whirl in "The Fox Woman from the Mountain" or "Hunting for Hidden Treasure"; we would shout and scream as we tottered around on stilts in the forbidden boy-game of "Riding the High-stepping Bamboo Horse" or the hopping game of "The One-legged Cripples."

But no outdoor play of our short summers nor any indoor game of our long winters was so dear to me as were stories. The servants knew numberless priest tales and odd jingles that had come down by word of mouth from past generations, and Ishi, who had the best memory and the readiest tongue of them all, possessed an unending fund of simple old legends. I don't remember ever going to sleep without stories from her untiring lips. The dignified tales of Honourable Grandmother were wonderful, and the happy hours I spent sitting, with primly folded hands, on the mat before her—for I never used a cushion when Grandmother was talking to me—have left lasting and beautiful memories. But with Ishi's stories everything was different. I listened to them, all warm and comfortable, snuggled up crookedly in the soft cushions of my bed, giggling and interrupting and begging for "just one more" until the unwelcome time would arrive when, Ishi, laughing but stern, would reach over to my night lantern, push one wick down into the oil, straighten the other, and drop the paper panel. Then, at last, surrounded by the pale, soft light of the shaded room, I had to say good-night and settle myself into the *kinoji*, which was the proper sleeping position for every samurai girl.

CHAPTER-4

The Old and the New

I WAS about eight years old when I had my first taste of meat. For twelve centuries, following the introduction of the Buddhist religion, which forbids the killing of animals, the Japanese people were vegetarians. In late years, however, both belief and custom have changed considerably, and now, though meat is not universally eaten, it can be found in all restaurants and hotels. But when I was a child it was looked upon with horror and loathing.

How well I remember one day when I came home from school and found the entire household wrapped in gloom. I felt a sense of depression as soon as I stepped from the "shoe-off" entrance, and heard my mother, in low, solemn tones, giving directions to a maid. A group of servants at the end of the hall seemed excited, but they also were talking in hushed voices. Of course, since I had not yet greeted the family, I did not ask any questions, but I had an uneasy feeling that something was wrong, and it was very hard for me to walk calmly and unhurriedly down the long hall to my grandmother's room.

"Honourable Grandmother, I have returned," I murmured, as I sank to the floor with my usual salutation. She returned my bow with a gentle smile, but she was graver than usual. She and a maid were sitting before the black-and-gold cabinet of the family shrine. They had a large lacquer tray with rolls of white paper on it and the maid was pasting paper over the gilded doors of the shrine.

Like almost every Japanese home, ours had two shrines. In time of sickness or death, the plain wooden Shinto shrine, which honours the Sun goddess, the Emperor, and the nation, was sealed with white paper to guard it from pollution. But the gilded Buddhist shrine was kept wide open at such a time; for Buddhist gods give comfort to the sorrowing and guide the dead on their heavenward journey. I had never known the gold shrine to be sealed; and besides, this was the very hour for it to be lighted in readiness for the evening meal. That was always the pleasantest part of the day; for after the first helping of our food had been placed on a tiny lacquer table before the shrine, we all seated ourselves at our separate tables, and ate, talked and laughed, feeling that the loving hearts of the ancestors were also with us. But the shrine was closed. What could it mean?

I remember that my voice trembled a little as I asked, “Honourable Grandmother, is—is anybody going to die?” I can see now how she looked—half amused and half shocked.

“Little Etsu-ko,” she said, “you talk too freely, like a boy. A girl should never speak with abrupt unceremony.”

“Pardon me, Honourable Grandmother,” I persisted anxiously; “but is not the shrine being sealed with the pure paper of protection?”

“Yes,” she answered with a little sigh, and said nothing more.

I did not speak again but sat watching her bent shoulders as she leaned over, unrolling the paper for the maid. My heart was greatly troubled.

Presently she straightened up and turned toward me.

“Your honourable father has ordered his household to eat flesh,” she said very slowly. “The wise physician who follows the path of the Western barbarians has told him that the flesh of animals will bring strength to his weak body, and also will make the children robust and clever like the people of the Western sea. The ox flesh is to be brought into the house in another hour and our duty is to protect the holy shrine from pollution.

That evening we ate a solemn dinner with meat in our soup; but no friendly spirits were with us, for both shrines were sealed. Grandmother did not join us. She always occupied the seat of honour, and the vacant place looked strange and lonely. That night I asked her why she had not come.

“I would rather not grow as strong as a Westerner—nor as clever,” she answered sadly. “It is more becoming for me to follow the path of our ancestors.”

My sister and I confided to each other that we liked the taste of meat. But neither of us mentioned this to any one else; for we both loved Grandmother, and we knew our disloyalty would sadden her heart.

The introduction of foreign food helped greatly to break down the wall of tradition which shut our people away from the world of the West, but sometimes the change was made at a great cost. This could not be otherwise; for after the Restoration many samurai suddenly found themselves not only poor and at the same time separated entirely from the system that had given them support; but also, bound as firmly as ever by the code of ethics that for centuries had taught them utter contempt for money. The land was flooded, during those first years, with business failures; for many of these men were young, ambitious, and eager to experiment with new customs.

Such a one was Mr. Toda, a friend and neighbour, who often came to shoot on our archery grounds with my father, or to take horseback rides with him in the mountains. I liked Mr. Toda very much, and could not understand why Grandmother seemed to feel that his ideas were too progressive and informal.

One day when he and Father were having a game of archery, they stopped to argue about some business plan. I was near by, trying to ride on the back of my father's big white dog, Shiro. After I had had a more severe tumble than usual, Mr. Toda picked me up and stood me very near the grassy bank against which was placed the large round target with its broad rings of black and white. Putting the big bow in front of me, he held my arms while I shot. The arrow struck the target.

"Best done!" he shouted. "You will make a great warrior, Little Mistress! You are your father's son, after all!"

My father laughed as he told the story that night. I felt very proud, but Mother looked thoughtful and Grandmother shook her head sadly.

"Your honourable father trains you in so boy-like a manner," she said turning to me, "that I fear fate must search long for your unfound husband. No genteel family wants an ungentle bride."

And so, even in our pleasant family, there was a continual hidden battle between the old and the new.

Mr. Toda was a man of independent thought, and after several vain attempts to adjust himself to new conditions and at the same time retain his dignity, he decided to throw dignity aside and engage in some business that would bring material results. This was just at the beginning of the talk about the strength-giving properties of foreign food. Since Mr. Toda owned a good-sized estate which at that time nobody would accept even as a gift, he converted it into a grass farm and sent to a far-away coast for some cattle. Then, with a few experienced men as assistants, he once more ventured into the business world; this time as a dairy man and a butcher.

The aristocratic family of Mr. Toda did not approve at all of this new occupation; for in the old days, only *eta* (the outcast class) ever handled bodies from which life had gone. For a while almost everyone looked upon him with a sort of curious horror, but gradually faith in meat as a strengthening food gained ground, and the families who used it on their tables grew steadily in number. So the business prospered.

The simpler part of his work—the selling of milk—was also successful, but it also had serious drawbacks. Most of the common people believed that cow's milk would influence the nature of those who drank it, and on this subject they gossiped much. We children heard from servants that Mrs. Toda's new-born baby had a tiny horn on its forehead and that its fingers were clubbed together like cows' hoofs. These tales were not true, of course. But fear has a strong influence on our lives for happiness or misery, and in the Toda household there was real and desperate anxiety about many trifling things.

The majority of intellectual men of that day, though broad thinkers themselves, allowed the women of their families to remain narrow and ignorant; and so it was that the constant friction between the old and new ideas ended finally in a tragedy. The proud old grandmother of the Toda house, feeling keenly what in her eyes was disgrace to the family name, chose the only way to right a wrong that a helpless Japanese knows—sacrifice. If one must die for a principle, it is not hard to find a way; so one day the grandmother was laid to rest with the ancestors whose honour she had died to uphold.

Mr. Toda was an unflinching man, who honestly believed that he was right in carrying out his progressive ideas, but to his mother's silent protest he yielded. He sold his business to a wealthy fish dealer, who steadily became wealthier, for the use of meat and milk constantly increased.

The spacious grounds where Mr. Toda's cattle had leisurely browsed were left vacant a long time. We children on our way home from school used to peep fearfully through the cracks in the black board fence and talk in whispers as we gazed at the desolate land covered with coarse grass and tall weeds. We always, in some way, associated that lonely place with the wandering soul of Mrs. Toda, who by going on the unknown journey had accomplished what here she was helpless to do.

One day my father came home and told us that Mr. Toda was now guard to a farmer landlord in an adjacent province. His good fortune was due to the fact that, for several years after the Restoration, the new government had much trouble in handling its numerous, previously separately governed provinces, and there was much lawlessness everywhere. To the landlord of many small farms the Restoration was not the tragedy it was to the samurai, for Echigo was famous for its abundant rice crops, and farmer storehouses were often filled with treasure. But it was a common thing for desperate robbers to raid these storehouses and sometimes even to murder the owners. Wealthy farmers had to be guarded, and since the restrictions of feudal days, which had rigidly regulated the style of living of the various classes, no longer existed, those farmers could enjoy their riches with out interference from the Government, and it became the fashion for them to hire ex-samurai—once their superiors—as guards. Partly on account of the dignity of their former station, which everyone of less honourable rank respected, and partly because of their skilled military training, the samurai were well fitted for this duty.

In his new business Mr. Toda was treated as a sort of honourable policeman-guest. He received a good salary, always formally presented folded in white paper and labelled: "An appreciation tribute." Of course, this position could not be permanent; for government authority gradually penetrated even to our remote district and made the farmers safe.

We next heard that Mr. Toda had become a teacher in a test school of the newly organized public-school system. His associate teachers were mostly young men proud to be called progressive, and affecting a lofty disdain for the old culture of Japan. The old samurai was sadly out of place, but being of philosophical bent and not without a sense of humour, he got along very well until the Department of Education made a rule that no one should be accepted as a teacher unless he held a normal-school diploma. To go through the required schooling and be examined by those whom he considered only conceited youths of shallow brain would have been too humiliating to a man of Mr. Toda's age, learning, and culture. He refused and turned his attention to one of his most elegant accomplishments—penmanship. He made beautiful ideographs for the trade-marks so frequently seen on the curtains that hang from the eaves of Japanese shops. He also copied Chinese poems for folding-screens and roll pictures and even wrote inscriptions for the banners of Shinto shrines.

Changes came to our family which separated us from the Todas, and it was several years before I learned that they had moved to Tokyo, Mr. Toda trusting with brave confidence that the new capital, with its advanced ideas, would treat him fairly. But, after all, he was a gentleman of feudal days, and the capital was overflowing with wild enthusiasm for everything new and supreme contempt for everything old. There was nowhere a place for him.

One day, years after, while I was a schoolgirl in Tokyo, I was passing through a crowded street when my eyes were caught by a beautifully written sign: "Instructor in the Cultural Game of *Go*." Between the strips of the lattice door I saw Mr. Toda, sitting very straight with samurai dignity, teaching *go*, a sort of chess, to a number of new rich tradesmen. They were men who had retired, as our older people do, leaving their business to sons or heirs and devoting their time to practice in *go*, tea ceremony, or other cultural occupation. Mr. Toda looked aged and poor, but he still had his undaunted air and half-humorous smile. Had I been a man I should have gone in, but for a young girl to intrude on his game would have been too rude, so I passed on.

Once more did I see him a few years later. Early one morning when I was waiting for a horse-car on a corner near an office building there passed an old man who had the slight droop of the left shoulder that always marks the man who once wore two swords. He went into the building, in a moment reappearing in the cap and coat of a uniform, and taking his stand at the door, opened and closed it for the people passing in and out. It was Mr. Toda. A number of supercilious young clerks in smart European dress pushed hastily by without even a nod of thanks. It was the new foreign way assumed by so-called progressive youths.

It is well for the world to advance, but I could not help thinking how, less than a generation before, the fathers of these same youths would have had to bow with their foreheads to the ground when Mr. Toda, sitting erect on his horse, galloped by. The door swung to and fro, and he stood with his head held high and on his lips the same half humorous smile. Brave, unconquered Mr. Toda! He represented thousands of men of the past, who, having nothing to offer the new world except the wonderful but unwanted culture of the old, accepted with calm dignity the fate of failure—but they were all heroes!

CHAPTER-5

Falling Leaves

THE day before Nagaoka's last "Castle Sinking Celebration," Kin took me to walk along the edge of the old castle moat. Years before, part of it had been levelled up, and was now occupied by neat little rice farms; but most of it was still only a marshy waste that was gradually being filled with rubbish from the town. In one place an angle of the wall projected out pretty far, forming a protected pond where was clustered a crowded mass of velvety lotus leaves. Kin said that the water of the moat used to be very deep and as clear as a mirror; and that, here and there, were large patches of lotus leaves, which, in the blooming season, looked like unevenly woven brocade with a raised pattern of white-and-pink blossoms.

"What did the castle look like, Kin? I want to hear again," I said, looking across the dykes to the ruined walls and piles of heaped-up stones on the top of the hill.

"Like all castles, Etsu-bo Sama," she replied, "except that this was ours."

It was not often that Kin's gay spirits were sobered, but she stood gazing gravely across at the ruins, saying nothing more.

I turned my face toward the hill and closed my eyes, trying to see, in my mind, the picture so often painted for me by the loyal lips of Jiya or Ishi. A great square mass of stone and plaster with narrow, white-barred windows and tiers of curving roofs artistically zig-zagging over each other in such a manner that an object thrown from any corner would find an unobstructed path to the ground; and high above the deep eaves and many-pointed roofs, on each end of the curving roof-ridge, a bronze fish with up-lifted tail shining rich and dark in the sunshine. Below, at the base of the pine-topped dykes, slept in dark quietude the waters of the moat—called "the bottomless" by simple-hearted people—whose clear waters reflected the six-sided stones of the "tortoise-back" wall.

"Come, Etsu-bo Sama, we must go."

I opened my eyes with a jerk. Nothing of the picture was there except the dykes that once formed a protection from flying arrows and shooting spears, and now were only hilly, peaceful vegetable gardens.

"All of this ground beyond," said Kin, with a wide sweep of her hand as we started toward home, "was once covered with beautiful gardens of noble retainers whose mansions were gathered about the outer wall of the castle. Now all that beauty is crushed into hundreds of plain little farms; and some of them, like ours, are ploughed by the unused hands of vassals of the 'ancient glorious'!"

Kin was quiet all the way home, and I walked soberly by her side, with my bright anticipations for the morrow's celebration somewhat dampened.

"Castle Sinking" is a term used in Japanese literature to describe the sublime desolation of the useless castle of a conquered people. The new government was both wise and generous in its endeavour to help its subjects adjust themselves to the puzzling situation which confronted them at the close of the war, but Nagaoka people were slow to forget. Many still believed that to have dragged the god-descended Emperor from his palace of holiness and peace, only to plunge him into a material world of sordid duties, was sacrilege; and that the failure of the shogun power to march steadily on its rightful way was a sorrowful thing for Japan.

I was many years younger than the time of the Restoration, but its memories were with me all through my childhood, for I was born not so long after those years of desolation and bitterness but that the everyday talk of the town was of the awful days that had left so many homes without a master. In my babyhood I heard war-songs as frequently as lullabies, and half of my childhood stories were tales of heroes on the battlefield. From the gateway of my home could be seen the ruined walls and half-filled moat of the castle, our godowns were filled to the roof with weapons and belongings of my father's retainers, and I scarcely ever went on to the street that I did not meet some old person who, as I passed, would stand humbly aside, bowing and bowing, with respectful and tearful murmurings of the "glories of the past." Ah me! Death had stepped many times between the strain of those days and the hesitating progress of my childhood's time, and yet the old spirit of dutiful loyalty to the overlord was not yet quenched.

May 7, 1869, was the day on which all power was removed from Nagaoka castle by the new Government, and after the bitterness of the first few years had passed, the anniversary of that day was always observed by the samurai families of the town. To the newcomers and to the tradespeople, the celebration was only an interesting episode, but to those who took part it was a tribute to the dying spirit of chivalry. The morning after my walk with Kin by the castle moat, I wakened with an excited feeling that something was going to happen. And indeed, it was a day of busy happenings! For breakfast everybody ate black rice—rice husked but not whitened, such as is used by soldiers during the haste of battle marches—and in the afternoon a sham battle was held on Yukuzan plain back of the shrine dedicated to the Nagaoka daimios.

What a gay assemblage there was that day! Most of the aristocracy were poor and much of their valuable armour had been disposed of, but everybody had retained some, and each one appeared in what he had. I can even now see the procession as it started, with my father as leader. He sat very straight on his horse, and, to my childish eyes, looked very grand in his cloth garment with close-wrist sleeves and bloomer-like skirt, over which rattled and clanged the lacquer-scaled breastplate with its cross-stitching of silk cord and its great gold crest. Of course, his own horse was gone, as well as its elaborate trappings, but Mother's ingenuity had decorated a plain harness with cords and tassels twisted from strips of silk, thus transforming a tenant's farm horse into somewhat the appearance of a war steed; and in place of the swords Father was no longer allowed to carry, he wore two sharpened bamboos stuck through his sash. A great crowd of people gathered by the stone bridge at the end of the town to see the little army start out. The spectators had clothed themselves as far as they could in ancient dress, and as they waited, the men all sitting with crossed legs in warrior fashion, they made a courageous-looking company.

Then the drum sounded, and my father raised his *saihai*—a stick with dangling papers which his ancestors had carried to guide their followers—and rode away, followed by a long train of men in armour as for war. They crossed the fields, climbed the mountain, and, after each warrior had made salutation at the temple, they gathered on the plain for the battle, following it with an exhibition in archery, fencing, spear-throwing, and athletic sports of various kinds.

Our men servants went to Yukuzan plain to watch the sports, but the women were busy all day preparing for the home-coming. Straw mats were spread on the grass and many fires were kindled in the garden over which, tied to a tripod of strong branches, swung large iron kettles holding game seasoned with *miso*, which with bran-rice forms the food of soldiers in camp. About twilight the little army came riding back. We children, dressed in our best attire, ran out to the big gateway and waited between the two tall lantern stands with the welcoming lights. When Father saw us he opened his iron war-fan and swung it back and forth, as one would wave a handkerchief in greeting, and we bowed and bowed in reply.

"Your honourable father looks to-day as he used to look in the prosperous time," said Mother, half sadly, "and I am thankful that you, his daughter, have seen him so."

The men piled their heavy regalia in a corner of the garden, and sat around the kettles, eating and laughing with the freedom of camp life. Father did not change his clothes, except to throw back his war hat, where it hung by its silk cord, encasing him, front and back, in two Inagaki crests; "thus boldly identifying myself to both friends and enemies," he said, laughing. Then, sitting on a high garden stone, he told war stories to us children, as we crowded close to each other on a straw mat before him.

That was our last celebration in memory of the castle sinking of Nagaoka. On the next May 7th the plain was flooded from a drenching downpour, and the year following, Father was in ill health. The men did not care for the sports without their old lord as leader, so the celebration was postponed to a day that never came.

Father never entirely recovered from the effects of the hard years of the Restoration. Each one as it passed left him looking less like the sturdy, ambitious youth—for he was only thirty at that time—who had held the reins of excited Nagaoka during those desperate days, but his brave, cheerful spirit remained unchanged. Even through the first erratic years of Japan's struggle to gain a foothold in the new world, when people were recklessly throwing off the old and madly reaching out for the new, Father had gone on his way, calm and unexcited. He held, with the most progressive men of his day, a strong belief in the ultimate success of Japan's future, but—and in this he received little sympathy—he also retained a deep reverence for the past. Father, however, was much liked, and he generally could turn aside undesirable comments or lengthy arguments by the aid of a keen sense of humour, which had a way of breaking through his stateliness and dignity like a gleam of unexpected sunshine; and so, without title or power, he held, as of old, his place as leader.

One autumn day, Father's physician, who was a very progressive man and as much friend as physician, suggested that Father should go to Tokyo and consult some doctors of a new hospital renowned for its successful use of Western methods. Father decided to go, and of course he took Jiya with him.

With Father and Jiya both gone, I was desolate. I still feel the heart-pull of those lonely days. Sister was preparing for her marriage, which was to take place in the fall, and her time was taken up with many things. I don't know what I should have done but for my good Shiro, who was equally lonely with me. Shiro really belonged to me, but of course I never called him mine, for it was considered rough and unladylike for a girl to own a dog. But I was allowed to play with him, and every day, as soon as my lessons were over, we would wander around together. One day we had visited the archery ground and were on the long walk where Father liked to trudge up and down for exercise, when suddenly Shiro galloped away from me toward a little house just within the gateway, where Jiya lived alone. Jiya's wife had died before I could remember, but he was a capable housekeeper, and any afternoon during the summer that I might go to his neat porch I would find a square lacquer box holding the most delicious things that a little girl could possibly want to eat between meals—a sweet potato baked in ashes and sprinkled with salt; or some big, brown chestnuts baked until their jackets had burst, disclosing the creamy richness of the dainty that was waiting for my fingers.

I hurried after Shiro and found him pushed close against the porch, his tail wagging and his nose eagerly sniffing in the corner where the lacquer box used to stand.

"Oh, no, no, Shiro!" I mournfully said. "The lacquer box is gone. Jiya is gone. Everybody is gone."

I sat down on the edge of the porch and Shiro snuggled his cold nose into my long sleeve. We were two as disconsolate creatures as could be found, and as I buried my hand in his rough white fur, I had to struggle hard to remember that a samurai's daughter does not cry.

Suddenly I recalled the saying, "To unreasonably relax is cowardice." I bounded up. I talked to Shiro. I played with him. I even ran races with him in the garden. When at last I returned to the house I had reason to suspect that the family felt disapproval of my wild conduct, but because I was all dearness to my father I escaped reproof for his sake. Everyone had a tender heart in those days; for the heaviness of dread was upon us all.

One day Shiro fell sick, and would eat nothing I put into his bowl. I had a childish feeling that if he would eat he would get well, but that day happened to be the death anniversary of an ancestor, and was therefore a day of fasting. We had only vegetables for dinner, and so there were no good scraps for Shiro. As always when in trouble, I went to Ishi. She knew we ought not to handle fish on a fast day, but she pitied my anxiety and smuggled me some fish bones from somewhere. I took them to a distant part of the garden and crushed them between two flat stones. Then I mixed them with bean soup from the kitchen and took them to the kindling shed where Shiro was lying on his straw mat. Poor Shiro looked grateful, but he would not get up; and thinking that perhaps he was cold, I ran to my room and brought my crêpe cushion to cover him.

When this became known to my grandmother, she sent for me to come to her room. The moment I lifted my face after bowing I knew this was not one of the times when I was to be entertained with sweet bean-cake.

"Little Etsu-ko," she said (she always called me "Etsu-ko" when she spoke sternly), "I must speak to you of something very important. I am told that you wrapped Shiro with your silk cushion."

Startled at her tone, I meekly bowed.

"Do you not know," she went on, "that you are guilty of the utmost unkindness to Shiro when you do inappropriate things for him?"

I must have looked shocked and puzzled, for she spoke very gently after that, explaining that since white dogs belong to the order next lower than that of human beings, my kindness might postpone for another lifetime Shiro's being born in human shape.

According to transmigration belief, the boundary line between the orders of creation must be strictly maintained. If we place an animal above its proper position we may prevent its advance in the next incarnation. Every devout Buddhist is absolutely submissive to Fate , for he is taught that hardship in his present life is either the atonement for sins committed in the last existence, or the education necessary to prepare him for a higher place in the life to come. This belief has held Japan's labouring class in cheerful resignation through ages of hardship, but also it has taught us to look with such indifference upon the sufferings of creatures below us in the order of creation that we have become, as a nation, almost sympathy-blind.

As quickly as possible to be polite, I thanked my grandmother and hurried to beg Shiro's pardon. I found him covered very comfortably with a matting of soft rice-straw suitable to his station. Out in the garden two coolies were engaged in burning the crêpe cushion. Their faces were very grave.

Poor Shiro! He had the best care we could give him, but the next morning his body was asleep under the straw matting and his spirit had passed on to the next state, which I pray was not lower because of my kindly meant mistake. He was buried in the sunniest corner of the garden beneath a big chestnut tree where many an autumn morning he and I had happily tossed and caught the fallen brown nuts. It would never have done for Shiro's grave to be publicly marked, but over it my father quietly placed, on his return, a small gray stone, in memory of his little girl's most faithful vassal.

Alas! Before the chestnut burrs were spilling their brown nuts over Shiro's grave, my dear father had been laid to rest in the family burial ground at Chokoji, and one more tablet had been placed in the gilded shrine before which every morning and evening we bowed in love and reverence.

CHAPTER-6

A Sunny New Year

OURS was a lonely house the winter after Father's death. The first forty-nine days when "the soul hovers near the eaves" was not sad to me, for the constantly burning candles and curling incense of the shrine made me feel that Father was near. And, too, everyone was lovingly busy doing things in the name of the dear one; for to Buddhists, death is a journey, and during these seven weeks, Mother and Jiya hastened to fulfil neglected duties, to repay obligations of all kinds and to arrange family affairs so that, on the forty-ninth day, the soul, freed from world shackles, could go happily on its way to the Land of Rest.

But when the excitement of the busy days was over and, excepting at the time of daily service, the shrine was dark, then came loneliness. In a childish, literal way, I thought of Father as trudging along a pleasant road with many other pilgrims, all wearing the white robes covered with priestly writings, the pilgrim hats and straw sandals in which they were buried—and he was getting farther and farther from me every day.

As time passed on we settled back into the old ways, but it seemed that everybody and everything had changed. Jiya no longer hummed old folk-songs as he worked and Ishi's cheerful voice had grown so lifeless that I did not care for fairy tales any more. Grandmother spent more time than ever polishing the brass furnishings of the shrine. Mother went about her various duties, calm and quiet as usual, but her smile was sad. Sister and I sewed and read together, but we no longer wasted time in giggling and eating sweets. And when in the evening we all gathered around the fire-box in Grandmother's room, our conversation was sure to drift to mournful topics. Even in the servants' hall, though talking and laughter still mingled with the sounds of spinning and grinding of rice, the spirit of merriment was gone.

During these months, my greatest pleasure was going to the temple with Mother. Toshi, the maid, always walked behind, carrying flowers for the grave.

During these months my greatest pleasure was going to the temple with Mother or Ishi. Mother's special maid, Toshi, always walked behind, carrying flowers for the graves. We went first to the temple to bow our respects to the priest, my much-honoured teacher. He served us tea and cakes and then went with us to the graves, a boy priest going along to carry a whitewood bucket of water with a slender bamboo dipper floating on the top. We made bows to the graves and then, in respect to the dead, poured water from the little dipper over the base of the tall gray stones. So loyal to the past are the people of Nagaoka that, many years after my father's death, I heard my mother say that she had never visited his grave when she had not found it moist with "memory-pourings" of friends and old retainers.

On February 15th, the "Enter into Peace" celebration of Buddha's death, I went to the temple with Toshi, carrying as a gift to the priest a lacquer box of little dumplings. They were made in the shapes of all the animals in the world, to represent the mourners at Buddha's death-bed, where all living creatures were present except the cat. The good old priest, after expressing his thanks, took a pair of chopsticks and, lifting several of the dumplings on to a plate, placed it for a few minutes in front of the shrine, before putting it away for his luncheon. That day he told me with deep feeling that he must say farewell, since he was soon to go away from Chokoji for ever. I could not understand, then, why he should leave the temple where he had been so long and which he so dearly loved; but afterward I learned that, devout and faithful though he was to all the temple forms, his brain had advanced beyond his faith, and he had joined the "Army of the Few" who choose poverty and scorn for the sake of what they believe to be the truth.

One evening, after a heavy snowfall, Grandmother and I were sitting cozily together by the fire-box in her room. I was making a hemp-thread ball for a mosquito net that was to be woven as part of my sister's wedding dowry, and Grandmother was showing me how to put my fingers deftly through the fuzzy hemp.

"Honourable Grandmother," I exclaimed, suddenly recalling something I wanted to say, "I forgot to tell you that we are going to have a snow-fight at school tomorrow. Hana San is chosen to be leader on one side and I on the other. We are to——"

I was so interested that again I lost my thread and it matted. I gave it a quick jerk and at once found myself in sad trouble.

"Wait!" said Grandmother, reaching out to help me. "You should sing 'The Hemp-Winding Song.'" As she straightened my tangled thread, her quavery old voice sang:

"Watch your hand as it winds hemp thread;
If it mats, with patience wait;
For a thoughtless move or a hasty pull
Makes smaller tangles great."

"Don't forget again!" she added, handing back the untangled bunch of hemp.

"I was thinking about the snow-fight," I said apologetically.

Grandmother looked disapproving. "Etsu-bo," she said, "your eldest sister, before she was married, made enough hemp thread for both the mosquito nets for her destined home. You have now entered your eleventh year and should aim to be more maiden-like in your tastes."

"Yes, Honourable Grandmother," I replied, feeling with humiliation how true her words were. "This winter I will wind plenty of hemp thread. I will make many balls, so Ishi can weave the two nets for Sister's dowry before New Year's."

"There is no need for such haste," Grandmother replied, smiling at my eagerness, but speaking gravely. "Our days of sorrow must not influence your sister's fate. Her marriage has been postponed until the good-luck season when the ricefields bow with their burden."

I had noticed that fewer shop men had been coming to the house, and I had missed the frequent visits of tall Mr. Nagai and his brisk, talkative little wife, the go-between couple for my sister. So that was what it meant! Our unknown bridegroom would have to wait until autumn for his bride. Sister did not care. There were plenty of things to be interested in and we both soon forgot all about the delayed wedding in our preparations for the approaching New Year.

The first seven days of the first month were the important holidays of the Japanese year. Men in pleated skirts and crest coats made greeting calls on the families of their friends, where they were received by hostesses in ceremonious garments who entertained them with most elaborate and especial New Year dishes; little boys held exciting battles in the sky with wonderful painted kites having knives fastened to their pulling cords; girls in new sashes tossed gay, feathery shuttlecocks back and forth or played poem cards with their brothers and brothers' friends, in the only social gatherings of the year where boys and girls met together. Even babies had a part in this holiday time, for each wee one had another birthday on New Year's Day—thus suddenly being ushered into its second year before the first had scarcely begun.

Our family festivities that year were few; but our sorrow was not allowed to darken too much the atmosphere of New Year, and for the first time since Father's death we heard sounds of merriment in the kitchen. With the hot smell of steaming rice and the "Ton-g—click! Ton-g—click!" of *mochi*-pounding were mingled the voices of Jiya and Ishi in the old song, "The Mouse in the House of Plenty," which always accompanies the making of the oldest food of Japan—the rice-dough called *mochi*.

"We are the messengers of the Good-luck god,
The merry messengers.
We're a hundred years old, yet never have heard
The fearful cry of cat;
For we're the messengers of the Good-luck god,
The merry messengers."

About two days before New Year, Ishi came into the kitchen looking for me. I was sitting on a mat with Taki, who was here to help for New Year time, and we were picking out round beans from a pile in a low, flat basket. They were the "stones of health" with which the demons of evil were to be pelted and chased away on New Year's Eve. Jiya, in ceremonious dress, would scatter them through the house, closely followed by Taki, Ishi, and Toshi, with Sister and Etsu-bo running after, all vigorously sweeping, pushing, tossing, and throwing; and while the rolling beans went flying across the porches into the garden or on to the walks, our high-pitched voices would merrily sing, over and over:

"Good luck within!
Evil, go out! Out!"

Ishi had some errands to do and Mother had said that I might go with her to see the gay sights. How well remember that wonderful sunshiny winter day! We crossed the streets on paths cut between walls of frozen snow only three feet deep; for we had but little early snow that winter, and no tunnels were made until after New Year. The sidewalk panels were down in some places, just like summer time, and the shops seemed very light with the sky showing. On each side of every doorway stood a pine tree, and stretched above was a Shinto rope with its ragged tufts and dangling zig-zag papers. Most of the shops on that street were small, with open fronts, and we could plainly see the sloping tiers of shelves laden with all the bright attractions of the season. In front of every shop was a crowd, many of the people having come from near-by villages, for the weather had been unusual, and Nagaoka had hopefully laid in a supply of New Year goods that would appeal to the simple taste of our country people.

To me, many of the sights, familiar though they were, had, in the novelty of their surroundings, the excitement and fascination of a play. At one place, when Ishi stopped to get something, I watched a group of ten- or twelve-year old boys, some with babies on their backs, clattering along on their high, rainy-day clogs. They stopped to buy a candy ball made of puffed rice and black sugar, which they broke, each taking a piece and not forgetting to stuff some scraps in the mouths of the babies that were awake. They were low-class children, of course, to eat on the street, but I could taste that delicious sweet myself, as my eyes followed them to the next shop, where they pushed and jostled themselves through a crowd toward a display of large kites painted with dragons and actors' masks that would look truly fearful gazing down from the sky, In some places young girls were gathered about shops whose shelves held rows of wooden clogs with bright-coloured toe-thongs; or where, beneath low eaves, swung long straw cones stuck full of New Year hairpins, gay with pine leaves and plum blossoms. There were, of course, many shops which sold painted battledores and long split sticks holding rows of five or ten feathery shuttlecocks of all colours. The biggest crowds of all were in front of these shops, for nobody was too poor or too busy to play *hana* on New Year days.

That was a wonderful walk, and I've always been glad I took it, for it was the only time I remember of my childhood when we had sunshiny streets at New Year time.

Notwithstanding our quiet house, the first three days of the New Year Mother was pretty busy receiving calls from our men kinsfolk and family friends. They were entertained with every-vegetable soup, with *miso*-stuffed salmon, fried bean-curd, seaweed of a certain kind, and frozen gelatin. *Mochi*, as a matter of course, was in everything, for mochi meant "happy congratulations" and was indispensable to every house during New Year holidays. With the food was served a rice-wine called *toso-sake*, which was rarely used except on certain natal occasions and at New Year time. Toso means "fountain of youth," and its significance is that with the new year, a new life begins.

The following days were more informal. Old retainers and old servants called to pay respect, and always on one day during the season Mother entertained all the servants of the house. They would gather in the large living room, dressed in their best clothes. Then little lacquer tables with our dishes laden with New Year dainties were brought in and the rice served by Sister and myself. Even Mother helped. There were Taki, Ishi, Toshi, and Kin, with Jiya and two menservants, and all behaved with great ceremony. Kin, who had a merry heart, would sometimes make fun for all by rather timidly imitating Mother's stately manner. Mother always smiled with dignified good nature, but Sister and I had to quench our merriment, for we were endeavouring to emulate Kin and Toshi in our deep bows and respectful manners. It was all very formally informal and most delightful.

On these occasions, Mother sometimes invited a carpenter, an old man who was always treated in our family as a sort of minor retainer. In old Japan, a good carpenter included the profession of architect, designer, and interior decorator as well as of a worker in wood, and since this man was known in Nagaoka as "Master Goro Beam"—the complimentary title of an exceptionally clever and skilful master-carpenter—and, in addition, was the descendant of several generations of his name, he was much respected. I was very fond of Goro. He had won my heart by making for me a beautiful little doll-house with a ladder-like stairway. It was my heart's pride during all the paper-doll years of my life. On the first New Year's Day that Goro came after Father's death, he seemed quiet and sad until Mother had served him *toso-sake;* then he brightened up and grew talkative. In the midst of the feast he suddenly paused and, lifting his *toso-sake* cup very respectfully to the level of his forehead, he bowed politely to Mother, who was sitting on her cushion just within the open doorway of the next room .

"Honourable Mistress," he began, "when your gateway had the pine decoration the last time, and you graciously entertained me like this, my Honourable Master was here."

"Yes, so he was," Mother replied with a sad smile. "Things have changed, Goro."

"Honourable Master ever possessed wit," Goro went on. "No ill-health or ill-fortune could dull his brain or his tongue. It was in the midst of your gracious hospitality, Honourable Mistress, that Honourable Master entered the room and assured us all that we were received with agreeable welcome. I had composed a humble poem of the kind that calls for a reply to make it complete; and was so bold as to repeat it to Honourable Master with the request that he honour me with closing words. My poem, as suitable for a New Year greeting, was a wish for good luck, good health, and good will to this honourable mansion.

"The Seven—the Good-fortune gods—
Encircle this house with safely-locked hands;
And nothing can pass them by.

"Then Honourable Master"—and Goro deeply bowed—"with a wrinkle of fun on his lips, and a twinkle of fun in his eyes, replied as quickly as a flash of light:

"Alas! and alas! Then from this house
The god of Poverty can never escape;
But must always stay within."

Goro enjoyed his joke-poem so much that Mother united her gentle smile with the gay laughter of his companions who were always ready to applaud any word spoken in praise of the master they had all loved and revered.

But bright-eyed Kin whispered to Ishi and Ishi smiled and nodded. Then Taki and Toshi caught some words and they, too, smiled. Not until afterward did I know that Kin's whisper was:

"The gods of Poverty are sometimes kind.
They've locked their hands with the Good-luck gods
And prisoned joy within our gates."

Thus lived the spirit of democracy in old Japan.

CHAPTER-7

The Wedding That Never Was

THE pleasant days of New Year barely lasted through the holidays. We usually left the *mochi* cakes on the *tokonoma* until the fifteenth, but it was everywhere the custom to remove the pines from the gateways on the morning of the eighth day. There was a tradition (which nobody believed, however) that during the seventh night the trees sink into the earth, leaving only the tips visible above the ground. Literally, this was true that year, for when we wakened on the morning of the eighth, I found the three-foot paths filled and our whole garden a level land of snow about four feet deep. Our low pines at the gateway were snowed under, and we saw nothing more of them until spring.

Every coolie in Nagaoka was busy that day, for the snow was unexpected and heavy. More followed, and in a few weeks we children were going to school beneath covered sidewalks and through snow tunnels; and our beautiful New Year was only a sunshiny memory.

One afternoon, as I was coming home from school, a postman, in his straw coat and big straw snow-shoes, came slipping down through a tunnel opening, from the snowy plain above.

"*Maa!* Little Mistress," he called gaily, when he saw me, "I have mail for your house from America."

"From America!" I exclaimed, greatly surprised; for a letter from a foreign land had never come to us before. It was an exciting event. I tried to keep the postman in sight as he hurried along the narrow walk between the snow wall and the row of open-front shops. Occasionally he would call out "A message!"—"A message!" and stop to put mail into an outstretched hand. The path was narrow and I frequently was jostled by passing people, but I was not far behind the postman when he turned into our street. I knew he would go to the side entrance with the mail; so I hurried very fast and had reached Grandmother's room and already made my bow of "I have come back," before a maid entered with the mail. The wonderful letter was for Mother, and Grandmother asked me to carry it to her.

My heart sank with disappointment; for my chance to see it opened was gone. I knew that, as soon as Mother received it, she would take it at once to Grandmother, but I should not be there. Then Grandmother would look at it very carefully through her big horn spectacles and hand it back to Mother, saying in a slow and ceremonious manner, "Please open!" Of course she would be agitated, because it was a foreign letter, but that would only make her still more slow and ceremonious. I could see the whole picture in my mind as I walked through the hall, carrying the big, odd-shaped envelope to Mother's room.

That evening after family service before the shrine, Grandmother kept her head bowed longer than usual. When she raised it she sat up very straight and announced solemnly, with the most formal dignity, almost like a temple service, that the young master, who had been in America for several years, was to return to his home. This was startling news, for my brother had been gone almost since I could remember and his name was never mentioned. To call him the "young master" was sufficient explanation that the unknown tragedy was past, and he reinstated in his position as a son. The servants, sitting in the rear of the room, bowed to the floor in silent congratulation, but they seemed to be struggling with suppressed excitement. I did not stop to wonder why. It was enough for me to know that my brother was coming home. I could scarcely hold the joy in my heart.

I must have been very young when my brother went away, for though I could distinctly recall the day he left, all memory of what went before or came immediately after was dim. I remember a sunny morning when our house was decorated with wondrous beauty and the servants all wore ceremonial dress with the Inagaki crest. It was the day of my brother's marriage. In the *tokonoma* of our best room was one of our treasures—a triple roll picture of pine, bamboo, and plum, painted by an ancient artist. On the platform beneath was the beautiful Takasago table where the white-haired old couple with rake and broom were gathering pine needles on the shore. Other emblems of happy married life were everywhere, for each gift—and there were whole rooms full—was decorated with small figures of snowy storks, of gold-brown tortoises, or beautiful sprays of entwined pine, bamboo, and plum. Two new rooms, which had been recently built, were full of beautiful lacquer toilet cases and whitewood chests with iron clasps. They had come the day before, in a procession of immense trays swinging from poles on the shoulders of coolies. Each was covered with a cloth bearing a crest not ours.

Ishi and I wandered from room to room, she explaining that the bride for the young master would soon be there. She allowed me one peep into the wedding room. It was all white and plain and empty except for the offerings to the gods on the *tokonoma* and the little table with the three red cups for the sacred promise.

Ishi was continually running to look out toward the big entrance gate, and of course wherever she went I was close by, holding to her sleeve. The whole house was open. The sliding doors of every room were pushed back and we could see clear to the big open gateway at the end of the stone walk. Just beneath its narrow thatch was looped a dark-blue curtain bearing the Inagaki crest and on each side were tall slender stands holding lanterns of congratulation. Near one of the stone posts was the "seven-and-a-half-times" messenger in his stiff-sleeved garment. He had returned from his seventh trip to see if the bridal procession was coming, and though the day was bright with sunshine, was just lighting his big lantern for his last trip to meet it halfway—thus showing our eagerness to welcome the coming bride.

Presently Ishi said that the procession was almost here and I saw the servants hurrying toward the entrance, all smiling, but moving with such respectful quiet that I could hear plainly the creaking of the bride's palanquin and the soft thud of the jinrikisha men's feet as they came up the hill.

Then suddenly something was wrong. Ishi caught my shoulder and pulled me back, and Brother came hurriedly out of Father's room. He passed us with long, swinging strides, never looking at me at all, and, stepping into his shoes on the garden step, he walked rapidly toward the side entrance. I had never seen him after that day.

The maiden my brother was to have married did not return to her former home. Having left it to become a bride, she was legally no longer a member of her father's family. This unusual problem Mother solved by inviting her to remain in our home as a daughter; which she did until finally Mother arranged a good marriage for her.

In a childish way I wondered about all the strangeness, but years had passed before I connected it with the sudden going away at this time of a graceful little maid named Tama, who used to arrange flowers and perform light duties. Her merry laugh and ready tongue made her a favourite with the entire household. Tama was not a servant. In those days it was the custom for daughters of wealthy tradesmen to be sent to live for a short time in a house of rank, that the maiden might learn the strict etiquette of samurai home life. This position was far from menial. A girl living with a family for social education was always treated with respectful consideration.

The morning after my brother went away I was going, as usual, to pay my morning greetings to my father when I met Tama coming from his door, looking pale and startled. She bowed good morning to me and then passed quietly on. That afternoon I missed her and Ishi told me that she had gone home.

Whatever may have been between my brother and Tama I never knew; but I cannot but feel that, guilt or innocence, there was somewhere a trace of courage. My brother was weak, of course, to prolong his heart struggle until almost the last moment, but he must have had much of his father's strong character to enable him, even then, to break with the traditions of his rigid training and defy his father's command. In that day there could be only a hopeless ending to such an affair, for no marriage was legal without the consent of parents, and my father, with heart wounded and pride shamed, had declared that he had no son.

It was not until several years later that I heard again of my brother. One afternoon Father was showing me some twisting tricks with a string. I was kneeling close beside his cushion, watching his rapidly moving hands and trying to catch his fingers in my own. Mother was sitting near with her sewing, and all three of us were laughing.

A maid came to the door to say that Major Sato, a Tokyo gentleman whom my father knew very well, had called. I slipped back by Mother. She started to leave the room, but Father motioned her not to go, and so we both remained.

I shall never forget that scene. Major Sato, speaking with great earnestness, told how my brother had gone to Tokyo and entered the Army College. With only his own efforts he had completed the course with honour and was now a lieutenant. There Major Sato paused.

My father sat very still with his head held high and absolutely no expression on his stern face. For a full minute the room was so silent that I could hear myself breathe. Then my father, still without moving, asked quietly, "Is your message delivered, Major Sato?"

"It is finished," was the reply.

"Your interest is appreciated, Major Sato. This is my answer: I have daughters, but no son."

Mother had sat perfectly quiet throughout, with her head bowed and her hands tightly clasped in her lap. When Father spoke she gave a little shudder but did not move.

Presently Father turned toward her. "Wife," he said very gently, "ask Ishi to bring the *go* board, and send wine to the honourable guest."

Whatever was in the heart of either man, they calmly played the game to the end, and Mother and I sat there in the deep silence as motionless as statues.

That night when Ishi was helping me undress, I saw tears in her eyes.

"What troubles you, Ishi?" I asked. "Why do you almost cry?"

She sank to her knees, burying her face in her sleeves, and for the only time in my life I heard Ishi wail like a servant. "Oh , Little Mistress, Little Mistress," she sobbed, "I am not sad. I am glad. I am thankful to the gods that I am lowly born and can cry when my heart is filled with ache and can laugh when my heart sings. Oh, my dear, dear Mistress! My poor, poor Master!" And she still sobbed.

That was all long ago, and now, after many years, my brother was coming back to his home.

The snow went away, the spring passed and summer was with us. It seemed a long, long wait, but at last came a day when the shrine doors were opened early in the morning and the candles kept burning steadily hour after hour, for Grandmother wanted the presence of the ancestors in the welcome to the wanderer, and as the trip from Tokyo was by jinrikisha and *kago* in those days, the time of arrival was very uncertain. But at last the call "Honourable return!" at the gateway brought everyone except Grandmother to the entrance. We all bowed our faces to the floor, but nevertheless I saw a man in foreign dress jump from his jinrikisha, give a quick look around, and then walk slowly up the old stone path toward us. He stopped at one place and smiled as he pulled a tuft of the little blossoms growing between the stones. But he threw it away at once and came on.

The greetings at the door were very short. Brother and Mother bowed, he speaking gently to her and she looking at him with a smile that had tears close behind. Then he laughingly called me "the same curly-haired, round-faced Etsu-bo."

His foreign shoes were removed by Jiya, and we went in. Of course, he went to the shrine first. He bowed and did everything just right, but too quickly, and some way I felt troubled. Then he went to Grandmother's room.

Immediately after greetings were over, Grandmother handed him Father's lacquer letter-box. He lifted it to his forehead with formal courtesy; then, taking out the letter, he slowly unrolled it and, with a strange expression, sat looking at the writing. I was shocked to feel that I could not know whether that look meant bitterness, or amusement, or hopelessness. It seemed to be a combination of all three. The message was very short. In a trembling hand was written: "You are now the head of Inagaki. My son, I trust you." That was all.

That evening a grand dinner was served in our best room. Brother sat next the *tokonoma*. All the near relatives were there, and we had the kind of food Brother used to like. There was a great deal of talking, but he was rather quiet, although he told us some things about America. I watched him as he talked. His strange dress with tight sleeves and his black stockings suggested kitchen people, and he sat cross-legged on his cushion. His voice was rather loud and he had a quick way of look ing from one person to another that was almost startling. I felt a little troubled and uncertain—almost disappointed; for in some puzzling way he was different from what I wanted him to be. But one thing I loved at once. He had the same soft twinkle in his eyes when he smiled that Father had. Every time I saw that, I felt that however different from Father he might look—or be—he really had the lovable part of Father in his heart. And in spite of a vague fear, I knew, deep, deep down, that whatever might happen in the days, or years, to come, I should always love him and should always be true to him. And I always have.

CHAPTER-8

Two Ventures

MY BROTHER'S coming introduced an entirely new and exciting element into our home. This was the letters which he occasionally received from friends in America. The letters were dull, for they told of nothing but people and business; so after the first few I lost all interest in them. But the big, odd-shaped envelopes and the short pages of thick paper covered with faint pen-writing held a wonderful fascination. None of us had even seen a pen or any kind of writing-paper except our rolls of thin paper with the narrow envelopes. We could write a letter of any length, sometimes several feet, on that paper. We began at the right side and, using a brush, wrote in vertical lines, unrolling from the left as we wrote. The graceful black characters standing out against a back ground all white, but shaded by the varying thickness of the paper into a mass of delicate, misty blossoms, were very artistic. In later years we had flowered paper in colours, but when I was a child only white was considered dignified.

Brother always used the large, odd-shaped envelopes for letters to America; so I supposed that kind was necessary. One day he asked me to hand to the postman a letter enclosed in one of our narrow envelopes, embossed with a graceful branch of maple leaves. I was greatly surprised when I saw that it had an expensive stamp on the corner and was addressed to America.

"Honourable Brother," I hesitatingly asked, "will Government allow this letter to go?"

"Why not?"

"I thought only big envelopes could be used for letters to America."

"Nonsense!" he said crossly. And then he added in a kind tone, "I haven't any more, and those I sent for to Tokyo, haven't come."

And so the delicate maple leaves went to America and my girlish heart was pleased. It was the first pleasant bond between the two countries of which I had known.

There was nothing definite in my mind against America, but I was so constantly hearing allusions to the disagreeable experiences of almost all persons who had dealings with foreigners that I had a vague feeling of distaste for the unknown land. This impression was strengthened by odd stories told by servants of "red-faced, light-haired barbarians who had no heels and had to prop up their shoes with artificial blocks."

It was said that animals were eaten whole by these strange people, and that the master of a lordly house often entertained his guests by cutting up a cooked eagle in their presence. It was also rumoured that the cheap red blankets extensively imported at that time were dyed with the blood of stolen infants. One report, which was widespread, in city and country alike, was that the peculiar animal odour of foreigners was caused by the eating of flesh. This probably originated from the unfamiliar odour of wool noticed in the damp clothing of foreign sailors. Since we had neither sheep nor woollen cloth in Japan, the unfamiliar odour was naturally associated with the person who carried the scent about with him. The name has clung, and even yet it is not uncommon for country people, inquiring in a store for woollen cloth, to ask for "animal-smelling goods."

Brother denied very few of these tales. I think many of them he believed, even after having lived in America. Apparently he had met while there very few people except those engaged in buying and selling. Once Grandmother said, with a sigh, "Your honourable brother seems to have learned only the ways of tradesmen in far-away America. But," she added thoughtfully, "perhaps it is a land where only tradesmen live."

He had been to America, but we did not realize that he had seen only one small portion of one coast city in that great land.

As time passed on, Brother seemed to withdraw from our family life, and yet he did not fall into the life of the people of Nagaoka. He was different from everybody. Sometimes he looked troubled and anxious, but more often he was only restless and dissatisfied. At such times he frequently came and sat beside me as I sewed or studied, and I think he talked more freely to me than to any one else. Occasionally, though not often, he spoke of himself, and gradually I learned much of what his life had been since he left home.

His going to America was due to the craze for foreign business which had struck Tokyo so forcefully about the time Brother left the army. Many young men, confident of rapid and brilliant success, were launching out in various directions, and someone induced Brother to invest all he had in what was represented to be a large export company having offices in

America. He was offered a partnership if he would take charge of the business there. Like most men of his rank, he had no realization of his own ignorance of business methods; so he accepted and set sail for America. On reaching his destination he found that he had been defrauded. The export company was only a small toy-shop situated in a crowded Japanese district and kept by the wife of a workman who knew nothing of the promised partnership.

Astonished and disappointed, Brother made his way to a near-by hotel—a pretty poor place, he said—where many Japanese men were talking and playing games. They were mostly workmen or cheap clerks of a humble class with almost no education. But they were most respectful to him, and, though the surroundings were uncongenial, he knew no other place to go. In a short time he had spent all his money, and, knowing nothing of any kind of work, and almost nothing of the English language, he easily drifted downward into the life of those around him.

Some men would have pushed up through the mud and found light, but my brother knew little of foreigners, he had no ambitions regarding them, and what he saw of them where he was only repelled him.

Sometimes he left the crowded district where he lived and strolled through wide streets where there were tall buildings and big stores. There he saw foreign people, but they either paid no attention to him or looked at him as he himself would look at a coolie at home. This amused him; for, to him, the strange-looking men who hurried by him, talking in loud voices and smoking large, ill-smelling tobacco rolls, or chewing horrible stuff that they blew out of their mouths on to the street, were wholly disgusting. The women were queerly dressed creatures who stared, and laughed with their mouths open. Nothing seemed delicate or refined, only big and strong and coarse. Everything repelled his artistic soul; so he drifted back to his uncongenial—but understandable—surroundings.

Then Fate stepped in. My brother was hurt by an accidental blow on the head, which sent him to a hospital for three blessed, cool, clean weeks. The day he was dismissed and, sick at heart, was slowly walking toward the only place he knew to go—his old quarters—he turned a corner and suddenly came face to face with a young man, vigorous and brisk, walking with a quick step. The man laughed aloud as both abruptly came to a standstill; then, seeing how pale and ill Brother looked, he turned and walked with him.

However shabbily my brother might be dressed, he always had the bearing of a gentleman, and recognizing this, the young man, whose name was Matsuo, insisted on taking Brother to his own room. A few days later he found a place for him in a store where he himself was foreman, and the acquaintance thus begun ripened into a warm and lasting friendship.

Had this help been given when Brother first reached America, the high-bred, delicately reared youth, although over-indulged and unwisely trained for practical life, might have won his puzzling way through all the strangeness; but it was now too late. That accidental blow on the head had caused a damage, which, though not apparent at first, gradually developed into a trouble that unfitted him for steady work; and my poor brother was never the same again. But Matsuo was steadfastly kind.

Then came a message from Major Sato in Tokyo, saying Father was ill and wanted his son to return home. Of what was in my brother's heart then I know nothing, but for many weeks he delayed his reply. Then he came.

That autumn our year of mourning was over, and Brother, being home to take the place of Father, Sister's marriage was planned for harvest time. The season, however, was early. Rice patches throughout Echigo were bowing with rich promise early in October, but of course, nobody was ever married in the no-god month, so the first good-luck day in November was chosen.

It is during October that the marriage gods all meet in Idzumo temple to join the names of those who are to wed. One of the favourite stories for grandmothers and nurses to tell little girls is about a youth of olden time who was so unfortunate as to have no parents or elder brother. There being no one to arrange a marriage for him, he grew to the age of twenty and was still a bachelor.

One October day he decided to visit Idzumo temple to see if his name was coupled with that of any maiden. So, taking with him, as a gift, the first rice-sheaf of his harvest, he started on his long day's journey. As he approached the temple steps he heard voices. Names were being called like counting: "He; she." "He; she." He recognized the name of a young man he knew; then another, and another—each paired off with the name of a young woman.

"*Maa! Maa!*" whispered the astonished youth, "I have intruded upon a meeting of the gods."

But his interest was too great to allow him to retreat. Creeping between the ornamental posts that supported the floor, he listened, guiltily, but with anxious hope.

Another two names! Another! "He; she." " He; she"—but alas! not his own.

Finally a voice of authority announced, "These are planned. Our last day is almost gone and our work for the year is ended."

"Wait a moment," said another voice. "There is Taro. Again he is left. Cannot we find a maiden for him?"

The youth's heart gave a bound, for he was Taro.

"Oh, troublesome!" impatiently cried a god. "Again comes that name!"

"We need not haste. He has no one to arrange for him," said another.

"His name must go uncoupled for another year," came from a distant corner. "There is no maiden left."

"Wait!" spoke the first voice. "In Chestnut Village a girl has just been born in the house of the village master. The family is of higher class, but let us give her to Taro. Then our work will be done."

"Yes! yes!" cried all the gods. "Put the names together and we will hasten to the duties of our own shrines."

"Our work for the year is ended," spoke the voice of authority.

The youth crept away, excited and indignant, and sorely diappointed.

As he trudged slowly along the road on his homeward way, both disappointment and indignation grew, but when he came in sight of Chestnut Village and saw the comfort able house of the village master with its thick thatch and large screen heavy with drying sheafs of rice, his anger lessened and he thought, "After all, it is not so bad!" He walked slowly by the open door. A child's bed of cushions was just within. He saw a baby's face and a tiny close-shut hand.

"Twelve years, at least, to wait!" he suddenly cried. "I will not have it so! I will defy the gods!" On the *tokonoma* was a sword-rest holding the single sword of a humble vassal. Grasping it, he made a quick thrust through the cushions, and bounding through the door, he hurried on his way.

Years passed. Fate was kind and Taro prospered, but no bride could he find. More years passed. At last, patiently accepting bachelorhood as a punishment for his defiance of the gods, he became resigned.

Then a surprising thing happened. A go-between called with the offer of a bride—beautiful, industrious, dutiful. Taro was delighted. Negotiations were carried through; the bride came; the marriage took place and the young wife proved all that the happy Taro could wish. One warm day, when she was sewing on the porch, she loosened her collar folds and Taro saw an odd curving scar on her neck.

"What is it?" he asked.

"That is a strange mystery," said the bride, smiling. "When I was only a babe, my grandmother heard me cry, and coming, found my father's sword on the floor and I with this curving cut across my neck and shoulder. No one was near, and it was never learned how it happened. My grandmother said that I was marked by the gods for some wise purpose. And so it must be," concluded the wife as she leaned again over her sewing.

Taro walked thoughtfully away. Again he saw the baby face and the tiny close-shut hand; and he realized how hopeless it is to try to thwart the decree of the gods.

When Ishi told us this story, she always closed with, "And so you see it is useless not to accept gratefully the will of the gods. What is planned must be obeyed."

When the day of Sister's wedding came, we were all greatly excited; but the real excitement of a Japanese marriage is at the house of the bridegroom, as it is there that the wedding takes place. However, the ceremony of leaving home is always elaborate, and for several days our entire house was filled with the sound of people ordering and people obeying. Then came a day when Taki, Ishi, and Toshi were busy for hours, all three folding bedding and packing bridal chests; and the next day the procession of bridal belongings went swinging out of our gateway and on over the mountain to Sister's home-to-be.

Two days later Sister went away. The hairdresser came very early that morning, for the bride's hair had to be arranged in the elaborate married style with wonderful ornaments of tortoise-shell and coral. Then her face and neck were covered with thick white powder and she was dressed in a robe and sash of white—the death colour—because marriage means the bride's death to her father's family. Beneath this was a garment of scarlet, the dress of a new-born babe, typical of her birth into her husband's family. Mother had on her beautiful crest dress, and Brother looked like Father in the ceremonious pleated linen skirt and stiff shoulder-piece of the *kamishimo*. I was so glad to see him look like Father.

Just as the bridal palanquin was brought to the door, we all went to the shrine for Sister to say farewell to the spirit of our ancestors, for, after marriage, she would belong no longer to our family, but to her husband's. She bowed alone before the shrine. Then Mother slipped over the mat to her side and presented her with a beautiful mirror-case, the kind that all Japanese ladies wear with ceremonial dress. Sister's was beautiful mosaic-work of crêpe in a pattern of pine, bamboo, and plum. It had been made by our great-grandmother's own hands. Inside it was a small mirror. A brocade-covered crystal hung from it on a silk cord and, on the edge of the case, slipped under the band, was a long silver hairpin. In olden days this was a dagger. These are emblematic of the mirror, the jewel, and the sword of the Imperial regalia.

As Mother handed the mirror-case to Sister, she said the same words that every mother says to a bride. She told her that now she was to go forth bravely to her new life, just as a soldier goes to battle. "Look in the mirror every day," she said, "for if scars of selfishness or pride are in the heart, they will grow into the lines of the face. Watch closely. Be strong like the pine, yield in gentle obedience like the swaying bamboo, and yet, like the fragrant plum blossoming beneath the snow, never lose the gentle perseverance of loyal womanhood."

I never saw my mother so moved, but poor Sister looked only blank and expressionless beneath the stiff white powder.

We all bowed deeply at the door. Sister entered the palanquin and the next moment was hidden behind the reed screen of the little window. Her own nurse, who should have come next, had married and gone far away, so Ishi took her place and entered the first jinrikisha. The go-between and his wife were in the next two, and then came Brother and Mother. The procession started, Toshi sprinkled salt on the doorstep just as if a corpse had been carried out, and mingling with the sound of rolling wheels and the soft thud of trotting feet came Grandmother's trembly old voice singing the farewell part of the wedding-song:

"From the shore
A boat with lifted sail
Rides toward the rising moon.
On waves of ebbing tide it sails,
The shadow of the land falls backward,
And the boat sails farther—farther——"

So ended Sister's life as an Inagaki; for however often she might visit us after this, and however lovingly and informally she might be treated, she would never again be anything but a guest.

Long afterward Sister told me of her trip to her new home. It was only a few hours long, but she had to go over a mountain, and the palanquin jolted fearfully. She said her greatest anxiety was to keep her head, laden with the heavy shell bars, from bumping against the cushions and disarranging her elaborately dressed hair. Finally the carriers were trotting along evenly on a smooth road, then they came to a stop and Ishi pushed up the reed screen of the window.

"Young Mistress," she said, "we have reached the halting place where we are to rest before presenting ourselves to the house of the honourable bridegroom."

Mother and Ishi helped Sister out, and they all went into a good-sized but simple farmhouse. They were received most graciously by the hostess, who was a distant relative of the bridegroom's family. There they had dinner, each person being served with red rice and a small fish, head and all—meaning Congratulation. Ishi freshened up Sister's dress, looked over her sash, examined her hair, and retouched her powdered face. Then the procession moved slowly on, up a long sloping hill. At the top they were met by the "seven-and-a-half-times" courier and soon reached the big gateway with its crest banner and lanterns of welcome. She was conscious of being on a stone path when the carriers placed the palanquin to the ground. She could see nothing, but she knew that in a moment the little window in the front would be opened and the bridegroom's face would appear. Then he would strike the top of the palanquin with his fan, which would mean Welcome.

There was usually no delay, but this bridegroom was a bashful youth, only seventeen, and they had to go for him. Sister said that in those few minutes of waiting, she, for the first time, was frightened. Then she heard swift footsteps and the next moment the little reed screen was jerked open. She ought to have sat quietly, with her eyes cast modestly down, but she was startled and gave one quick glance upward. In that instant's time she saw a pale, pock-marked face with a broad low brow and close-pressed lips.

Down went the screen and, without a second's pause, "clap! clap!" came a nervous slap of the fan above her head.

The palanquin was lifted and carried to the door.

Sister, within, sat strangely calm, for in that instant of lifted screen her fright had slipped away—for ever.

The door was reached. The palanquin was lowered to the ground. Sister was helped out, and as she entered her life home, two old voices completed the wedding-song with the words of welcome:

"On the sea
A boat with lifted sail
Rides toward the rising moon.
On the waves of the flowing tide it comes.
The shadow of the past lies far behind,
And the boat sails nearer—nearer
To the shore called Happy Life."

CHAPTER-9

The Story of a Marionette

ON THE first day of Ura Bon, when I was twelve years old, Ishi brought a new ornament for my hair and placed it just in front of my big, stand-up bow-knot. It was a silver shield set in a mass of small, loose silver flowers, and looked very beautiful against the shiny black background.

"It was sent to you by Honourable Yedo Grand mother," she said. "She had it made from melted ancient coins, and it is very wonderful."

I turned my face in the direction of Tokyo and bowed a silent "Thank you" to the kind invisible donor. Just who Honourable Yedo Grandmother was I did not know. Each year, ever since I could remember, I had received a beautiful gift from her for our midsummer festival of Ura Bon, and, in a vague way, I was conscious that our family had some close connection with her; but I gave it no thought. All little girls had grandmothers. Some had two and some still more. Of course, grandmothers on the mother's side lived elsewhere, but it was not unusual for a father to have both his mother and grandmother living in his home. Old people were always welcome, their presence giving dignity to the family. The house of a son who had the care of three generations of parents was called "the honoured seat of the aged."

Ura Bon—(A Welcome to Souls Returned)—was our festival to celebrate the annual visit of O Shorai Sama, a term used to represent the combined spirits of all our ancestors. It was the most dearly loved of our festivals, for we believed that our ancestors never lost their loving interest in us, and this yearly visit kept fresh in all our hearts a cheerful and affectionate nearness to the dear ones gone.

In preparing for the arrival of O Shorai Sama the only standards were cleanliness and simplicity; everything being done in an odd primitive fashion, not elaborated, even in the slightest degree, from Bon festivals of the most ancient time.

For several days everyone had been busy. Jiya and another man had trimmed the trees and hedges, had swept all the ground, even under the house, and had carefully washed off the stepping stones in the garden. The floor mats were taken out and whipped dustless with bamboo switches, Kin and Toshi, in the meantime, making the air resound with the "pata-pata-pata" of paper dusters against the *shoji*, and the long-drawn-out "see-wee-is-shi" of steaming hot padded cloths pushed up and down the polished porch floors. All the woodwork in the house—the broad ceiling boards, the hundreds of tiny white bars crossing the paper doors, the carved ventilators, and the mirror-like post and platform of the *tokonomas*—was wiped off with hot water; then every little broken place in the rice-paper *shoji* was mended, and finally the entire house, from thatch to the under-floor ice-box, was as fresh and clean as rain-water falling from the sky.

Mother brought from the godown a rare old *kakemono*, one of Father's treasures, and after it was hung Kin placed beneath it our handsomest bronze vase holding a big loose bunch of the seven grasses of autumn—althea, pampas, convolvulus, wild pink, and three kinds of asters, purple, yellow, and white. These are mostly flowers, but Japanese designate all plants that grow from the ground in slender, blade-like leaves, as grasses.

The shrine was, of course, the most important of all, as it was there the spirit guest lived during the days of the visit. Jiya had gone to the pond before dawn to get lotus blossoms, for it is only with the first rays of sunrise that the "puff" comes, which opens the pale green buds into snowy beauty. Before he returned, the shrine had been emptied and cleaned, and the bronze Buddha reverentially dusted and returned to his place on the gilded lotus. The tablet holding the ancestors' names, and Father's picture, which Mother always kept in the shrine, were wiped off carefully, the brass open-work "everlasting light" lantern filled afresh with rape-seed oil, the incense burner, the candle stands, the sacred books, and our rosaries, all arranged in place, and the ugly fish-mouth wooden drum, which is typical of woman's submissive position, rubbed until the worn place on the red lacquer was a shiny brown. Then Jiya covered the floor before the shrine with a fresh, rudely woven mat of pampas grass and placed on either side a vase holding bunches of the seven grasses of autumn.

But the most interesting time of all came when Honourable Grandmother and I sat down before the shrine to prepare the decorations of welcome. I always loved to help her do this. Ishi and Toshi brought us some odd-shaped vegetables they had found in the garden, a handful of dried hemp stems from which the bark had been removed, and yards and yards of *somen*—a sort of soft, pliable macaroni. Honourable Grandmother took a crooked-necked cucumber, one end of which was shaped something like a lifted head, and made it into a horse, using corn silk for mane and tail and hemp stems for stiff little legs. Of a small, plump eggplant she made a water buffalo, with horns and legs of hemp stems, and twisting some half-dried *somen* into harness for both little animals, she placed them in the shrine. I made several horses and buffaloes too. While we were working, Jiya came in with some small lotus leaves, the edges of which were beginning to dry and turn up like little curved dishes, and a few very small yellow and red balls, a new kind of fruit, which I now know were tomatoes.

After Ishihad filled the lotus-leaf dishes with vegetables and every kind of fruit except the furry peach, Honourable Grandmother looped the *somen* across the top of the shrine in a series of graceful festoons, hanging on it at intervals small purple eggplants and the tiny yellow and red tomatoes.

Then Ishi brought the kitchen "row-of-steps," and climbing up, hung the white Bon lantern high above every thing. It was only a white paper cube, twisted about with a braid of paper having loose ends; but when it was lighted the heat made it constantly whirl, and the many ends of paper rising, falling, and waving looked like a flock of tiny fluttering birds. It was very beautiful.

The meaning of the decorations and the queer little vegetable animals has been lost in the mist of past years, but the lotus-leaf shape of the dishes was because the lotus is a sacred flower. The Buddhist bible tells this story of Buddha's time of temptation when he was living as a hermit on the Mount of Snow.

One day, at the hour of dawn, he was sitting in meditation, when he heard a strange, sweet song. As he listened wonder and joy crept into his heart, for in the notes of the melody was slowly unfolding the plan of salvation. Suddenly it ceased. In vain he waited. All was silence. Hurrying to the edge of a precipice he peered into the mists of the valley and there saw a horrible demon who turned a taunting face toward the disappointed and anxious prophet. Earnestly the Buddha begged for the remainder of the song, but the demon said that he could sing no more until his hunger was satisfied with human flesh and his thirst with human blood. Then would he sing the mystic plan, until the knowledge of salvation had reached all humankind.

The Buddha's dearest vision that he himself should bring the message to the world faded into nothingness, and eagerly he cried, "Satisfy thy hunger with my flesh, and quench thy thirst with my blood; but continue thy song until every soul is saved!" and casting off his robe he sprang from the rock.

A sudden gleam of sunshine lighted the valley and touched the waters of a pool where was floating a lotus with spreading leaves and one unopened bud. As the holy prophet fell through the air, the bud burst suddenly into bloom, and on its snowy petals softly sank the one who was to give to more than one third of the world a faith far better than any they had known.

The raised centre of the lotus, even now, is called *utena*, which means "seat," and lotus blossoms, either natural or artificial, are always before every Buddhist shrine.

Just before sunset we were all ready, for twilight was the hour of welcome. O Shorai Sama was always spoken of as a vague, impersonal figure who came riding on a snow-white steed from "the land of darkness, the shores of the unknown, the place of the dead."

Like all children I had always looked forward with pleasure to the visit of the ancestors, but after Father's death, I felt a deep personal interest, and my heart was beating with excitement, as the family met at the shrine. Each one, even the servants, wore a new dress—simple and inexpensive, but new. As twilight deepened, the shrine lantern was lighted, the *shoji* pushed back, and the entrance doors opened; thus leaving a free path from the outside road all the way to the shrine.

Then we started, walking two by two through the open door, across the hall, down the step of the "shoe-off" place and along the stone walk to the big entrance gates, which were open wide. In the centre of the gateway Jiya had criss-crossed a little pile of hemp stems—just thirteen—around a tiny heap of fluffy dried grass. When we reached this we parted, Jiya and Yoshita going on one side of the path, and on the other, Honourable Grandmother, Mother, myself, and Ishi, Kin, and Toshi. Then, all respectfully stooping, we bowed our heads and waited. Brother was in Tokyo, so Honourable Grandmother, with Ishi's help, struck the fire of purity with flint and steel, and the dropping sparks lighted the hemp stems into a blaze of welcome.

All the town was silent and dusky except for hundreds of tiny fires, for one was blazing at every gateway. As I bowed, my longing heart seemed to pull my father to me. Through the distance I could hear the sound of soft, galloping feet, and I knew the snow-white steed was nearing. The moment's blaze of the hemp-stem fire was dying, a faint breath of warm August wind struck my cheek, and peace crept into my heart. Slowly we rose and with bowed heads walked back, on the outside edges of the path, two by two—but wide apart—leaving the sacred space of the walk between. When we reached the shrine Mother struck the gong and we all bowed with the dignified cheerfulness of our usual greeting to a welcome guest. We seemed so few since even the year before, and how cordially our hearts welcomed the presence which we knew would bring into our home cheerful companionship for the happy and helpful comfort for the sorrowful.

The next two days the town was full of lanterns. Everybody carried one, every house was decorated with them, every street was lined with them, and at night the cemeteries were filled with glow-worm lights; for every grave had above it a tiny white lantern swinging from an arch made from stems of pampas grass. It was a happy time for all Japan, and the one day in the year when no life was taken of fish, fowl, or even insect. The fishermen idly wandered about arrayed in holiday garments, the chickens cackled and crowed in their bamboo cages, and the little crickets, which children love to keep in tiny cages, sang their shrill song in the trees without the approach of a single sticky-topped pole. And charity extended loving arms to the farthest limit. No priest passed with an empty begging bowl; pampas-woven baskets of food were hidden beneath lotus leaves on the graves, waiting for the poor to carry away when the Bon lights had burned out; and even the sinners in hell, if their hearts longed for salvation, were given another chance during the merciful days of Bon.

Our home was filled with an atmosphere of pleasant thoughts, unselfish acts, and happy laughter; for we felt that our kind guests enjoyed our simple pleasures of new clothes, company courtesies, and our daily feasts with them of the shrine food consisting of fruits, vegetables, and rice dumplings. Honourable Grandmother's face grew more peaceful each hour, Mother's beamed with calm content, the servants were chattering and smiling all the time, and my heart was full of quiet joy.

In the shadows before sunrise of the fourth day, Jiya went for lotus blossoms, and Mother placed fresh food before the shrine. When the brightening air outside began to quarrel with the soft white lantern inside we gathered for the farewell.

The past days had been happy ones and I think we all felt sad when, after the last deep bows, Mother rose and lifted the pampas mat from before the shrine. She doubled and flattened it, then tied the ends with grass, thus forming a rude little canoe, and fixed a hemp-stem arch in the centre. The lotus-leaf dishes of food were placed within, and some balls of rice and uncooked dough added, as O Shorai Sama's gift to the birds. Then the little vegetable animals and all the decorations of the shrine were put in, the white fluttering lantern was swung from the arch, and, with Jiya carrying the little canoe, Mother and I, followed by Ishi and Toshi, went to the river.

Morning was just dawning, but the streets were full of people and the air crowded with circling birds who seemed to know that a treat was before them. When we reached the bank, all except Jiya took their places on the bridge and watched him make his way down the slippery steps cut in the bank, and join the throng below. Each person was holding a little canoe with its burden of food and tiny swinging lantern.

"Look," whispered Ishi, as Jiya lifted his hands to strike the flint and steel to light our little lantern, "our honourable ancestors will embark on the first tide warmed by the sunrise."

The silence was unbroken except for the loud cries of the birds, then a sudden ray of sunlight shot across a distant mountain and hundreds of figures stooped and launched the little canoes. All stood watching as they whirled and drifted along in the midst of the storm of darting birds screaming their thanks. One upset.

"My O Shorai Sama has stepped off and is now in the unknown land!" said an old lady, and waiting no longer, she climbed the bank and contentedly made her way home.

As daylight brightened we could see the little boats far in the distance rising and falling, the tiny white lanterns swinging back and forth. We waited until the sun broke into brilliance; then, as the light came racing down the mountain-side, a soft, deep murmur rose from the bowing figures all along the shores.

"Farewell, O Shorai Sama," we all gently called. "Come again next year. We will be waiting to welcome you!"

The crowd scattered, and with satisfied faces, made their way homeward.

Mother and I walked happily along, with Ishi, Toshi, and Jiya chatting pleasantly behind us. The anxious look that Mother's face had lost during the last few days did nor come back, and I felt that Father had really been with us bringing comfort and help to us all; and now he had gone, leaving behind him, not loneliness, but peace.

That afternoon, as Ishi was putting away my flower hair-ornament, she pointed to the shield of polished silver set in the midst of the flowers. A crest was carved deeply in it, and the cut edges sparkled like jewels.

"It is not the Inagaki crest," I said.

"No, it is the birth crest of Honourable Yedo Grandmother," said she, closing the little box and putting it away. "It is very wonderful work. Everything Honourable Yedo Grandmother has ever given you is especially beautiful or rare."

"Honourable Yedo Grandmother never sends a gift to my father or to my mother," I said.

"No. To no one but you," Ishi replied. "She always remembers you on the festival to welcome and honour the ancestors of the Inagaki."

I remembered long afterward that a faint wonder passed through my mind at that time that I should be the one member of the family who ever received a gift from Honourable Yedo Grandmother, but it lasted only a moment. A Japanese child rarely asked what was not told, and there were so many taken-for-granted things in Japanese life, anyway, that I gave the matter no further thought.

Not until I was grown did I learn that Honourable Yedo Grandmother was my father's own mother, and that my dear Honourable Grandmother, to whom I owed so much, was in reality my great-grandmother.

When my grandfather died suddenly, leaving Father, at the age of seven, as his heir, Honourable Grandmother became the mistress of her dead son's home and the mother of his child. That the young widow, Father's mother, did not remain in her own home, was one of the tragedies of our family system, which, wise as it was when made, has resulted in many wrongs, as must always be the case when the world moves too swiftly and customs slowly lag behind.

The Restoration of 1868 was not a sudden event. There had been political agitation for years, in which the world of Japan was divided into two factions—those who believed that the Imperial power should include both sacred and secular duties, and those who believed the shogun, as military ruler, should take all national burdens from the shoulders of the sacred Emperor.

My grandfather believed in the restoration of Imperial power, but his wife's father, being a *hatamoto*—body-guard of the shogun—was, of course, a strong advocate of the opposing party. Personally, the two men were friends, but each was strongly loyal to his own principles and to his overlord.

Grandfather's death took place very suddenly when he was in Tokyo (then called Yedo) on official duty. It is said that he was taken violently and mysteriously ill just after being elaborately entertained at the mansion of his father-in-law. At the feast were present a number of ardent politicians. That my grandfather understood the political significance of the gathering was shown, when, after his death, it was discovered that he had gone to the feast wearing beneath his usual ceremonial dress his white death robe.

In those days, when the heart of Japan was beating violently and she was pushing hard against the set, but questioned, control of ages, such an event was not so unusual; nor was my grandfather's quiet acceptance of his fate so rare. It was only samurai loyalty to a cause, and samurai bravery in accepting defeat. Standards differ in different countries, but everywhere we are expected to be loyal and to be brave.

But the tragedy of it came to the girl wife—my grandmother, who was little more than twenty years old when she became a widow. Under ordinary circumstances she would have been the honoured widow-mother of the seven-year-old heir—my father; but because of the well-understood though outwardly ignored situation, there was but one thing for this proud, deeply humiliated woman to do. Whether she was the sacrifice of her father's ambition, or of his loyalty, I do not know, but she "humbly abdicated" from her husband's family, and changing her name Inagaki to the death name, returned to her former home. According to the ideals of that time, this was the most dishonoured position that any samurai woman could hold. It was scorned as would be that of a soldier who goes bravely to the battlefield and cowardly returns home before fighting has begun.

For a few years the young widow lived a quiet life in her father's home devoting her time to classic literature and cultural attainments; then she was offered an important position as lady official in the mansion of the daimio of Satsuma.

This was just the time when Satsuma was playing a conspicuous part in history. It was this daimiate which, single-handed, challenged the entire British Eastern Squadron, after the young samurai of the clan had killed Mr. Richardson, a British merchant who boldly crossed the ceremonial procession of their overlord. Satsumawas the most powerful daimio in Japan and his home, like all high-rank houses during feudal days, was divided into two distinct departments: the State and the Home. The government of the Home Department was entirely under lady officials; and in large mansions with many retainers these lady officers had to be as efficient as the officials of the State Department. Among these able retainers my grandmother occupied an honoured place.

Very soon her special gifts were recognized and she was chosen as governess to the little girl-princess, a position which she held until her charge became a bride-elect and required teachers for wifehood training. Then my grandmother, generously pensioned for life, was "honourably released," this farewell being poetically worded "the regretted disappearance of the full moon behind folds of cloud, leaving in her wake soft, wide spreading shafts of light, to remain with us always, as gentle and lasting memories."

I never saw Honourable Yedo Grandmother with my human eyes, but I can see her always when I look into my heart. Living in the largest daimio mansion in Japan, surrounded by wealth and luxury, in the midst of daily expressed appreciation of her culture and her natural gifts and with the respect and affection of her much-loved young princess always with her, yet her thoughts turned to the little granddaughter whom she never saw. It was not altogether the call of love, though I like to think that that was there also.

Her life work, through no fault or neglect of her own, had been taken from her, but her broken duty she held firmly in her heart; and unflinchingly reaching out—as is the samurai way—she, as long as she lived, faithfully sent each year one of her closest personal possessions to the little granddaughter who was said to resemble her, even to her curly hair, to be worn in a welcome greeting to the spirits of the Inagaki family to whom she could no longer bow, but to whom her duty was due. Her helplessness was tragedy. Her efforts were pathos. But to her best, and to the last, she was true.

Standards of duty differ on opposite sides of the world, but Japanese people never finch at its call. Many a boy and girl not yet in their teens, many a man and woman at the time of brightest promise, many of the aged have gone alone to a distant province, and among strangers have become of them—body, brain , and spirit. But even among beautiful surroundings, if duty lies behind, undone, nothing, while life lasts, can break the heart pull, the brain planning, the soul prayer to reach, even partially, the lost goal. Such is the deep-hidden soul of Japan.

When the young princess bade farewell to my grand mother, she presented her, as the highest token of grateful and affectionate appreciation, something which she herself had worn—a dress bearing her own crest. Many years afterward, for the Bon festival when I was ten years old, my grandmother sent this choice treasure to me. I well remember that day. Ishi had taken me to my room to dress for the evening of welcome. Hanging over one of the large lacquer frames on which we spread our clothing to air or to wait until we were ready, was a beautiful summer dress of pale blue linen decorated with an exquisite design of the seven grasses of autumn. It seemed to me the most beautiful thing that I had ever seen in my life.

"Oh, Ishi," I cried, "is this beautiful dress for me?"

"Yes, Etsu-bo Sama. Honourable Yedo Grandmother has sent it to you for the festival."

It was too large for me and Toshi had to take deep tucks at the shoulders and waist. When I dressed I went to show myself to Honourable Grandmother and Mother, then I went to Father's room.

"I have come!" I announced, kneeling outside the closed door, ready to open it.

"Enter !" came the response from within.

I pushed back the *shoji*. Father was reading. He looked up with a smile; then what was my surprise to see him, after one glance at me, quickly slip from his cushion and with slow dignity dramatically announce, "Enter the Princess of Satsuma!".

Then he made a deep bow.

Of course my own little head was down to the floor in an instant, and though when I lifted it he was laughing, still I felt, in some subtle way, that there was something deeper beneath his smile than just his humorous obeisance to the crest of a superior clan: a combined pride and grief, and perhaps pain also—like the cruel ache in the heart of a strong man whose sword arm is helpless.

CHAPTER-10

The Day of the Bird

BROTHER had been at home a year when the letters from his friend in America began coming more frequently. After each one Grandmother, Brother, and Mother would have long talks, and not all of them were happy ones. In a vague way I sometimes thought these discussions had something to do with me; and one day was a little troubled when a long conference ended by Brother's abruptly coming out of the room with only a short bow that was almost rude. He started swiftly toward the door, then turning, came back and stood by my side, looking steadily at me for a moment. But he went on without saying a word.

Several weeks later a thick, heavy letter came, one with many stamps; and after another talk in Grandmother's room, Brother sent Jiya out with the long lacquer box tied with a cord which I knew held a "rounding letter" for all the relatives. Jiya would wait at each place for it to be read before carrying it on to the next place. That afternoon I noticed Mother was very thoughtful and quiet; and Grandmother sat by her fire-box, silent and stern, with her long, slender pipe in her hand. The tiny bowl held only three puffs, and, after refilling it twice, she always put it away, but she seemed to have forgotten it that day and sat holding it a long time.

The next day there was a meeting of the family council.

It has always been a Japanese custom to decide important family problems by calling an assembly of the older relatives. There had been family councils ever since I could remember, but, being the youngest of the family, and a girl, I was not concerned in them, and I never gave more than a passing thought as to whether this time it would mean the selling of another piece of land or of one of our roll pictures. We had been selling things all my life. Sister and I were so accustomed to seeing the second-hand man go into the big plaster storehouse with old Jiya that we made a practice of playing a guessing game as to whether he would come out with a small package in his hand or a big bundle on his shoulders. Mother used to look troubled when a group of men came to look at things, but Father would laugh and say, "Useless beauty had a place in the old life, but the new asks only for ugly usefulness."

But one thing Father never laughed about. Whenever negotiations were pending in regard to land he was always watchful. The outside limits of our once large estate had gradually been withdrawn within the wall, and year by year they were closing in nearer to the house; but Father would never part with any portion of the garden over looked by Grandmother's room. After his death Brother was equally considerate; so as long as she lived, Grandmother could gaze out upon the garden, the stream, and the little slope of azaleas against the background of feathery bamboo just as she had done for years.

This family council was the largest that had been held since Father's death. Two gray-haired uncles were there with the aunts, besides two other aunts, and a young uncle who had come all the way from Tokyo on purpose for this meeting. They had been in the room a long time, and I was busy writing at my desk when I heard a soft "Allow me to speak!" behind me, and there was Toshi at the door, looking rather excited .

"Little Mistress," she said with an unusually deep bow, "your honourable mother asks you to go to the room where the guests are."

I entered the big room. Brother was sitting by the *tokonoma*, and next to him were two gray-haired uncles and the young uncle from Tokyo. Opposite sat Honourable Grandmother, the four aunts, and Mother. Tea had been served and all had cups before them or in their hands. As I pushed back the door they looked up and gazed at me as if they had never seen me before. I was a little startled, but of course I made a low, ceremonious bow. Mother motioned to me, and I slipped over beside her on the mat.

"Etsu-ko," Mother said very gently, "the gods have been kind to you, and your destiny as a bride has been decided. Your honourable brother and your venerable kindred have given much thought to your future. It is proper that you should express your gratitude to the Honourable All."

I made a long, low bow, touching my forehead to the floor. Then I went out and returned to my desk and my writing. I had no thought of asking, "Who is it?" I did not think of my engagement as a personal matter at all. It was a family affair. Like every Japanese girl, I had known from babyhood that sometime, as a matter of course, I should marry, but that was a far-away necessity to be considered when the time came. I did not look forward to it. I did not dread it. I did not think of it at all. The fact that I was not quite thirteen had nothing to do with it. That was the attitude of all girls.

The formal ceremony of the betrothal took place some months later. It was not an elaborate affair, like a wedding, but was very important; for in old-fashioned families the betrothal was considered as sacred as the marriage itself, and indeed it could not be nearly so easily broken as might be the marriage tie.

There was an air of quiet excitement in the whole house that day. The servants, who always felt a personal interest in everything that happened in the family, had hung weather dolls of folded paper on the *nanten* bush near the porch, to insure sunshine, and were jubilant over the result; and even Mother, who always seemed more calm when she was excited, went around giving unnecessary directions to various maids. "Be careful in powdering Etsu-ko Sama's face," I heard her say to Ishi. "Get the paint smooth." And when the hairdresser arrived Mother made a second trip to the room to give a special order that Etsu-ko Sama's hair must be pulled *straight*.

As soon as I was dressed, I went to Grandmother's room for morning greetings. Her kindly smile was more gentle than usual, and we had a pleasant talk before breakfast was announced. As we were leaving the room she reminded me that it was the Day of the Bird.

"Yes, I know," I said. "A betrothal ceremony always takes place on the Day of the Bird. Honourable Grandmother, why is it?"

"Be not ambitious to be vain !" she said, smiling and resting her arm on my shoulder as we walked down the porch . "This day was chosen by your relatives with the kind wish that good fortune will bless your life with silks and brocades as plentiful as are the feathers of the birds."

Matsuo's aged uncle, Mr. Omori, had arrived from Kyoto a few days before and had been entertained at the home of the go-between. The ceremony had to take place in the waxing rather than the waning of the day; so about the middle of the forenoon, when I went into the best room, I found the others already assembled. Matsuo's uncle was seated on a cushion near the *tokonoma*. He sat very straight and had a pleasant face. I liked him. Grandmother, Brother, Mother, and the two go-betweens were there, and I sat beside Mother. The woman go-between brought to me a small white table with a square of crêpe over it, on which was Matsuo's crest. It was the engagement gift from his family, and I was looking for the first time upon the crest that I should have to wear all my life; but I did not seriously realize it. Another tray held other gifts, the most important of which was a pair of folding fans, signifying a wish for constantly widening happiness.

Then Toshi brought into the room two trays and set them before Mr. Omori. It was my family's gift to Matsuo.

Of course, I had been told exactly what to do; so I lifted the square of crêpe from my table, displaying a roll of magnificent brocade for a sash. On Mr. Omori's tables were the essential pair of fans and a wide-pleated silk skirt called *hakama*—the regulation dress for a Japanese gentleman. These have been the betrothal gifts from time immemorial.

I bowed most formal thanks, and Mr. Omori did the same. Then the gifts were placed on the *tokonoma*, and everybody, even Grandmother, made a slight bow and murmured, "Congratulations!"

Soon after, the maids brought the small tables for our dinner, placing those for the gentlemen on one side of the room and those for the ladies on the other. Then Toshi, with her tray, took her place in the open space at the end of the two lines, each person made a slight bow, and the dinner commenced. The conversation was general and the guests seemed to have a pleasant time, but, of course, I was very quiet and dignified.

The most interesting part of the day to me came after everyone had gone and Ishi was taking off my dress. She eyed my head very closely. "*Maa! Maa!* Etsu-bo Sama," she said. "It was such luck that to-day was cold and dry. Your hair has not one bit of a crinkle!"

For once my unruly hair had not disgraced my family, and giving a sigh of relief, I placed my head carefully upon my little wooden pillow and went contentedly to sleep.

After my betrothal my life was a sort of make-believe game, for my education as a wife began that very day. I had already received the usual training in cooking, sewing, and various household duties, as well as flower-arranging, tea-serving, and other womanly accomplishments; but now I had to put these things into practice as if I were already in my husband's home. I was expected to select without assistance the proper flowers, the suitable roll picture and *tokonoma* ornament, and see that the house was always arranged according to certain established rules.

Every moment my life was filled with training and preparation. The object was not explained to me, for this education was a taken-for-granted part of every betrothal; and it happened in my case that no special explanation was necessary other than that I had to be careful not in any way to show disrespect to wood-sorrel since Matsuo's crest was conventionalized wood-sorrel. Except that I had to learn to like tuna, which was a favourite dish of Matsuo's and which I had never cared for, my diet was not affected at all by my betrothal. Sister had a long training, for she had been betrothed five years, including the year of postponement on account of Father's death. As her expected husband's crest was conventionalized plum, she never, during the five years, tasted plum, even in jelly. It would have been disrespectful.

The hardest thing I did that year was to learn how to make a sleeping cushion. I loved to sew and was rather skillful with the needle, but I had never made anything by myself. Ishi or Toshi had always helped me. But every Japanese housewife had to know how to make cushions, for they were our chairs and our beds; so Mother said that I must make a sleeping-cushion entirely alone. This was a difficult thing for any one to do, and my sleeves were wet with foolish tears when for the fourth time I pulled out the threads and turned the immense cushion inside out, in order to refit the corners, which, in spite of my persistent efforts, *would* stay twisted.

Another of my duties was the preparation, on anniversaries and at festival times, of a shadow table for my absent fiancé. On these days I myself cooked the food which Brother told us Matsuo especially liked. His table was placed next to mine and I arranged for it to be always served before my own. Thus I learned to be watchful for the comfort of my prospective husband. Grandmother and Mother always spoke as if Matsuo were present, and I was as careful of my dress and conduct as if he had really been in the room. Thus I grew to respect him and to respect my own position as his wife.

Most of the memories of that time are like faint heart-throb phantoms now, but one always stands out clear and strong. That has to do with a birthday. Japanese people do not, as a rule, observe individual birthdays. Instead, it is the custom to celebrate New Year as a birthday for each person of the nation. This gives a double meaning to the day and makes New Year the most joyously celebrated of any festival of the year. But in our house one especial birthday was always honoured. That was Matsuo's. This was not on my account. From the time Mother had learned of his kindness to Brother, never did a January 8th pass that we did not have an elaborate dinner with a table for Matsuo in the place of honour as our guest. Mother always kept up this custom, and in later years, when in a far-distant land, I have thought with a mist in my eyes of the birthday table in my mother's home in the mountains of Japan.

During these months Mother and I came closer to each other than we had ever been before. She did not confide in me—that was not Mother's way—but it seemed that an invisible cord of sympathy was drawing our hearts together. I had always greatly admired my mother, but there was a little awe mixed with my admiration. Father had been my comrade and my friend as well as my wise adviser; and my whole heart was filled with tender love for my dear, patient, unselfish Ishi. But Mother was aloft, like the sun, flawless and steady, filling the home with life-giving warmth, yet too far away to be treated familiarly. So I was surprised one day, when she came quietly to my room and told me there was something she wanted to speak to me about before she told Grandmother. Our house had received word from the go-between that Matsuo had removed to a city in the eastern part of America, and had gone into business for himself. On this account he had decided not to return to Japan for several years, and asked that I be sent to him there.

Mother always accepted inevitable circumstances with calm resignation, but this was a very unusual and puzzling situation. For generations Japanese mothers, believing that the destined home for every girl is settled by the gods, have sent their daughters as brides to distant provinces; so my going to America was not a matter of deep concern. But for a bride to go into a home where there was neither mother-in-law nor an elder sister of wisdom-age to train her in the ways of the new household, was a serious problem. And this was not a case that could be referred to the family council; for I was as much bound to Matsuo as if I were already married, and in his affairs the Inagaki family had no authority. In this strange situation Mother turned to me, and for the first time in my life I was consulted in a family matter. I think I changed from girl to woman in that hour of conversation with my mother.

We decided that, at least for the present, there was but one problem for us to face. That was how to prepare for an unknown life in a strange land. In this my relatives could take no part. Of course, all were excited and each one volunteered advice; but the only practical suggestion came from Brother. He said I must have an English education. That meant that I should have to be sent to school in Tokyo.

All that winter the household was busy getting me ready for school. The pathos of these preparations I did not realize; nor, I think, did any of us. Mother spent evening after evening bending her stately head over wonderful embroidered garments, ripping out, stitch by stitch, the exquisite work of hands folded in rest generations ago. Then Ishi would dye the silk and make it into plain garments suitable for my school life.

And many things were sold. Grandmother and Mother consented to any sacrifice, though sometimes their faces were sad; but Brother seemed to have lost all feeling for the precious old belongings and would part with them without one expression of regret.

"Treasures are a useless care," he often said. "In a poor house like ours there is no need to keep dozens of chests of retainers' armour. They had their place in the past, but hereafter the sons of our ancestors must fight on the battlefield of commerce. Business is the key to wealth, and in this new world wealth is the only power."

I thought little of it then, but now it aches me to remember the sword-hilt ornaments of exquisite workmanship in gold and silver and bronze that were sold for almost nothing; and I can see, even now, how the great scales of the dealer in old iron tipped heavily with the weight of swords that once were the pride of our humblest retainers.

One cold evening I went into Grandmother's room and snuggled down beside her cushion, close to the fire-box, just as I used to do in the days which were beginning to seem to me far in the past. We had grown somewhat apart that year. I was no longer the little child she could make happy with sweets, could train in politeness and teach useful lessons by means of fairy lore; and I felt that, much as she loved me, the new conditions that my future faced were beyond her old-fashioned comprehension. But I learned that night, while I talked with her, that samurai training will prepare one for any future.

As we sat in the quiet room, lighted only by the soft glow of the charcoal fire, she told me how, that very day sixty years before, she, as a bride, had left her home in a distant province to come to her husband in Nagaoka. Most brides of her rank revisited their homes each year in a long procession of grandeur, but, though messengers were sent with inquiries and gifts every New Year and summer-festival season, Grandmother never, after she entered the marriage palanquin, saw her home or her people again. In those days of slow travel, distance was counted by time rather than miles, and hers was a long trip. She left home on the night of a full moon, and another full moon was in the sky when she was carried through the entrance gate of her husband's home.

"I was just your age—fourteen," she said, "and sometimes as the procession passed through strange provinces, climbing over mountains and crossing wide rivers, I wondered many things. It was farther than Kyoto that I came, and at the gateway of each province there were long waits while the officials of the procession exchanged papers and received permission for us to pass. At these times my nurse always came and remained beside my palanquin, and the spear-retainers and 'six-shoulders' of coolie carriers were with us; so I did not fear. But the world seemed very strange and large to me. And the people I came to live among were very different from my own. The customs were new; even the language had an accent and idioms that seemed peculiar. It was like a foreign land. And so, of late, I have thought much of you and the unknown country to which your fate is taking you. Remember, Etsu-bo," and her voice was strangely tender, "where you live is a small matter. The life of a samurai, man or woman, is just the same: loyalty to the overlord; bravery in defence of his honour. In your distant, destined home, remember Grandmother's words: loyalty to your husband; bravery in defence of his honour. It will bring you peace."

CHAPTER-11
My First Journey

THAT was one of the long Nagaoka winters. For five months we saw only snow. In the early spring our relatives in Tokyo had written that arrangements had been made for my school. From that time I had been waiting impatiently for the mountain roads to become safe from avalanches; for just as soon as we could travel Brother was to take me to the capital.

At last the dykes were dry—that was where the snow always melted first—and we had a "gathering-green" picnic as a farewell to my companions in Nagaoka. One sunny morning a group of us, with purple scarfs on our heads and kimonos tucked up over our bright skirts, dotted the dyke slopes, each carrying a small basket and a bamboo knife and filling the air with laughter and merry calls as we hurried up and down the banks, trying to see how many different kinds of green each could find. Often in later years I recall that happy day as my last gay time at home as a girl.

Finally the mail carriers reported that the overhanging snow-cliffs had all fallen and the slopes were clear. Soon after came the day of our departure. With a heart half of elation, half of regret, I bade good-bye to Honourable Grandmother and Mother and with misty eyes was carefully tucked into my jinrikisha by Ishi. Then, between lines of bowing friends, our two jinrikishas and a baggage-laden horse led by a coolie started on the eight-days' journey to Tokyo.

Most of the way we travelled in jinrikishas, changing them at certain towns, but occasionally we had to go on horseback. My saddle was a high box-seat; so Brother and the coolie rigged up a double-basket held by bands across the horse's back. I sat in one part, and baggage filled the other. As we went around the steep, curving road on the mountain side, I could lean over and look far, far down to the fisher villages on the coast. But it was more interesting, as we got farther along, to look across the deep valley to the sloping hillsides with their terraces of ricefields—odd-shaped patches fitted in like the silk pieces of a Buddhist priest's robe. In every little village of thatch-roofed huts was a shrine set high in the midst of a few trees, and, half-hidden in a hollow beside a stream, was whirling the great narrow wheel of a rice-mill. The air was so clear that I could plainly see the awkward lunge of a water-buffalo as he dragged a wooden plough along the furrows of one of the rice-patches, and I could even distinguish a scarlet flower stuck between the folds of the towel knotted about the head of the coolie behind. In those days no one ever wore a living flower, except to carry it to the dead; so I knew he was taking it home for the house shrine. I wondered what kind of a home he had.

I think it was our third day when I noticed that we were leaving the snow country. No longer did the towns have their sidewalks roofed, and these thatches bore no rows of avalanche stones. The houses looked bare and odd—like a married woman's face with newly shaved eyebrows. But we were not entirely beyond the sight of snow, for as we skirted Myoko Mountain we saw a good many drifts and patches. The jinrikisha men said snow lasted there until July.

"From the top," said Brother, "you can see Fujiyama——"

My heart thrilled, and I foolishly turned my head, feeling for a moment that I was really near the sacred mountain which my eyes had never expected to behold. And then, with a deeper, warmer thrill, I heard the conclusion of his sentence:

"—and then, if you turn and look in the opposite direction, you can see the plains of Echigo."

"We are very far away from home," I replied in a small voice.

Brother gave a quick look at my grave face; then he laughed.

"Also, if you look just beyond, you can see the Isle of Sado. If Matsuo should not come up to expectations, here's some advice for you."

And his merry voice broke into an old song:

"Nikuiotoko ni kisetae shima wa
Royagoshi ni Sado ga shima."

I was shocked that Brother should sing a common servant's song, and doubly shocked that he should joke so lightly about serious things; so my face was still grave as we rolled along in our jinrikishas.

The Isle of Sado used to be a place of exile for criminals and was considered by common people as the end of the world. This joking song, which is popular among peasant girls, is literally a threat to present to a disliked suitor, not the pleated garment which is the usual gift of the bride to a groom, but instead, a convict's garb: meaning, "I pray the gods will send the unwelcome one across the raging seas to the end of the world."

We spent our fifth night at Nagano in the temple of Zenkoji where lived the royal nun beneath whose high-lifted razor I had walked, years before, in a procession of gaily clad little girls, for a Buddhist ceremony of consecration.

The next morning, soon after we started, Brother halted and allowed my jinrikisha to roll up to his side. "Etsu-bo," he asked, "when did they give up making a priestess of you?"

"Why—I don't know," I said, surprised.

He gave a little scornful laugh and rode on to his place ahead leaving me silent and thoughtful.

I had spoken the truth when I said I did not know. I had always accepted my education with no thought of results. But Brother's laugh had startled me, and, rolling along that mountain road, I did a good deal of thinking. At last I believed that I understood. I know my father had never approved, although he acquiesced in Honourable Grandmother's wish that I should be educated for a priestess; and when, after my brother's sad departure, he had quietly substituted studies which would be of benefit should I ever hold the position of his heir, I think Honourable Grandmother, aching with sympathy for her proud, disappointed son, laid aside her cherished hope, and the plan was silently abandoned.

In the province of Shinano, an hour or so from Nagano, my jinrikisha man pointed across the river to a small wooded mountain.

"Obatsuyama, it is," he said.

How my mind went back to Ishi and her mother-love story which tells of a time long, long ago, when there lived at the foot of this mountain a poor farmer and his aged widowed mother. They owned a bit of land which supplied them with food and their humble lives were peaceful and happy.

At that time Shinano was governed by a despotic ruler who, though a brave warrior, had a great and cowardly shrinking from anything suggestive of fading health and strength. This caused him to send out a cruel proclamation. The entire province was given strict orders immediately to put to death all aged people.

Those were barbarous days, and the custom of abandoning old people to die was not uncommon. However, it was not a law, and many of the helpless old lived as long as nature allowed in comfortable and welcome homes. The poor farmer loved his aged mother with tender reverence, and the order filled his heart with sorrow. But no one ever thought a second time about obeying the mandate of a daimio, so with many deep and hopeless sighs the youth prepared for what at that time was considered the kindest mode of death.

Just at sundown, when his day's work was ended, he took a quantity of the unwhitened rice which is the principal food of the poor, cooked and dried it, and tying it in a square of cloth he swung the bundle around his neck along with a gourd filled with cool, sweet water. Then he lifted his helpless old mother to his back and started on his painful journey up the mountain.

The road was long and steep. He plodded steadily on, the shadows growing deeper and deeper, until the moon, round and clear, rose above the mountain-top and peered pityingly through the branches upon the youth toiling onward, his head bent with weariness and his heart heavy with sorrow. The narrow road was crossed and recrossed by many paths made by hunters and wood-cutters. In some places they mingled in a confused puzzle, but he gave no heed. One path or another, it mattered not. On he went, climbing blindly upward—ever upward—toward the high, bare summit of what is now known as Obatsuyama, the mountain of the "Abandoning of the Aged."

The eyes of the old mother were not so dim out that they noted the reckless hastening from one path to an other, and her loving heart grew anxious. Her son did not know the mountain's many paths, and his return might be one of danger, so she stretched forth her hand and snapping the twigs from the bushes as they passed, she quietly dropped a handful every few steps of the way, so as they climbed, the narrow path behind them was dotted at frequent intervals with tiny piles of twigs.

At last the summit was reached. Weary and heartsick, the youth gently released his burden and silently prepared a place of comfort, as his last duty to the loved one. Gathering fallen pine needles he made a soft cushion, and tenderly lifting his old mother thereon, he wrapped her padded coat more closely about the stooping shoulders and with tearful eyes and an aching heart said farewell.

The trembling mother voice was full of unselfish love as she gave her last injunction.

"Let not thine eyes be blind, my son. The mountain road is full of danger. Look carefully and follow the path which holds the piles of twigs. They will guide thee to the familiar way farther down."

The son's surprised eyes looked back over the path, then at the poor old shrivelled hands all scratched and soiled by their work of love. His heart smote him and, bowing to the ground, he cried aloud:

"Oh, Honourable Mother, thy kindness thrusts my heart! I will not leave thee. Together we will follow the path of twigs, and together we will die!"

Once more he shouldered his burden (how light it seemed now!) and hastened down the path, through the shadows and the moonlight, to the little hut in the valley.

Beneath the kitchen floor was a walled closet for food, which was covered over and hidden from view. There the son hid his mother, supplying her with everything needful and continually watching and fearing.

Time passed and he was beginning to feel safe, when again the despot sent forth heralds bearing an unreasonable and useless order; seemingly as a boast of his power. His demand was that his subjects should present him with a rope of ashes. The entire province trembled with dread. The order must be obeyed; yet who in all Shinano could make a rope of ashes?

One night, in great distress, the son whispered the news to his hidden mother.

"Wait!" she said, "I will think."

On the second day she told him what to do.

"Make a rope of twisted straw," she said, "then stretch it upon a row of flat stones and burn it there on a windless night."

He called the people together and did as she said, and when the blaze had died, behold, upon the stones, with every twist and fibre showing perfect, lay a rope of whitened ashes.

The daimio was pleased at the wit of the youth, and praised him greatly, but demanded to know where he had obtained his wisdom.

"Alas! Alas!" cried the farmer, "the truth must be told!" and with many deep bows he related his story.

The daimio listened, then meditated in silence. Finally he lifted his head.

"Shinano needs more than the strength of youth," he said gravely. "Ah, that I should have forgotten the well-known saying, 'With the crown of snow, there cometh wisdom!'"

That very hour the cruel law was abolished, and the custom drifted into so far a past that only the legend remains.

As we went farther on, I found the customs so different from those of Nagaoka that I felt as if I were already in a strange land. At one place, long before we reached the village, we heard a hoarse voice calling, "*Ma-kat-ta? Ma-kat-ta?*" (Is it sold ? Is it sold ?) and as we rolled through the one narrow, crowded street we saw an auctioneer standing high in the midst of dozens of bamboo baskets of beans, carrots, greens, and bamboo shoots; while lying around him, in ungainly confusion, were every size and shape of purple eggplant and long, sprawling, delicious lotus roots.

Brother looked back and laughed.

"Who is he? What were all the people doing?" I asked, as soon as we reached the end of the long street and rolled out on to the public road.

"It is a vegetable auction," Brother explained. "Merchants buy in quantities, and every morning the things are auctioned off by the basketful. Weren't those fine lotus roots? If we hadn't had breakfast only a couple of hours ago I'd believe I was hungry."

At another place we went by a house where death had entered. Before the door stood a funeral palanquin into which coolies with big hats and crest-coats were just lifting the heavy wooden bucket containing the body. Over it was thrown a small kimono of scarlet and gold, showing that the dead child must have been a little daughter. The dress would have been white for a son. Around stood a number of white-robed mourners with white towels folded over their hair. As we passed, I caught a glimpse of a screen placed upside down and the lighted candles of a tiny shrine.

At one place, where the road ran close to a broad river with bold bluffs coming down, in some places, almost to the water, we saw a number of odd floating rice-mills with turning paddle-wheels that looked like a fleet of boats standing motionless in a hopeless struggle against a strong tide. I wondered where, in that rocky country, were enough people to eat all the rice that was being ground; but when we turned away from the river we suddenly found ourselves in a silk-culture district, where our road ran through village after village, each having its own mulberry plantation.

The town where we expected to spend the night was only a few hours ahead when the sky began to darken with a threatening storm. Brother was casting anxious looks backward when his jinrikisha man told him that in the next village was a large house where travellers had sometimes been kept for a night. So we hurried there, the last quarter of an hour being a bouncing, breathless race between men and clouds. The men won, whirling us up to the door, into which we ran unannounced, just as the storm broke with a downpour which it would have been hard to struggle through on the road.

It was an odd house where we had found shelter; but I know that even my honourable father, on his journeys in ancient days, never, on any occasion, received a more cordial welcome or more kindly treatment than did we and our perspiring, laughing, boasting men at the end of our exciting race.

CHAPTER-12
Travel Education

THE large, well-cared-for house in which we had taken refuge that stormy night was crowded full of busy workers. With the exception of the living rooms of our host, his wife, and two daughters, the entire house was full of skeleton frames containing tiers and tiers of bamboo trays, each holding a network screen covered with silk worms. There must have been thousands and thousands of them. I had been accustomed to silkworms all my life. Ishi's home had been in a weaving village, and my elder sister had many silk villages on her three-mountain estate; but I never before had spent a night in sound of the continual nibbling of the hungry little creatures. It filled the whole house with a gentle rustling, exactly like the patter of raindrops on dry leaves, and I dreamed all night of dripping eaves. The next morning I awakened with a depressed feeling that I was to have a day's ride in a close-shut jinrikisha, and was surprised, when I pushed back one of the wooden panels at the porch edge, to find that the sun was shining.

While I was standing there, one of the daughters, about my age, came out carrying a straw mat of silkworm waste to throw on a pile in the yard for the mulberry stems and rice hulls of silkworm waste make the best fertilizer in the world—and she stopped to bow good-morning. Then she stood there in the June sunshine with her sleeves looped back and her bare feet in straw sandals, and I squatted on the edge of the porch in my home-dyed night kimono, and we got acquainted.

She told me that she took care of six trays of silkworms all by herself. She seemed to know everything about them, and she loved them.

"They're clean," she said, "and dainty about food, and intelligent about their own affairs—just like people."

I was so interested in all the surprising things I heard that I was still listening when a girl came to fold away my bed cushions, and I had to hurry to get dressed.

“Well,” said Brother, after my room had been cleaned, and breakfast brought in, “how do you like living in a boarding house?”

“The boarders are very noisy,” I replied; “and, from what our hostess’s daughter told me, they are very particular. She says they cannot endure one particle of dust. Even a withered leaf will sometimes cause one to ‘tie on his blue neckerchief’ and creep to the outer edge of the tray.”

“Have you seen our host’s grandmother?” asked Brother.

“No, I didn’t know there was a grandmother.”

“She went early to her cushions last night; probably to escape the bustle and annoyance of our abrupt arrival. We will pay our respects to her before we leave.”

When breakfast was over, our host took us to the grandmother’s room. She was a very old lady with a reserved manner and a face of more than usual intelligence. As soon as she bowed I knew that she had been trained in a samurai house, and when I saw the crest of a *naginata* on the wall-rest above the *shoji*, I knew why Brother had wanted me to come to this room.

A *naginata* is a long, light spear with curved blade, which samurai women were taught to use, partly for exercise and partly for defence in case of necessity. This one bore the crest of one of our northern heroes. He was a traitor, but nevertheless he was a hero. When he was killed, his daughter was one of the group—three of them women—who defended the sorely pressed castle during the last desperate hours of hopeless struggle. The old lady told us, with modest pride, that she had been a humble attendant of the daughter and was with her at that dreadful time. The *naginata* was a memory gift from her honourable and beloved mistress.

Seeing that we were deeply interested, she brought out her other treasure—a slender, blunt knife called a *kogai*, which, with the throwing-dagger, forms part of the hilt of a samurai’s long sword. In very ancient days Japanese warfare was a science. Artistic skill was always displayed in the use of weapons, and no soldier was proud of having wounded an enemy in any other manner than the one established by strict samurai rule. The long sword had for its goal only four points: the top of the head, the wrist, the side, and the leg below the knee. The throwing-dagger must speed on its way, true as an arrow, direct to forehead, throat, or wrist. But the blunt little *kogai* had many uses. It was the key that locked the sword in its scabbard; when double it could be used as chopsticks by the marching soldier; it has been used on the battlefield, or in retreat, mercifully to pierce the ankle vein of a suffering and dying comrade, and it had the unique use in a clan feud, when found sticking upright in the ankle of a dead foe, of bearing the silent challenge, "I await thy return." Its crest told to whom it belonged and, in time, it generally was returned—to its owner's ankle. The *kogai* figures in many tales of romance and revenge of the Middle Ages.

I was glad to see Brother so interested, and was happy myself in watching the old lady's face flush and light up with her memories; but her closing words made me feel sorry. To some remark of Brother's she replied, "Youth is always listening eagerly for marching orders; but the aged can only look backward to sad memories and hopeless dreams."

As I mounted my jinrikisha and bowed again to the entire group of family and servants bowing in the doorway, I could not help sending a thought farewell to the busy little boarders. I had learned more about silkworms during that short rustling visit than in my fourteen years of life in a silkworm district. As we rolled along over a smooth, monotonous road my mind was busy, and I believe that then and there I first began to realize—vaguely—that all creatures, however insignificant, were "intelligent about their own affairs—just like people."

"Dear me!" I finally said to myself. "How much we learn when we travel!" and I pulled the jinrikisha robe over my lap and settled myself for the long ride ahead.

I think I must have gone to sleep, for I found myself crookedly but comfortably snuggled into almost a *kinoji* when I heard Brother's voice.

We were entering a good-sized town and he was leaning back and pointing across the tiled roofs to a castle on the hill beyond.

"This is Komoro," he called, "and there's where the foot-high dolls came from."

I smiled as my mind flew back to the Nagaoka home and pictured two enormous dolls of the festival set brought by our Komoro great-great-grandmother with her wedding dowry. In her day the Government permitted only the daughter of a daimio to own dolls a foot high, and her entire set must have been wondrously handsome. But in my time, when our living came principally from the visits of the second-hand man to our godown, the wonderful Komoro dolls, with their miniature furniture of gold and lacquer—the perfection of Japanese art of the Middle Ages—gradually found new homes. They went, I know, to no godown of Japan, but, through some shrewd dealer, into foreign hands and foreign lands and probably to-day are calmly resting in widely scattered homes and museums of Europe or America.

Two of the dolls had become defaced in someway, and thus, being unsaleable, they were placed as ornaments on the high *tokonoma* shelf in my room. I was very fond of acting out scenes of the stories that were told me, and I used to take down the dolls and use them as an audience while I strutted around the room representing an ancient samurai with some fearful duty to perform. The dolls' heads were movable, and thus supplied a splendid opportunity for a favourite revenge story of mine. Many a time I have placed my hand on one of the enamelled heads and, with my ivory paper knife as a sword, have struck fiercely at the doll, at the same instant lifting out the head from its collar of rich brocade; then, with stern, set face, I would hurriedly wrap the head in a purple square of crêpe and, tucking it under my arm, stride boldly off to an imaginary courtroom.

I suspect my father knew of this barbarous game of mine, for I always borrowed his purple crêpe *fukusa* for this purpose, feeling that something belonging to him would give dignity to the occasion; but I never heard Honourable Grandmother's step on the porch that I did not quickly restore the head to its brocade nest in order to save her another anxious fear that I was growing too bold and rough ever to find a husband.

As our jinrikishas rolled through the town I looked up at the castle with interest. And this was the home from which our Komoro grandmother had gone forth on her wedding journey to Nagaoka! Half buried in trees it stood, the gray, tipped-up corners of many roofs peeping through the branches. It looked like a broad, low pagoda towering above a slanting wall of six-sided stones—the "tortoise back" of all Japanese castles.

From Komoro to Nagaoka! It must have seemed a long trip to the young girl in the teetering bridal *kago!* I thought of what Honourable Grandmother had told me of her own month-long bridal trip. And then I looked ahead. The Idzumo gods, who plan all marriages, had decreed the same fate for many brides of our family, and, so far as my own future was planned, I seemed destined to follow in the footsteps of my ancestors.

At one place where we had to take *kagos* I disgraced myself. I dreaded a *kago.* The big basket swinging from the shoulders of the trotting coolies always made me dizzy and faint, but that day it was raining hard and the mountain path was too rough for a jinrikisha. I stood things as bravely as I could, but finally I became so sick that Brother had the baggage taken off the horse and, wedging me in between cushions on its back, covered me with a tent made of a straw mat and, disdaining comfort for himself, walked all the way up the mountain beside me, the coolie following with the two *kagos*.

At the top the sun was shining, and when I peeped out from my tent Brother was shaking himself as my poor Shiro used to do when drenched with rain. I ventured to apologize in a shamed voice.

"Kago sickness is a great absorber of pride, Etsu-bo. I'm afraid you have lost your right to be called your father's 'brave son.'"

I laughed, but my cheeks were hot.

As he helped me to the ground, Brother pointed toward a wide-spreading cloud of smoke floating lazily above a cone-shaped mountain.

"That's the signpost for the Robber Station," he said. "Do you remember?"

Indeed I did. Many times I had heard Father tell the story of the small hotel at the top of a mountain where the rates were so high that people called it the 'Robber Station.' I was a big girl before I learned that it was a very respectable stopping place and not a den of thieves where money was extorted from travellers as tribute.

We walked down the mountain, passing several cave shrines. In one I caught the twinkle of a burning lamp. It reminded me of the hermit caves of Echigo. This was my first long trip from home, and it was full of strange new experiences. Yet there seemed to be familiar memories connected with everything. I wondered vaguely if I should find it so in America.

One day, after a shower, as the man stopped to lower the top of my jinrikisha, a sudden burst of sunshine showed me, high up on the mountain-side, pressed flat against the green, an immense white *dai*, the Japanese character meaning "great." It looked as if it had been painted with a brush, but Jiya, who had once been there, had told me that it was made of strips of bamboo covered thickly with paper prayers tied on by pilgrim visitors to the temple on top of the mountain.

Near by was the rude little village where Miyo lived. She was Jiya's sister, and we spent the night in her house. It was a queer place, a sort of cheap hotel for country people. Miyo, with her son and his wife, met us at the door with deep bows and many a "*Maa! Maa!*" of surprise and pleasure. The wide entrance opened into a big room having a clay floor. Several casks bound with hoops of twisted bamboo were piled in one corner, and from the smoky ceiling hung a bulging bag of grain, bunches of *mochi* cakes and dried fish, and bamboo baskets containing provisions of various kinds.

We passed through a mob of chattering pilgrims who had just come down from the mountain, and, crossing the stones of a crude little garden, reached the rooms where Miyo lived. Everything was clean, but the paper doors were patched, the mats yellow with age, and the cloth bindings worn almost through. Miyo must have had a rather hard time in the past; for she was an independent character who, in violation of all tradition, had cast off a worthless husband and brought up her four children herself. Of course it was very low class to do a thing like that, but she was as brave as a man, and, since her husband had no parents, she had been able legally to keep the children herself.

Miyo had been a servant in our house when Brother was a child, and her delight in seeing the "Young Master" was pathetic. Her bare feet went pattering over the mats, slipping quickly into her sandals each time she crossed the door-sill to the kitchen. She hurried here and there, bringing us the best she had and offering everything with bows and apologies. One thing troubled her very much. She had only wooden trays with no feet, and she had never known my brother to eat off a low tray. In the days when she lived at our house, even an informal serving of cake was presented to him on a high lacquer stand, just as it was to Father. But she was ingenious, and presently she brought in a brassbound rice-bucket and with many bows and an anxious "Please grant your honourable pardon!" placed the tray on it before Brother. He laughed heartily and said that even a shogun had never received a similar honour.

We sat up very late and had a most interesting time. Brother talked of past days and of many things about our home, so little known to me that I felt as if I were reading some old, half-familiar book. I had never known him to be so free and merry as he was that evening. And Miyo, half laughter and half tears, talked rapidly, asking many questions and interrupting herself continually. She was reminding him of some incident of his childhood, when he abruptly asked: "What became of your 'own-choice' husband, Miyo?"

I thought that question was too cruel, but Miyo calmly replied: "Young Master, 'The rust of one's own sword can be brightened only by one's own effort.' I am still paying the penalty of my life mistake."

Very gravely she went across the room to a big chest and took out a small, flat package. It was a square of purple crêpe bearing our crest. With a serious face she unfolded it, showing a brocade charm bag such as we children used to wear to hold the paper blessing of the priest. The gold threads were a little ravelled and the heavy scarlet cord mellowed with age.

Miyo lifted it reverently to her forehead.

"The Honourable Mistress gave it to me," she said to Brother, "the night she let my lover and me through the water gate. It held square silver coins—all that I needed."

"Ah!" Brother exclaimed excitedly, "I know! I was a little boy. It was dark and I saw her coming back alone, carrying a lantern. But I never understood what it meant."

Miyo hesitated a moment; then she told us.

When she was employed in our house, she was very young, and because she was the sister of Father's faithful Jiya, she was allowed much freedom. A youthful servant, also of our house, fell in love with her. For young people to become lovers without the sanction of proper formalities was a grave offence in any class, but in a samurai house hold it was a black disgrace to the house. The penalty was exile through the water gate—a gate of brush built over a stream and never used except by one of the *eta*, or outcast, class. The departure was public, and the culprits were ever after shunned by everyone. The penalty was unspeakably cruel, but in the old days severe measures were used as a preventive of law-breaking.

Mother always rigidly obeyed every law of the household, but she saved Miyo from public disgrace by taking the lovers quietly, at midnight, and herself opening the big swinging gate for them to pass. No one ever knew the truth.

"It is said," concluded Miyo sadly, "that the hearts of those who pass the water gate are purified by the gods; but even so, the penalty of a law-breaker can never be evaded. In secret I have paid the penalty, and my children were saved from disgrace by the heavenly kindness of the Honourable Mistress of the Inagaki."

We all sat quiet for a moment. Then Brother said bitterly:

"The Honourable Mistress of the Inagaki was many times more merciful to the servants of her household than to her one and only son."

Impatiently he pushed his cushion aside and abruptly said good-night.

The next morning our road wound along the side of a mountain stream awkwardly threading its way through a series of angular gullies, finally ending abruptly in a swift, sloping leap into a wide, shallow river, which we crossed on a boat poled by coolies. This river was the scene of one of Jiya's most exciting stories. Father, on one of his hurried trips to Tokyo, had found it flooded and had ordered his coolies to place his palanquin on a platform and carry it on their heads through the whirling waves to the opposite shore. One man was drowned.

As our jinrikishas rolled along I thought of how often Father had gone over that road amidst the state and pomp of old Japan; and now his two dear ones—his eldest and his youngest—were following the same path in rented jinrikishas, simply garbed and with no attendants except a wheezy old coolie with a baggage horse. How strange it seemed.

At last we reached Takasaki—the place from which the celebrated "land steamer" started on its puffing way to Tokyo. That was the first time that I ever saw a railway train. It looked to me like a long row of little rooms, each with a narrow door opening on to the platform.

It was late in the afternoon, and I was so weary that I have little recollection of anything except a scolding from Brother, because I, feeling that I was entering some kind of a house, stepped out of my wooden shoes, leaving them on the platform. Just before the train started, they were handed in at the window by an official whose special duty it was to gather all the shoes from the platform before the starting of every train. I went to sleep at once, and the next thing I knew we were in Tokyo.

CHAPTER-13
Foreigners

MY TOKYO relatives had arranged for me to live with them and attend a celebrated school for girls, where English was taught by a man who had studied in England. This I did for several months, but my brother was not satisfied. The girls were required to give much attention to etiquette and womanly accomplishments; and since my uncle lived in a stately mansion, a great part of my time at home was occupied with trifling formalities. Brother said that I was receiving the same useless training that had been given him, and, since I was to live in America, I must have a more practical education.

Once more my poor brother was totally misunderstood by our kindred on account of his stubborn opposition to all advice; but finally Father's old friend, Major Sato, suggested a mission school that his wife had attended and which bore the reputation of being the best girls' school for English in Japan. This pleased Brother and, since it was a rule of the school that each pupil should have a resident guardian, Major Sato accepted the responsibility and it was arranged that, until the beginning of the next term, some weeks away, I should be a member of the Sato household. Major Sato's wife was a quiet, gentle lady, unassuming in manner, but with a hidden strength of character most unusual. Having no daughter, she accepted me as her own and in numberless kind ways taught me things of lasting value.

It was a five-mile walk to school from the Sato house. In very bad weather I was sent in Mrs. Sato's jinrikisha, but, true to my dear priest-teacher's training, I felt that it was almost a disgrace to consider bodily comfort when on the road to learning, so I usually walked.

Starting immediately after an early breakfast, I went down the hill and along an old temple road until I reached the broad street passing the palace of His Imperial Majesty. I always walked slowly there. The clear water of the moat, reflecting every stone of the sloping wall and the crooked pine trees above, formed a picture of calm, unhurried peace. It was the only place I had seen in Tokyo that gave me the familiar feeling of ceremonious dignity. I loved it. From there I came out upon the wide, sunshiny parade ground. There was a solitary tree standing just in the centre, where I always rested a few minutes; for beyond was a long climb through a series of narrow, crooked, up-hill streets crowded with children, almost every one having a baby on its back. These city children did not have the care-free manner of the street children of Nagaoka. They were older and graver, and although all were busy, some playing games, some chattering in groups, and some jogging along on errands, there was little noise except the "gata-gata" of their wooden clogs.

At the top of the hill was my school. It stood behind a long mound-wall topped with a thorn hedge. A big gateway opened into spacious grounds, where, in the midst of several trees, stood a long, two-storied wooden house with a tiled roof and glass windows divided into large squares by strips of wood. In that building I spent four happy years, and learned some of the most useful lessons of my life.

I liked my school from the first, but some of my experiences were very puzzling. Had it not been for the constant sympathy and wise advice of kind Mrs. Sato, my life might have been difficult; for I was only a simple country girl alone in a new world, looking about me with very eager, but very ignorant, eyes, and stubbornly judging everything by my own unreasonably high standards of conservative opinion.

All our studies, except English and Bible, were taught by Japanese men—not priests, but professors. Since they came only for their classes, we saw little of them. The foreign teachers were all women. I had seen one foreign man in Nagaoka, but, until I came to this school, I had never seen a foreign woman. These teachers were all young, lively, most interesting and beautiful. Their strange dress, the tight black shoes,the fair skin untouched by the cosmetics which we considered a necessary part of dressing, and the various colours of hair arranged in loose coils and rolls, were suggestive of dim visions I had had about fairyland. I admired them greatly, but their lack of ceremony surprised me. The girls, most of whom were from Tokyo, where living was less formal than in my old-fashioned home, made very short bows and had most astonishing manners in talking with one another; nevertheless, I had a certain interest in watching them. But the free actions of the teachers with the pupils and the careless conduct of the girls in the presence of the teachers shocked me. I had been taught such precepts as "Step not on even the shadow of thy teacher, but walk reverently three steps behind," and every day I saw familiar greetings and heard informal conversations that seemed to me most undignified on the part of the teacher and lacking in respect on the part of the pupil.

And there was another thing which troubled me greatly. Friendly smiles and small attentions from teachers seemed to be liked by these city girls, but I shrank indescribably from personal advances made to myself. My rigid training held me back from being even mildly responsive to either teachers or schoolmates, and it was a long time before the strangeness wore away and I found myself joining with the girls in their games and beginning to feel acquainted with my teachers. This was helped along greatly by certain democratic rules in the school, which, though not enforced, were encouraged, and became the fashion. One of these was giving up the use of the honorific "Sama" and substituting the less formal prefix, "O"; thus placing the girls on a plane of social equality. Another, which greatly interested me, was the universal agreement to give up arranging the hair in Japanese style. All wore it alike, pulled back from the face and hanging in a long braid behind. This change was a mixed pleasure. I was no longer a martyr to the "gluing-up process" of scented oil and hot tea, but as I was the only curly-haired girl in the school I could not escape a certain amount of good-natured ridicule.

These things I accepted with ease, but my my shoes were a real annoyance. All my life I had been accustomed to leave my shoes at the door whenever I stepped inside a house, but here, in the school, we wore our sandals all the time, except in the straw-matted dormitory. I was slow to adapt myself to this, and it was months before I conquered the impulse to slip back my toes from the cord when I reached the door of the class room. The girls used to wait outside, just to laugh at my moment's hesitation.

These changes in my life-long habits, combined with the merry ridicule of the girls, made me feel that I was one of them, and that Etsu-bo had slipped entirely out of the old life and was now fitted happily into the new. Nevertheless, there were times when, aroused from deep study by someone suddenly calling, "O Etsu San!" and, after a dazed moment of adjusting myself to the new name, I would hurry down the hall, my sandals sounding a noisy "clap-clap" on the floor, and my head feeling light with the cool looseness of unbound hair, I would be vaguely conscious, somewhere within me, of an odd fear that Etsu-bo was nowhere.

However, this feeling could never last long; for there was a dreaded something which constantly reminded me that I was still a daughter of Echigo. My pronunciation of certain sounds, which was different from that of Tokyo, caused considerable amusement among the girls. Also, I suppose I used rather stately and stilted language, which, combined with the odd Echigo accent, must have sounded very funny to city-bred ears. The girls were so good-natured in their mimicry that I could not feel resentment, but it was a real trial to me, for it touched my deep loyalty to my own province. Since I did not quite understand where the difficulty lay, I was helpless, and gradually got in the habit of confining my conversation to few remarks and making my sentences as short as possible.

Mrs. Sato noticed that I was growing more and more silent, and by tactful questioning she discovered the trouble. Then she quietly prepared a little notebook with a diagram of the troublesome sounds and, in the kindest way in the world, explained them to me.

Brother was there that evening, and he laughed.

"Etsu-bo," he said, looking at me rather critically, "there is not such good reason to be shamed by the accent of an honourable province as over your countrified dress. I must get you some different clothes."

I had already grown suspicious of the glances which my schoolmates had been casting at the sash that Toshi had so painstakingly made me of a piece of newly imported cloth called *a-ra-pac-ca*, so I was glad to accept the garments which Brother brought the next day. They were surprisingly gay, and the sash, with one side of black satin, reminded me of the restaurant waiters of Nagaoka, but the girls all said they had a "Tokyo air," so I wore them with a pride and satisfaction greater than I ever had felt about clothes—except once. That was many years before, when my father, on one of his visits to the capital, had seen in a store foreign clothes for a child and had brought them home for me. They were of dark blue cloth and very peculiar in shape. None of us knew they were clothes for a little boy. Ishi dressed me and I strutted about, cramped into a straitjacket of cold, tight, scratchy discomfort. But the family admired me the, servants watched me with in-drawn breaths of awe, and I was as proud as the "bird of many eyes," which is our symbol of vanity.

The more I saw of my teachers, the more I admired them. I had lost my feeling of repulsion at their lack of ceremony when I learned to understand the hidden dignity that lay beneath their individual differences, and finally it began to dawn upon me that the honourable position of instructor was not inconsistent with being merry and gay. My Japanese teachers had been pleasantly courteous, but always lofty and distant in manner; while these smiling, swift-moving creatures ran with us in the gymnasium, played battledore and shuttlecock with us, and took turns in eating with us in our own dining room where Japanese food was served on trays as it was on our small tables at home.

Often on Friday evenings we were allowed to arrange a Japanese programme of entertainment. We would bring out our bright undergarments, which are the gayest part of Japanese dress, and hang them across the room, where they swayed in long curves suggesting the broad-striped and crest curtains stretched by ancient warriors in camp. Then we would borrow things of each other to make costumes for tableaux or character sketches of celebrated people. Sometimes a daring girl would select a teacher—but always a favourite—and pleasantly caricature her. Occasionally we gave a pantomime of an old historic drama, but we never acted with words. That would have been too bold and unladylike. Even in theatres, women's parts were taken by men, for our stage was not yet far removed from the time when actors were called "beggars on the shore."

The teachers were always present on these occasions, laughing, applauding, and praising our efforts as freely and happily as if they were girls of our own age. And at the same time, they were all busy knitting and sewing, or—most interesting of all the things in that wonderful school—darning stockings.

But in spite of my steadily increasing contentment there was one thing that was a constant ache to me. Neither at school nor near the Sato home was there a shrine. Of course, there were prayers at morning service in the school chapel, and they were very beautiful and solemn. I always felt as if I were in a temple. But they lacked the warm homeliness of our family gathering in Honourable Grandmother's quiet room with the lighted candles and curling incense of the open shrine; and the consciousness of the near-by protecting presence of the ancestors. This I missed more than anything else. And an added grief was that I could have no part in the service held on the twenty-ninth of each month in memory of my father's death-day.

Before I left home Mother had given me a very sacred thing. It was my father's death-name written on a certain kind of paper by my revered priest-teacher. Preciously I had carried this with me wherever I went, but after I became a boarder in the school I had a vague feeling that for me to keep it there permanently would be disloyal to the sacred name and also discourteous to the school; for it would be intruding something of the old into an atmosphere which belonged only to the new. I felt I could not keep it, and yet I could not part with it. I was sorely puzzled.

One week-end I went to visit Mrs. Sato. It was the twenty-ninth day of the month. We were sewing, and our cushions were drawn close to the open doors over looking the garden. I had dropped my work and was thinking, my unseeing eyes gazing out at a path of stepping-stones that ran between two little hills and around a big stone lantern before disappearing in a group of small trees.

"What are you thinking, O Etsu San San?" asked Mrs. Sato. "You look worried."

Turning, I saw real concern in her face. Perhaps under the influence of the school my reserve was beginning to melt. At any rate, I told her of my trouble.

At once she was all sympathy.

"I am ashamed that we have no shrine," she said; "for we have not even the excuse of being Christians. We are nothing. It is the fashion lately to adopt the Western way, and we have no house shrine. But there is one in the nun's house at the end of the garden."

"The nun's house at the end of the garden!" I repeated in great astonishment.

She explained that the land on which they lived had once belonged to an old temple where priestesses were in charge, which, on account of the changing times, had grown very poor. The property had been sold to Major Sato on condition that a little thatched hut, once belonging to a temple servitor, should be allowed to remain as the home of a very old and very holy nun, who wished to spend her life in this much-loved spot.

That evening we went to see her, walking over the stepping-stones between the little hills and around the stone lantern to where, through the foliage, I could see a small house surrounded by a low brush fence. Faint candlelight twinkled through the paper doors, and I heard the gentle, familiar "ton-ton, ton-ton" of the soft wooden drum and the low chanting of Buddhist words. I bowed my head, and in the darkness homesick tears came to my eyes.

Mrs. Sato opened the humble bamboo gate.

"Pardon. May we enter?" she called gently.

The chanting ceased. The door slid back, and a kindly looking, very aged nun in a gray cotton robe welcomed us most cordially.

The room was simply furnished except that on one side stood a very beautiful temple shrine of gilded lacquer. It was darkened by age and constant incense smoke. Before the gilded Buddha lay a pile of worn chanting-books and the small wooden drum we had heard.

The nun was gentle and sweet like my grandmother, and it was easy for me to explain my trouble and show her the paper holding the sacred name. Lifting it to her forehead, she took it to the shrine and reverently placed it before the Buddha. Then we had a simple service, such as we used to have in Honourable Grandmother's room at home, and when I came away I left the precious paper in the safe keeping of her shrine. After that, on the last Friday of every month, I used to visit the holy nun and listen to her soft voice chant the service in memory of Father's death-day.

CHAPTER-14

Lessons

OUR time in school was supposed to be equally divided between Japanese and English, but since I had been already carefully drilled in Japanese studies, I was able to put my best efforts on English. My knowledge of that language was very limited. I could read and write a little, but my spoken English was scarcely understandable. I had, however, read a number of translations of English books and more valuable than all else—I possessed a supply of scattered knowledge obtained from a little set of books that my father had brought me from the capital when I was only a child. They were translations, compiled from various sources and published by one of the progressive book houses of Tokyo.

I do not know whose idea it was to translate and publish those ten little paper volumes, but whoever it was holds my lasting gratitude. They brought the first shafts of light that opened to my eager mind the wonders of the Western world, and from them I was led to countless other friends and companions who, in the years since, have brought to me such a wealth of knowledge and happiness that I cannot think what life would have been without them. How well I remember the day they came! Father had gone to Tokyo on one of his "window toward growing days" trips.

That was always an important event in our lives, for he brought back with him, not only wonderful stories of his journey, but also gifts of strange and beautiful things. Mother had said that he would be home at the close of the day, and I spent the afternoon sitting on the porch step watching the slow-lengthening shadows of the garden trees. I had placed my high wooden clogs on a stepping-stone just at the edge of the longest shadow, and as the sun crept farther I moved them from stone to stone, following the sunshine. I think I must have had a vague feeling that I could thus hasten the slanting shadow into the long straight line which would mean sunset.

At last—at last—and before the shadow had quite straightened, I hurriedly snatched up the clogs and clattered across the stones, for I had heard the jinrikisha man's cry of "*Okaeri!*" just outside the gate. I could scarcely bear my joy, and I have a bit of guilt in my heart yet when I recall how crookedly I pushed those clogs into the neat box of shelves in the "shoe-off" alcove of the vestibule.

The next moment the men, perspiring and laughing, came trotting up to the door where we, servants and all, were gathered, our heads bowed to the floor, all in a quiver of excitement and delight, but of course everybody gravely saying the proper words of greeting. Then, my duty done, I was caught up in my father's arms and we went to Honourable Grandmother, who was the only one of the household who might wait in her room for the coming of the master of the house.

That day was one of the "memory stones" of my life, for among all the wonderful and beautiful things which were taken from the willow-wood boxes straddled over the shoulders of the servants was the set of books for me. I can see them now. Ten small volumes of tough Japanese paper, tied together with silk cord and marked, "Tales of the Western Seas." They held extracts from "Peter Parley's World History," "National Reader," "Wilson's Readers," and many short poems and tales from classic authors in English literature.

The charm of delight that rare things give came to me during days and weeks—even months and years—from those books. I can recite whole pages of them now. There was a most interesting story of Christopher Columbus. It was not translated literally, but adapted so that the Japanese mind would readily grasp the thought with out being buried in a puzzling mass of strange customs. All facts of the wonderful discovery were stated truthfully, but Columbus was pictured as a fisher lad, and somewhere in the story there figured a lacquer bowl and a pair of chopsticks.

These books had been my inspiration during all my years of childhood, and when, in my study of English at school, my clumsy mind began to grasp the fact that, hidden beneath the puzzling words were continuations of stories I knew, and of ideas similar to those I had found in the old familiar books that I had loved so well, my delight was unbounded. Then I began to read eagerly. I would bend over my desk, hurrying, guessing, skipping whole lines, stumbling along—my dictionary wide open beside me, but I not having time—to look and yet, in some marvellous way, catching ideas. And I never wearied. The fascination was like that of a moon-gazing party, where, while we watched from the hillside platform, a floating cloud would sail across the glorious disk , and we—silent, trembling with excitement—would wait for the glory of the coming moment. In the same way, a half-hidden thought—elusive, tantalizing—would fill me with a breathless hope that the next moment light would come. Another thing about English books was that, as I read, I was constantly discovering shadowy replies to the unanswered questions of my childhood. Oh, English books were a source of deepest joy!

I am afraid that I should not have been so persistent, or so successful in my English studies, could I have readily obtained translations of the books I was so eager to read. Tokyo bookshops, at that time, were beginning to be flooded with translations of English, French, German, and Russian books; and these generally, if not scientific treatises, were classics translated, as a rule, by our best scholars; but they were expensive to purchase and difficult for me to obtain in any other way. To read, even stumblingly, in the original, the books in the school library was my only resource, and it became one of my greatest pleasures.

Excepting English, of all my studies history was the favourite; and I liked and understood best the historical books of the Old Testament. The figurative language was something like Japanese; the old heroes had the same virtues and the same weaknesses of our ancient samurai; the patriarchal form of government was like ours, and the family system based upon it pictured so plainly our own homes that the meaning of many questioned passages was far less puzzling to me than were the explanations of the foreign teachers.

In my study of English literature, it seems odd that, of all the treasures that I gathered, the one which has been most lasting as a vivid picture is that of Tennyson's "Dora." Probably this was because of its having been used by a famous Japanese writer as the foundation of a novel called "Tanima no Himeyuri"—Lily of the Valley. The story of Dora, being a tale of the first-born of an aristocratic family disinherited because he loved a rustic lass of humble class; and the subsequent tragedy resulting from the difference in training of different social circles, was a tale familiar and understandable to us. It was skilfully handled, the author, with wonderful word pictures, adapting Western life and thought to Japanese conditions.

"The Lily of the Valley" appeared at just the time when the young mind of Japan, both high and humble, was beginning to seek emancipation from the stoic philosophy, which for centuries had been the core of our well-bred training, and it touched the heart of the public. The book rushed with a storm of popularity all through the land and was read by all classes; and—

which was unusual—by both men and women. It is said that Her Imperial Majesty became so interested in reading it that she sat up all one night while her court ladies, sitting silent in the next room, wearily waited.

I think it was my third year in school that a wave of excitement over love stories struck Tokyo. All the schoolgirls were wildly interested. When translations were to be had we passed them from hand to hand through the school; but mostly we had to struggle along in English, picking out love scenes from the novels and poems in our school library. Enoch Arden was our hero. We were familiar with loyalty and sacrifice on the part of a wife, and understood perfectly why Annie should have so long withstood the advances of Philip, but the unselfishness ofthe faithful Enoch was so rare as to be much appreciated.

The hearts of Japanese girls are no different from those of girls of other countries, but for centuries, especially in samurai homes, we had been strictly trained to regard duty, not feeling, as the standard of relations between man and woman. Thus our unguided reading sometimes gave us warped ideas on this unknown subject. The impression I received was that love as pictured in Western books was interesting and pleasant, sometimes beautiful in sacrifice like that of Enoch Arden; but not to be compared in strength, nobility, or loftiness of spirit to the affection of parent for child, or the loyalty between lord and vassal.

Had my opinion been allowed to remain wordless, it probably would never have caused me annoyance, but it was destined to see the light. We had a very interesting literature society which held an occasional special meeting, to which we invited the teachers as guests. With an anxious pride to have a fine entertainment, we frequently planned our programme first and afterward selected the girls for the various tasks. The result was that sometimes the subject chosen was beyond the capacity of the girl to handle. At one time this rule brought disaster to me, for we never shirked any duty to which we were assigned.

On this occasion I was asked to prepare a three-page essay in English, having one of the cardinal virtues for a subject. I puzzled over which to select of Faith, Hope, Charity, Love, Prudence, and Patience; but recalling that our Bible teacher frequently quoted "God is Love," I felt that there I had a foundation, and so chose as my topic, "Love." I began with the love of the Divine Father, then, under the influence of my late reading, I drifted along, rather vaguely, I fear, on the effect of love on the lives of celebrated characters in history and poetry. But I did not know how to handle so awkward a subject, and reached my limit in both knowledge and vocabulary before the three pages were filled. Faithfulness to duty, however, still held firm, and I wrote on, finally concluding with these words: "Love is like a powerful medicine. When properly used it will prove a pleasant tonic, and some times may even preserve life; but when misused, it can ruin nations, as seen in the lives of Cleopatra and the beloved Empress of the Emperor Genso of Great China."

At the close of my reading one teacher remarked, "This is almost desecration."

It was years before I understood what the criticism meant.

For a while my great interest in English reading filled all my hours of leisure, but there came a time when my heart longed for the dear old stories of Japan, and I wrote to my mother asking her to send me some books from home. Among others she selected a popular classic called "Hakkenden," which I especially loved. It is the longest novel ever written in the Japanese language, and our copy, Japanese-bound and elaborately illustrated, consisted of 180 volumes. With great effort Mother succeeded in obtaining a foreign-bound copy in two thick volumes. I welcomed these books with joy, and was amazed when one of the teachers, seeing them in my bookcase, took them away, saying they were not proper books for me to read.

To me, "Hakkenden," with its wonderful symbolism, was one of the most inspiring books I had ever read. It was written in the 18th Century by Bakin, our great philosopher-novelist, and so musical is the literature, and so lofty the ideals, that frequently it has been compared, by Japanese of learning, to Milton's "Paradise Lost" and the "Divine Comedy" of Dante. The author was a strong believer in the unusual theory of spiritual transmigration, and his story is based on that belief.

The tale is of the daimio Satomi, who, with his almost starving retainers, was holding his castle against a besieging army. Knowing that the strength of the enemy lay alone in their able general, he desperately offered everything he possessed, even to his precious daughter, to any one brave enough to destroy his enemy. Satomi's faithful dog, a handsome wolf-hound named Yatsubusa, bounded away, and the next morning appeared before his master, carrying by its long hair the head of Satomi's foe. With their leader gone the enemy was thrown into confusion, and Satomi's warriors, with a mighty rush, put them to flight. Thus was the province restored to peace and prosperity. Then, so bitterly did Satomi regret his promise that he was enraged at the very sight of the faithful animal to whom he owed his good fortune. But his beautiful daughter, the Princess Fuse, pitied the wronged animal.

"The word of a samurai, once uttered, cannot be recalled," she said. "It is my duty to uphold the honour of my father's word."

So the filial daughter went with Yatsubusa to a mountain cave where she spent her time in praying to the gods that a soul might be given to the brave animal; and with every murmured prayer the noble nature of the dumb Yatsubusa drew nearer to the border line of human intelligence.

One day there came to the mountain a loyal retainer of Satomi. He saw, just within the cave, the Princess Fuse sitting before the shrine holding an open book. Before her, like a faithful vassal, Yatsubusa listened with bowed head to the holy reading. Believing he was doing a noble deed, the retainer lifted his gun and fired. The bullet, swift and strong, was guided by fate. It passed directly through the body of Yatsubusa and on, piercing the heart of the Princess Fuse.

At that instant the freed spirit of the Princess, as eight shining stars in a floating mist, rose from her body and floated softly through the sky to the eight corners of the world. Each star was a virtue: Loyalty, Sincerity, Filial Piety, Friendship, Charity, Righteousness, Courtesy, and Wisdom.

Fate guided each star to a human home, and in course of time, into each of these homes a son was born. As they blossomed into manhood, Fate brought the youths together, and the reunited eight virtues become heroic vassals, through whom came glory to the name of Satomi. So the spirit of the filial daughter brought honour to her father's name.

I could not understand why this miracle-story, filled with lofty symbolism, could be more objectionable than the many fables and fairy tales of personified animals that I had read in English literature. But, after much pondering, I concluded that thoughts, like the language, on one side of the world are straightforward and literal; and on the other, vague, mystical, and visionary.

At the end of my school life my beloved books were returned to me. I have them now—battered, loose-leafed, and worn—and I still love them.

As time passed on, I learned to like almost everything about my school—even many of the things which at first I had found most trying; but there was one thing which from the very first I had enjoyed with my whole heart. The school building was surrounded by large grounds with tall trees. A small lawn near the principal doorway was well cared for, but beyond was an extensive stretch of weedy grass and untrained shrubbery. There were no stone lanterns, no pond with darting gold-fish, and no curving bridge; just big trees with unbound branches, uncut grass, and—freedom to grow.

At my home there was one part of the garden that was supposed to be wild. The trees were twisted like wind-blown mountain pines; the stepping-stones marked an irregular path across ground covered with pine needles; the fence was of growing cedar peeping between uneven rods of split bamboo, and the gate was of brushwood tied with rough twine. But someone was always busy trimming the pines or cutting the hedge, and every morning Jiya wiped off the stepping-stones and, after sweeping beneath the pine trees, carefully scattered fresh pine needles gathered from the forest. There the wildness was only constant repression, but here at the school everything was filled with the uplifting freshness of unrestrained freedom. This I enjoyed with a happiness so great that the very fact that such happiness could exist in the human heart was a surprise to me.

One section of this wild ground the teachers divided into small gardens, giving one to each of the girls and providing any kind of flower seeds we wanted. This was a new delight. I already loved the free growth of the trees, and the grass on which I could walk even in my shoes; but this "plant-what-you-please" garden gave me a wholly new feeling of personal right. I, with no violation of tradition, no stain on the family name, no shock to parent, teacher, or townspeople, no harm to anything in the world, was free to act. So instead of having a low bamboo fence around my garden, as most of the girls had, I went to the kitchen and coaxed the cook to give me some dried branches used for kindling. Then I made a rustic hedge, and, in my garden, instead of flowers, I planted—potatoes.

No one knows the sense of reckless freedom which this absurd act gave me—nor the consequences to which it led. It had unloosed my soul, and I stood listening, while from a strange tangle of unconventional smiles and informal acts, of outspoken words and unhidden thoughts, of growing trees and untouched grass, the spirit of freedom came knocking at my door.

CHAPTER-15

How I Become a Christian

IN MY Nagaoka home, notwithstanding the love and care that surrounded me, my mind was always filled with unanswered questions. My education as a priestess had developed my mind, but it had grown in cramped silence; for, liberal as was my father in his views regarding my training, I was influenced by the home atmosphere of conservatism, and rarely spoke, even to him, of my inmost thoughts.

But occasionally this reserve was broken. Once, just after I had made many bows of farewell to the departing guests of the three-hundredth death celebration of an ancestor, I asked:

"Honourable Father, who is the first, the away-back, the very beginning of our ancestors?"

"Little daughter," Father gravely answered, "that is a presumptuous question for a well-bred girl to ask; but I will be honest and tell you that I do not know. Our great Confucius replied to his disciple concerning that very question, 'We know not life.'"

I was very young, but I well understood that I must in the future be more demure and womanly in my inquiries, and not ask questions with the freedom of a boy.

The influence of my school life in Tokyo had been subtle. Unconsciously I had expanded, until gradually I became convinced that asking questions was only a part of normal development. Then, for the first time in my life, I attempted to put into words some of the secret thoughts of my heart. This was gently encouraged by my tactful teachers; and, as time passed on, I realized more and more that they were wonderfully wise for women, and my confidence in them grew. Not only this, but their effortless influence to inspire happiness changed my entire outlook on life. My childhood had been happy, but it had never known one throb of what may be called joyousness. I used to gaze at the full moon sailing in the deep sky, with all the poetic ecstasy of the Japanese heart, but always, like a shadow, came the thought, "It will grow less from to-night." Our flower viewings were a delight to me, but invariably, as I travelled homeward, I sighed to myself: "The lovely blossoms will fall before the winds of to-morrow." So it was with everything. In the midst of gladness I unconsciously sent out a heart search for a thread of sadness. I ascribe this morbid tendency to the Buddhist teaching of my childhood; for there is a strain of hopeless sadness in all Buddhist thought.

But my life at school blew into my heart a breath of healthful cheerfulness. As the restraint which had held me like a vise began to relax, so also there melted within me the tendency to melancholy. It could not be otherwise; for the teachers, whether working, playing, laughing, or even reproving, were a continual surprise. In my home, surprises had been infrequent. People bowed, walked, talked, and smiled exactly as they had bowed, walked, talked, and smiled yesterday, and the day before, and in all past time. But these astonishing teachers were never the same. They changed so unexpectedly in voice and manner with each person to whom they spoke, that their very changeableness was a refreshing attraction. They reminded me of cherry blossoms.

Japanese people love flowers for what they mean. I was taught from babyhood that the plum, bravely pushing its blossoms through the snows of early spring, is our bridal flower because it is an emblem of duty through hardship. The cherry is beautiful and it never fades, for the lightest breeze scatters the still fresh and fragrant petals into another beauty of tinted, floating clouds; which again changes to a carpet of delicate white-and-pink shells—like my teachers, always changing and always beautiful.

Although I now know that my first impressions of American womanhood were exaggerated, I have never regretted this idealization; for through it I came to realize the tragic truth that the Japanese woman—like the plum blossom, modest, gentle, and bearing unjust hardship without complaint—is often little else than a useless sacrifice; while the American woman—self-respecting, untrammelled, changing with quick adaptability to new conditions—carries inspiration to every heart, because her life, like the blossom of the cherry, blooms in freedom and naturalness.

This realization was of slow growth, and it brought with it much silent questioning.

From childhood I had known, as did all Japanese people, that woman is greatly inferior to man. This I never questioned. It was fate. But as I grew older I so constantly saw that fate brings inconvenience and humiliation to blameless people that I fell into a habit of puzzling, in a crude, childish way, over this great unkind Power. At last a day came when my heart broke into open rebellion.

Ever since the hard days before the Restoration, my mother had been subject to occasional attacks of asthma, which we all were sincere in believing was due to some unknown wrong committed by her in a previous existence. Once when, after a breathless struggle, I heard her gasp, "It is fate and must be borne," I ran to Ishi and asked indignantly why fate made my mother suffer.

"It cannot be helped," she replied, with pitying tears in her eyes. "It is because of the unworthiness of woman. But you must be calm, Etsu-bo Sama. The Honourable Mistress does not complain. She is proud to bear silently."

I was too young to understand, but, with my heart pounding in hot rebellion against the powerful, mysterious injustice, I pulled myself into Ishi's lap and, convulsively clinging to her, begged her to tell me a story—quick—of clashing swords, and flying arrows, and heroes who fought and won.

Japanese children were not taught that rebellious thoughts, if unexpressed, are a wrong to the gods, so the resentment in my heart grew. But as it grew there slowly drifted into, and curiously blended with it, a blind wonder why my mother and Ishi, when hardship came for which they were not to blame, should submit to it, not only dutifully and patiently—that, of course, it was their place, as women, to do—but with pride. Something within me cried out that, however dutiful they might be in act, their *hearts* ought to rebel; yet I had known both unnecessarily to accept a humiliating blame that they knew was not theirs! That those two noble women should encourage self-humiliation I resented more bitterly than I did the hard decrees of fate.

Of course, this thought was not clear in my mind at that time. Then and for years after my idea of fate—for in fate I firmly believed—was of a vague, floating, stupendous power, for which I felt only resentful wonder.

Another puzzle came one midsummer airing day. It seems odd that it should have happened then, for airing days were the most care-free, happy time of the year for me. Then the godowns were emptied and long ropes stretched in the sunshine, on which were hung torn banners bearing our crest, old field-curtains used in the camps of our ancestors, ancient regalia of house officers, and many odd-shaped garments belonging to what Ishi's fairy tales called "the olden, olden time." Beneath the low eaves were piles of clumsy horse armour bound with faded ropes of twisted silk; and old war weapons—spears, battle-axes, bows, and sheaves of arrows—stood in out-of-the-way corners of the garden. All available space was utilized; even the bridge-posts and the stone lanterns were decorated with chain-silk armour and lacquer helmets with fearful masks.

The confusion was delightful. I loved it. And Father would walk around with me, showing me things and explaining their use, until, all perspiring and with eyes dazzled by the sun, we would go indoors and stumble through the cluttered-up halls to Honourable Grandmother's room. That seemed to be the only place in the house in order. Everywhere else were busy servants brushing, folding, or carrying, and at the same time all chattering gayly; for airing days, although bringing hard work, were a happy diversion in our rather monotonous household and always cordially welcomed by the servants.

When Father and I reached Honourable Grandmother's room we found ourselves suddenly shut away from all the turmoil into a place cool and quiet. I can see Father now, as, with a sigh of satisfaction, he closed the door behind him and, pushing aside the proffered cushion, bowed his thanks to Honourable Grandmother and seated himself on the cool straw mat beside the open doors overlooking the shady "wild garden." There he would sit, fanning himself and talking with Honourable Grandmother of old times.

Once, just after the noon meal of hot whale soup and eggplant, which was always served on airing days, Father went directly to his room. I was hurrying after him when I saw Jiya and another manservant in their stiff crestdresses crossing the garden from the godown. They were carrying, reverentially, a whitewood chest shaped like a temple box for sacred books. On the front, very large, was our crest, and around it was tied a straw rope with dangling Shinto papers. Many times I had seen that chest in the godown, standing alone on a whitewood platform. It held family heirlooms, some of them centuries old. The men were on their way to a certain room which Mother had prepared, where the chest would be opened in silence, and the sacred articles carefully examined by men in ceremonial garments.

I sat down listlessly on the edge of the porch, for I knew that Father, dressed in his stately *kamishimo* garments, would soon go to the room where the heirloom chest had been taken, and I should see him no more that afternoon. On airing days I generally followed him wherever he went, but across the threshold of that room I should not be allowed to step. I did not wonder why. It had always been so.

But as I sat alone on the porch I began to think, and after a while I hunted up Ishi.

"Ishi," I said, "I go everywhere else with Father. Why cannot I be with him in the room where they are airing the sacred things?"

"Etsu-bo Sama," she replied in the most matter-of-fact tone, as she shook out the long fringe of an old-fashioned incense ball, "it is because you were born a daughter to your father instead of a son."

I felt that her words were a personal reproach, and with the age-old, patient submission of the Japanese woman, I walked slowly toward Honourable Grandmother's room. It was comforting to turn my mind toward my stately, noble grandmother, to whom the entire household, even Father, looked up with reverence. Then, suddenly, like a breath of cold wind, came the thought that even my saintly grandmother would not dare touch the sacred things that were used to honour the Shinto gods. She always attended to the Buddhist shrine, but it was Father's duty to care for the white Shinto shrine. During his absence, Jiya or another manservant took his place, for no woman was worthy to handle such holy things, And yet the great god of Shinto was a woman—the Sun goddess!

That night I was bold enough to ask my father if his honourable mother was an unworthy woman like all others.

"What do *you* think, little Daughter?" he asked, after a moment's hesitation.

"It cannot be," I replied. "You honour her too greatly for it to be true."

He smiled and tenderly touched my head with his hand.

"Continue to believe so, little Daughter," he said gently. "And yet do not forget the stern teachings of your childhood. They form the current of a crystal stream that, as it flows through the ages, keeps Japanese women worthy—like your grandmother."

It was not until long, long afterward, when the knowledge of later years had broadened my mind, that I comprehended his hidden meaning that a woman may quietly harbour independent thought if she does not allow it to destroy her gentle womanhood. The night that this thought came to me I wrote in my diary: "Useless sacrifice leads to—only a sigh. Self-respect leads to—freedom and hope."

Beyond the wall on one side of our school was a rough path leading past several small villages, with ricefields and patches of clover scattered between. One day, when a teacher was taking a group of us girls for a walk, we came upon a dry ricefield dotted with wild flowers. We were gathering them with merry chattering and laughter when two village farmers passed by, walking slowly and watching us curiously.

"What is the world coming to," said one, "when workable-age young misses waste time wandering about through bushes and wild grass?"

"They are grasshoppers trying to climb the mountain," the other replied, "but the sun will scorch them with scorn. There can be only pity for the young man who takes one of those for his bride."

The men were rough and ignorant, but they were *men;* and though we all laughed, not one of the girls was far enough from the shackles of her mother's day not to feel a shadow of discomfort as we walked homeward.

The teacher paused as we came to the moss-covered stone wall of an old shrine and pointed to a near-by cherry tree, young and thrifty, growing out of the hollow of another tree whose fallen trunk was so old and twisted that it looked like a rough-scaled dragon. Beside it was one of the wooden standards so often seen in an artistic or noted spot. On the tablet was inscribed the poem:

> "The blossoms of to-day draw strength from the roots of a thousand years ago."

"This tree is like you girls," said the teacher, with a smile. "Japan's beautiful old civilization has given its strength to you young women of to-day. Now it is your duty to grow bravely and give to new Japan, in return, a greater strength and beauty than even the old possessed. Do not forget!"

We walked on homeward. Just as we reached our gate in the hedge wall one of the girls, who had been rather quiet, turned to me.

"Nevertheless," she said, defiantly, "the grasshoppers *are* climbing the mountain into the sunlight."

As I learned to value womanhood, I realized more and more that my love of freedom and my belief in my right to grow toward it meant more than freedom to act, to talk, to think. Freedom also claimed a *spiritual* right to grow.

I do not know exactly how I became a Christian. It was not a sudden thing. It seems to have been a natural spiritual development—so natural that only a few puzzles stand out clearly as I look back along the path. As I read, and thought, and felt, my soul reached out into the unknown; and gradually, easily, almost unconsciously, I drifted out of a faith of philosophy, mysticism, and resignation into one of high ideals, freedom, cheerfulness, and hope.

Of the wonder and glory of what I consider the greatest faith of the world I do not speak. Of that many know. And the selfish gain to me is beyond all words of all languages.

When I was sent to the mission school the fact that the teachers were of another religion was not considered at all. They were thought of only as teachers of the language and manners of America; so when I wrote to Mother, asking her consent to my becoming a Christian, I know she was greatly surprised. But she was a wise woman. She replied, "My daughter, this is an important thing. I think it will be best for you to wait until vacation. Then we will talk of it."

So I postponed being baptized, and when vacation came, I went to Nagaoka. The people there knew little of Christianity. The only impression most of them had was that it was a curious belief lacking in ceremony, whose converts were required to trample upon sacred things. There existed, especially among the old, a strong distaste against *Jakyo*, the evil sect, but it held no vital, forceful bitterness. The people of Nagaoka looked upon the stories of Japan's Christian martyrs as a distant and pitiful thing; but they had none of the shuddering horror felt in some communities of southern Japan, whose memories of the tragedies of four centuries ago had reason to live.

My mother, who had learned from Father to be tolerant of the opinions of others, had no prejudice against the new religion; but she believed that the great duty in life for sons and daughters consisted in a rigid observance of the ritual for ancestor-worship and the ceremonies in memory of the dead. When I first reached home her heart was heavy with dread, but when she learned that my new faith did not require disrespect to ancestors, her relief and gratitude were pathetic, and she readily gave her consent.

But Honourable Grandmother! My proud, loyal grandmother! It was impossible for her to understand, and I think my becoming a heretic was to her a lifelong sorrow. Her grief was my heaviest cross.

It was hard, too, to visit my relatives and friends. They looked upon me as a curiosity, and my mother was in a continual state of explanation and apology. One old aunt closed the doors of her shrine and pasted white paper over them that the ancestors might be spared the knowledge of my "peculiarity."

Another aunt, who invited me out to dinner, served no fish, feeling that, since I was so puzzlingly removed from ordinary life, I could not be feasted in the usual way. After discarding one plan after another, she finally concluded it would be both harmless and respectful for her to treat me as a priest.

All these things among the friends that I had known from babyhood hurt me. I could bravely have borne persecution, but to be set apart as something strange almost broke my heart. How I longed for my father! He would have understood, but I was alone in the midst of kindly ignorance. Everybody loved me, but they all looked at me in helpless pity.

At first I was unhappy, but my three months at home changed everything, both for my friends and for myself. When I returned to school I carried with me all the respect and love of the home friends that had always been mine, and which—thank God I have kept until now.

I think I am a true Christian. At least my belief has given me untold comfort and a perfect heart-satisfaction, but it has never separated me from my Buddhist friends. They have respect for this strange belief of mine; for they feel that, although I am loyal to the Christian God, I still keep the utmost reverence for my fathers and respect for the faith that was the highest and holiest thing they knew .

CHAPTER-16

Sailing Unknown Seas

ANOTHER happy year I spent in school. Then I returned to Nagaoka, realizing, myself, how little I knew, but in the eyes of my friends, an educated woman. This was an unenviable reputation—one which I knew I should have to live down if I wanted to stand well in the eyes of my old friends during these last months before I started for my new home in America. Each vacation I had had the same experience; for Nagaoka minds, although simple, loving, and true, were also stubborn; and no year could I begin where I had left off the year previous. My friends all loved me and they had become somewhat reconciled to my change of faith, but they could not help thinking, that, after all, I must be peculiar-minded to enjoy being so unlike other women. So again I had to accommodate myself to the discomfort of being received formally, and again patiently watch the gradual melting away of outward reserve until I could once more reach the faithful hearts beneath.

But finally I found myself settled into the old life, only now with the added excitement of my preparations for going to America.

As a Japanese marriage is a family matter it is not the custom for outsiders to present gifts; but the circumstances connected with mine were so unusual that many Nagaoka families sent large *mochi* cakes of red and white, most of them in the shape of storks or twin love-birds—emblems of congratulation and happy long life. Distant relatives, old retainers, and family servants, even those married and living at some distance, remembered me with weaves of silk and rolls of red and white *mawata*—the light, soft silk floss, so useful in every Japanese family as interlining for cloaks and dresses and for various delicate household purposes.

Most of these homely gifts were wholly inappropriate for life in America, but they expressed so much personal interest in me and loyalty to my father's family that I was deeply touched. And the dinners were many—most of them from relatives—where I, always seated next to Mother, in the place of honour, was served red rice and red snapper, head and all, and soup with seven, nine, or eleven vegetables.

All this was exciting in a quiet way; but the real excitement came when Brother, whose home was now in Tokyo, came up to be with us for my last weeks at home. He brought a letter from Matsuo, saying that a kind American lady, for the sake of a Japanese girl of my school in whom she was interested, had asked Matsuo to take me to her home when I arrived, and that we were to be married there. Mother read the letter with bowed head, and when she looked up, I was astonished to see the shadow of tears in her eyes. Poor Mother! Almost six years she had held, deep hidden in her heart, the shadowy dread that had assailed her when we first heard of Matsuo's decision to remain in America; for it was absolutely without precedent in Japanese life that a bride should go to a husband who had no mother or elder sister to guide and instruct the young wife in her new duties. This message was like a whisper of welcome from the thoughtful heart of a stranger; and that the stranger was a woman brought to Mother a feeling of safe, warm comfort. Lifting the letter to her forehead, she bowed in the ordinary form of expressing thanks, but said nothing, and not one of us realized that beneath her quiet manner a flood of grateful relief was sweeping away the anxiety of years. That night, as I passed her open door, I caught the fragrance of incense. The shrine was open. Matsuo's letter had been placed within, and before it the curling incense was carrying upward the deep thanks of a mother's heart.

Brother watched some of the preparations for my departure with evident disapproval.

"Those things are all right for a bride who is to live in Japan," he said, "but all nonsense for Etsu-bo. What will she do with a long crest-curtain and a doll festival set? Matsuo, being a merchant, will have to pay a big duty, and they're useless in America anyway."

At first. Honourable Grandmother and Mother listened in silence, but one day Mother gently but firmly protested.

"They may be useless," she said. "Of Etsu-ko's future I know nothing. But now she is a Japanese bride, going from her home to her husband. It is my duty to see that she goes as well prepared as is possible, according to the custom of her family. So it is decided."

Brother grumbled, but it is the women in a Japanese family who decide all things in connection with the "great interior," so the preparations went on according to rule. Mother, however, conceded some things to Brother's superior knowledge of America, and the rolls of silk and crêpe-brocade which came arranged in the shape of storks, pine trees, and the many beautiful emblems for a happy life, were given to sisters and other relatives; and my doll festival set, which every girl takes with her to her husband's home, was left behind.

The question of my personal trousseau was so important that a family council was called. Brother's ideas were positively startling. Most of the relatives were too honest to offer guessing suggestions, and none were well enough informed to make practical ones. Matters were in a rather puzzling and still undecided state when the Tokyo uncle, whose opinion the majority of the relatives looked upon with respect, sided with Brother in favouring the American costume.

"Among European people," he said, "it is considered extreme discourtesy to expose the body. Even men, whose liberty is of course greater than that of women, have to wear high collars and stiff cuffs. The Japanese dress, being low in the neck and scanty of skirt, is improper for wear among the European people."

Since most of my relatives knew almost nothing of foreign customs my uncle's statement made a great impression. Mother looked very anxious, for this was a new aspect of the subject, but Honourable Grandmother's loyal heart was wounded and aroused. To her, Japan was the land of the gods, and the customs of its people ought not to be criticized. Very quietly but with great dignity she protested.

"According to pictures," she said, "the pipe-shaped sleeves of the European costume lack grace. They are like the coats our coolies wear. It grieves me to think a time has come when my posterity are willing to humiliate themselves to the level of humble coolies."

Honourable Grandmother, being the most honoured one in the council, her opinion carried weight, and it was finally decided to prepare Japanese dress only, leaving my European clothes to be selected after I reached America. Brother had arranged that I should travel in the care of Mr. Holmes, an English tea merchant, a business friend of my uncle's, who, with his family, was returning to Europe by way of America.

At last the day came when all arrangements were complete, all farewells said, and Brother and I had again started together on a trip to Tokyo. But by this time the puffing land-steamer had, step by step, advanced over, and through, the mountains, and our former journey of eight days was now reduced to eighteen hours of jolting, rattling discomfort. We did not talk much, but sometimes at large stations we would get out for a few minutes of rest and change. At Takasaki we had just returned to our seats after a brisk walk up and down the platform when Brother anxiously stuck his head out of the window.

"What is it?" I asked.

"I am looking to see if you left your wooden clogs on the platform again," he replied with the old twinkle in his eye.

We both laughed, and the remainder of the trip was a pleasant three hours which I like to remember.

In Tokyo there were more dinners of red rice and whole fish, more useless, loving gifts, more farewells with warm heart throbs within and cool formal bows without, and then I found myself standing on the deck of a big steamer, with my brother by my side, and, on the water below, a waiting launch to take ashore the last friends of the passengers.

The third long, hoarse blast of the warning whistle sounded, and with an odd tightness in my throat I bent in a deep, long bow. Brother stood close to my sleeve.

"Little Etsu-bo," he said, with a strange tenderness in his voice, "I have been a poor brother, in whom you could not take pride; but I have never known an unselfish person—except you."

I saw his shadow bow, but when I lifted my head, he was in the crowd pressing toward the ship steps, his head held high and his laughing face lifted in a shout of farewell to Mr. Holmes.

After the first few days the voyage was pleasant, but Mrs. Holmes, who was not very strong, was ill most of the way over and her maid was busy with the care of the baby; so I spent much time on the deck alone, either gazing quietly out over the water or reading one of several Japanese magazines that had been given me just as I started. Mr. Holmes was most kind and attentive, but I was not used to men, and was so silent that he, knowing Japanese people, must have understood; for after the first day he would see me comfortably settled in my deck chair, then go away, leaving his own chair, next to mine, vacant except for the plate of fruit or cup of tea which he would have occasionally sent to me.

Because of my dress and the magazine, the passengers concluded that I could not understand English; and remarks about me or about Japanese were frequently made within my hearing by persons sitting near me. They were not unkind, but it seemed discourteous to be listening to words not meant for my ears, so one morning I took an English book up to the deck with me and was reading it when a lady, walking by, paused.

"I see you understand English," she said pleasantly, and remained for a little chat. She must have passed the news around, for after that I not only heard no more remarks about "the quiet little Jap," but, at various times, several ladies stopped for a short conversation. My place at the table was beside Mrs. Holmes. She rarely came, but I never felt alone, for the other passengers, seeming to feel responsible for the American lady's charge, were unceasingly kind in their attentions. Indeed there was an atmosphere of free action and cheerful speech among the passengers that was as refreshing as the salty, breezy air. Everyone said "Good-morning" to everyone else, friends or strangers, no one seemed to care. One day I saw two well-dressed ladies greet each other with a merry "Hello! Wonderful morning, isn't it? Let's take our constitutional together," and swinging into step, they marched off like a couple of soldier comrades. No bowing—no formal words. Everything was free and cordial. This lack of formality was very surprising, but it was most interesting, and it held a certain charm.

Of course I watched the dresses of these foreign ladies with the greatest interest. My uncle's remarks regarding the low neck and scanty skirt of the Japanese dress had astonished and troubled me very much, and since I was the only Japanese woman on the ship among some fifty or sixty American ladies, I felt responsible not to disgrace my nation. The Japanese dress is so made that it can be properly worn only when put on in one certain way, but I, inspired with a combination of girlish modesty and loyal patriotism, tried to pull the embroidered folds at the neck close up to my chin ; and I remained seated as much as possible so my scanty skirt would not be noticed.

The weather was unpleasant at the beginning of the voyage, and few ladies came on deck, but it was not long before the promenading commenced, and then I began to suspect that my uncle's opinion might not be wholly correct; but it was not until an evening entertainment where there was dancing that I entirely lost faith in his judgment. There the high collar and stiff cuffs of the gentlemen were to be seen, just as he had said; but I found that most of the ladies' dresses were neither high in the neck nor full in the skirt, and I saw many other things which mystified and shocked me. The thin waists made of lawn and dainty lace were to me most indelicate, more so, I think, unreasonable though it seemed, than even the bare neck. I have seen a Japanese servant in the midst of heavy work in a hot kitchen, with her kimono slipped down, displaying one entire shoulder; and I have seen a woman nursing her baby in the street, or a naked woman in a hotel bath, but until that evening on the steamer I had never seen a woman publicly displaying bare skin just for the purpose of having it seen. For a while I tried hard to pretend to myself that I was not embarrassed, but finally, with my cheeks flaming with shame, I slipped away and crept into my cabin berth wondering greatly over the strange civilization of which I was so soon to be a part.

I have no spirit of criticism in writing this. Indeed, after years of residence in this country I have so changed that I can look back with surprised amusement at my first impressions. The customs of all countries are strange to untrained eyes, and one of the most interesting mysteries of my life here is my own gradual but inevitable mental evolution. Now I can go to a dinner or a dance and watch the ladies in evening dress with pleasure. To me the scene is frequently as artistic and beautiful as a lovely painting, and I know those happy-faced women walking with the courteous gentlemen or swinging to the time of gay music are just as innocent and sweet of heart as are the gentle and hushed women of my own country over the sea.

My experiences in San Francisco were strange and puzzling, but delightful in their novelty. The astonishing little room at the Palace Hotel which we had no sooner entered than it began to rise upward, finally depositing us in a large apartment where we had a view as vast as from a mountain-top; the smooth white bathtub which could be filled with hot water without fuel or delay; the locked doors everywhere, for in Japan we never had a lock; all of these strange things, combined with the bewildering sense of the *bigness* of everything, was almost overpowering.

This sense of the enormous size of things—wide streets, tall buildings, great trees—was also pronounced inside the hotel. The ceilings were lofty, the furniture was large, the chairs were high and the sofas were wide, with the back far from the front. Everything seemed made for a race of giants; which, after all, is not so far from the truth, for that is what Americans are—a great people, with nothing cramped or repressed about them; both admirable and faulty in a giant way; with large person, generous purse, broad mind, strong heart, and free soul. My first impression has never changed.

We were in San Francisco only a few days, but everything was so hurried, so noisy, and so strange that my brain settled into a half-numb condition of non-expectancy. Then something happened. So simple, so homely a thing it was, that it stands out in my memory clear and separate from all else connected with my short stay in that wonderful city. A gentle, white-haired old minister, who had lived in Japan, came to make a friendly call. After the words of greeting he unwrapped a white box and placed it in my hand.

"I thought you would like a bit of home after your long trip," he said. "Look inside and see what it is." I lifted the cover and what was my surprise to see real Japanese food, fresh and delicious. I must, long before, have heard my brother say that Japanese food could be obtained in America, but it had made no impression upon me, and I was as astonished as if I had expected never again to behold Japanese food.

I looked up gratefully, and when I saw the humorous twinkle in his eye and kindliness in every feature of his smiling face, the strangeness of my surroundings melted away and there came my first throb of homesickness; for behind the gentle smile I saw the heart of my father. Years before, just after my father's death, Ishi had taken me to the Temple of the Five Hundred Buddhas, where stood row after row of big, carved images of stone or gilded wood. Every face was gentle, calm, and peaceful, and my lonely little heart searched each one, hoping to find my father's, for he too was now a Buddha. I did not know then that a longing heart will recognize its own reflection in only a trifle; and when at last I saw a face—gentle, dignified, and with a kindly smile, I felt that it pictured my father's heart, and I was satisfied. Just so I saw my father in the face of the old man whose kind heart had prompted the homely gift. I love to remember that smile as my welcome to the strange new country, which ever after was to be linked in my heart so closely to my own.

During the long ride across the continent I was reminded constantly of the revolving lanterns which were so fascinating to me as a child. The rapidly changing views from the train were like the gay scenes on the lantern panels that flitted by too quickly to permit of a clear image; their very vagueness being the secret of their charm.

Mr. and Mrs. Holmes came as far as a large city near my future home where they placed me in charge of a lady schoolteacher, a friend of Mrs. Holmes. Then they said good-bye and slipped out of my life, probably for ever. But they left a memory of kindness and consideration which will remain with me always.

When I was whirled into the dusky station of the city of my destination, I peered rather curiously from the car window. I was not anxious. I had always been taken care of, and it did not trouble me that I was to meet one I had never known before. On the crowded platform I saw a young Japanese man, erect, alert, watching. eagerly each person who stepped from the train. It was Matsuo. He wore a gray suit and a straw hat, and to me looked modern, progressive, foreign in everything except his face. Of course, he knew who I was at once but to my astonishment, his first words were, "Why did you wear Japanese dress?" There flashed into my mind a picture of the grave faces of the family council and my grandmother's words regarding pipe-sleeves. Yet here was I in a land of pipe-sleeves, gazing upon my future husband , a pipe-sleeved man. I laugh about it now, but then I was only a lonely, loose-sleeved, reproved little girl. Matsuo's disappointment in my dress was mostly on account of a much-honoured friend, Mrs. Wilson, the kind lady about whom Matsuo had written in the letter which for years was kept in Mother's shrine. With thoughtful kindness she had sent Matsuo in her carriage to meet me, and he, anxious that I should appear well in her eyes, was disgusted not to find me very up-to-date and progressive.

I silently took my place beside Matsuo in the shining carriage with its prancing black horses and uniformed coachman, and in absolute silence we rolled along the busy streets and up the long, sloping hill to a beautiful suburban home. I did not realize that the situation was perhaps as trying to him as to me; for I had never been so close to a man in my life, except my father, and I almost died on that trip.

The carriage turned into a road that circled a spacious lawn and stopped before a large gray house with a wide, many-columned porch. Outside the door stood a stately lady and a tall white-haired gentleman. The lady greeted me with outstretched hands and cordial words of welcome. I was too grateful to reply, and when I looked up into the noble, kindly face of the white-haired gentleman beside her, peace crept into my heart, for, behind his gentle smile, again I saw the heart of my father.

Those two good people will never know until they stand within the shining gates where heavenly knowledge clears our eyes how much their kindness, both before and after our wedding, meant to Matsuo and to me.

For ten restful days I was made welcome in that beautiful home; then came the second of "The Three Inevitables"—for, in Old Japan, marriage held its place equally with birth and death. My wedding took place on a beautiful day in June. The sun shone, the soft wind murmured through the branches of the grand old trees on the lawn, the reception room, with its treasures of art gathered from all lands, was fragrant with blossoms, and before a wonderful inlaid console table were two crossed flags—American and Japanese. There Matsuo and Etsu stood while the Christian words were spoken which made them one. By Matsuo's side was his business partner, a good kind man, and beside me stood one who ever since has proved my best and truest friend. So we were married. Everyone said it was a beautiful wedding. To me the room was filled with a blur of strange things and people, all throbbing with the spirit of a great kindness; and vaguely, mistily, I realized that there had been fulfilled a sacred vow that the gods had made long before I was born.

Our friend, Mrs. Wilson, was always kind to me, and I have been a happy and grateful guest in her beautiful home many, many times; but my permanent home was in an adjoining suburb, in a large, old-fashioned frame house set on a hill in the midst of big trees and lawns cut with winding gravel paths. The mistress of this house was a widowed relative of Mrs. Wilson, a woman in whom was united the stern, high-principled stock of New England with the gentle Virginia aristocracy. She invited us for a visit at first, because she loved Japan. But we were all so happy together that we decided not to separate; so for many years our home was there with "Mother," as we learned to call her. Close to my own mother in my heart of hearts stands my American mother—one of the noblest, sweetest women that God ever made.

From the love and sympathy and wisdom of this pleasant home I looked forth upon America at its best, and learned to gather with understanding and appreciation the knowledge that had been denied my poor brother in his narrow life in this same land.

CHAPTER-17

First Impressions

MY FIRST year in America was a puzzling, hurried push from one partially comprehended thought to another. Nevertheless it was a happy year. No Japanese bride is ever homesick. She has known from baby-hood that fate has another home waiting for her, and that there her destiny is to be fulfilled. Every girl accepts this in the same matter-of-course way that she accepts going to school. In marriage, she does not expect happiness without hardship any more than she expects school to be a playground with no study.

So I drifted on from week to week, occasionally having to remind myself that, even in America, the "eyelids of a samurai know not moisture," but, on the whole, finding the days full of new and pleasing experiences. I soon learned to like everything about my home, although, at first, the curtained windows, the heavy, dark furniture, the large pictures and the carpeted floors seemed to hem me in.

But I revelled in our wide porches and the broad lawn which swept in a graceful slope, between curving paths, down to the low stone wall. The battlemented top was like an elongated castle turret, and the big stone posts of the iron gates, half hidden from the porch by tall evergreens, seemed tome to have a protecting air. Then there was one big, crooked pine and an *icho* tree, standing side by side, which when the moon was just right, made a perfect picture of an old Japanese poem:

> "Between bent branches, a silver sickle swings aloft in youthful incompleteness, unknowing of its coming day of glory."

Oh, I did love all the outdoors of that home, from the very first moment that I saw it!

Much of my time was spent on one or the other of our three big porches, for Mother loved them almost as much as I did, and we used to go out the first thing after breakfast, she with her sewing and I with the newspaper.

In order to improve my English I read the paper every day, and I found it very interesting. I always turned first to the list of divorces in the court news. It was such a surprising thing to me that more women than men should be seeking for freedom. One day I told Mother that I felt sorry for the husbands.

"Why?" she asked. "It is as often the fault of the husband as the wife, I think. Isn't it so in Japan?"

"But after choosing for herself it must be hard for her wifely pride to acknowledge failure," I replied.

"How about the man?" said Mother.

> "He sees, and wants, and beckons;
> She blushes, and smiles, and comes—

or not, as she pleases. That is her part: to come or not to come."

"Why, I thought it was the custom in American marriages for the woman to select," I said, somewhat surprised; for I, with most Japanese people of that day, so interpreted the constant references in books and papers to the American custom of "women choosing their own husbands." It was one of many exaggerated ideas that we had of the dominant spirit of American women and the submissive attitude of American men. In the conversation that followed I heard for the first time that in this country the custom is for the worded request always to come from the man.

"It is like the folk tale that tells of the origin of our race," I said.

"That sounds as if it might be more interesting than the court items in the newspaper," laughed Mother. "Suppose you tell me about it."

"It's rather a long story from the beginning," I said; "but the important part is that a god and goddess named Izanagi and Izanami—our Adam and Ever—came from Heaven on a floating bridge and formed the islands of Japan. Then they decided to remain and build themselves a home. So they went to the Heavenly Post for the ceremony of marriage. The bride starting from the right and the bridegroom from the left, they walked around the Heavenly Post. When they met on the other side, the goddess exclaimed:

"'Thou beautiful god!'

"The god was displeased and said the bride had spoiled the ceremony, as it was his place to speak first. So they had to begin again. The goddess started again from the right of the Heavenly Post, and the god from the left; but this time, when they met, the goddess did not speak until she was spoken to.

"'Thou beautiful goddess!' Izanagi said.

"'Thou beautiful god!' replied Izanami.

"As this time the ceremony was properly performed, the husband and the wife built themselves a home, and from them came the nation of Japan."

"So it seems that Japanese and American marriages were originally not so unlike, after all," said Mother.

One of the most surprising things in America to me was the difficulty and often impossibility of my being able to do, as a wife, the very things for which I had been especially trained. Matsuo had come to this country when he was a boy in his teens, and was as unfamiliar with many Japanese customs as I was with those of America; so, with no realization on his part of my problems, I had many puzzling experiences connected with wifely duty. Some of these were tragic and some amusing.

At one time, for several evenings in succession, business detained Matsuo until a late hour. I was not well and Mother objected to my sitting up to await his return. This troubled me greatly; for in Japan it is considered lazy and disgraceful for a wife to sleep while her husband is working. Night after night I lay with wide-open eyes, wondering whom it was my duty to obey–my far-away mother who knew Japanese customs, or the honoured new mother, who was teaching me the ways of America.

I had another puzzling time when Mother was called away for a week by the death of a relative. Our maid, Clara, had heard Japan spoken of as "the land of cherry blossoms," and, thinking to please me, she made a cherry pie one night for dinner. In Japan cherry trees are cultivated for the blossoms only, just as roses are in America, and I had never seen cherry fruit; but the odour of the pie was delicious as it was placed before me to cut and serve.

"What is that?" asked Matsuo. "Oh, cherry pie! It's too acid. I don't care for it."

No Japanese bride is so disrespectful as to eat a dainty her husband cannot enjoy, so I gave orders for that beautiful pie to be eaten in the kitchen. But my heart followed it, and no pie that I have ever seen since has seemed worthy to compare with that juicily delicious memory.

Clara was always doing kind things for me, and one day I asked Matsuo what I could give her as a present. He said that in America money was always welcome; so I selected a new bill and, as we do in Japan, wrapped it in white paper and wrote on the outside, "This is cake."

How Matsuo did laugh!

"It's all right in America to give naked money," he said.

"But that is only for beggars," I replied , really troubled.

"Nonsense!" said Matsuo. "Americans consider money an equivalent for service. There is no spiritual value in money."

I meditated a good deal over that; for to a Japanese the expression of thanks, however deceitful the form it takes, is a heart-throb.

I liked our servants, but they were a never-ending surprise to me. Mother was kindness itself to the maid and to the man who worked on the place; but she had no vital interest in them, and they had no unselfish interest in us. In my home in Japan the servants were minor members of the family, rejoicing and sorrowing with us and receiving in return our cordial interest in their affairs. But this did not mean undue familiarity. There always existed an invisible line "at the doorsill," and I never knew a servant to overstep it or wish to; for a Japanese servant takes pride in the responsibility of his position. Clara attended to her duties properly, but her pleasures were outside the home; and on the days of her "afternoon out," she worked with such astonishing energy that it suggested no thought of anything but getting through. I could not help contrasting her with gentle, polite Toshi and her dignified bows of farewell.

But, on the other hand, Clara voluntarily did things for us which I should never have expected from any maid in Japan except my own nurse. One day I cringed with a feeling akin to horror when I heard Matsuo carelessly call out, "Clara, won't you take these shoes to the kitchen porch for William to clean?"

Such a request of a Japanese servant, other than the one whose duty it was to care for the sandals, would be considered an insult; but Clara picked up the shoes and carried them away, singing cheerily as she went. Life in America was very puzzling.

All Japanese girls are trained in housework, so naturally I was much interested in watching how everything was done in my American home. Mother encouraged my curiosity, saying that the inquiring mind is the one that learns; and Clara was always patient in explaining to "that sweet little Mrs. Sugarmoter." I was interested in the kitchen most of all, but the things to work with were so heavy, and were hung so high, and the shelves were so far up, that when I attempted to do anything there I found myself at a serious disadvantage. For the first time I sympathized with foreigners in Tokyo, who, it was said, frequently complained of the inconvenient "littleness" of everything. One of the schoolgirls used to tell us amusing tales about a foreign family to whom her father had rented his house. The man had to bow his head every time he passed through a doorway, and his wife thought it dreadful that the servant wanted to cut vegetables on a table six inches from the floor and to wash dishes without soap.

All the schoolgirls thought that that woman must have a peculiar mind, for we understood that foreigners used soap as we did a bran-bag—for bathing only. But after seeing how lavishly Clara used boiling water and soap in the kitchen, I realized that it was necessary, because so much grease and oil are used in American cooking. Our Japanese food was mostly vegetables. For fish we had special dishes and washed them with charcoal ashes.

One Friday, which was our cleaning day, I went into my room and was surprised to find Clara rubbing my bureau with an oiled cloth.

"What are you doing, Clara?" I asked.

"Oh, just cleanin' up a bit, Mrs. Sugarmoter," she replied .

To put something sticky on a thing to make it clean was incomprehensible. But when I examined my bureau later and found that it was dry and shiny, and *clean*, I was still more surprised. None of the wood of Japanese houses, outside or in, was ever varnished, oiled, or painted; and nothing was ever put on furniture except lacquer to preserve, or hot water to cleanse. Taki and Kin wiped the entire woodwork of the house every day with a cloth wrung out of hot water; and our porches were cleaned, morning and evening, by a servant, who, stooping over and pushing a steaming pad of folded cloth before her, ran quickly back and forth, from one end of the porch to the other, carefully following the line of the boards. The porches had gradually become so dark and polished that they reflected distinctly any person walking on them, and since they never were stepped on with outside shoes, they kept their satiny polish for years.

I was always interested in housework, but an exciting interest came at the time of house-cleaning. Then I wandered from room to room, watching with amazement and delight while William and Clara worked. I had never dreamed that the heavy cloth which covered the floors, fitting so neatly into each corner and around the projections, was nailed down and could be lifted up in one immense piece and carried out to be cleaned. Two men were required to do the work. Our floors in Japan were covered with mats that pushed together as tight as the pieces in a box of dominoes, but each mat was only six feet by three in size, and Jiya could easily handle them alone.

Matsuo and I had adjoining rooms, and when I went upstairs to see if the cloth had been taken from his floor also, I saw that the large mahogany closet, which I had supposed was a part of the house, had been pulled out bodily into the middle of the room. I was too surprised for words. And its back—and indeed the backs of all our beautiful furniture—was only rough boards; just such as I had seen in Japan on a cart being taken to the shop of a carpenter. It was most astonishing. I had never before seen any furniture that was not planed and polished all over—outside, inside, top, bottom, and back.

Mother explained that this American deceit originated in the practical idea of saving time and work. Thus I received my first insight into the labour problem.

It was during house-cleaning that Mother and I had our first heart-to-heart talk. She was looking over some trunks of clothing in the attic, and I was sitting near, holding a big cake of camphor, from which I broke off small pieces and wrapped them in tissue paper for her to place between the folds of the garments. She was showing me an army coat which her grandfather had worn in the War of 1812. The open trunks, the disarranged clothing, the familiar odour of camphor in the air, reminded me of the airing-days at home. I could see so well Grandmother's room where Father and I always went to get away from the ropes of swaying garments and the confusion of busy servants brushing and folding.

"What are you thinking of, Etsu?" asked Mother, with a smile. "Your eyes look as if they were seeing things five thousand miles away."

"More than that," I answered, "for they are looking into a past before I was born."

I leaned over and stroked the big collar of the old army coat on Mother's lap. In some way it seemed, just then, the nearest to my heart of anything in America.

"In our godown also, Mother," I said, "are sacred mementoes to which war memories cling. There is a pile of thin-leaved books written in my father's hand, which are dear treasures to us all. You do not know, Mother, but my father was a prisoner once—held as hostage for a long time in an army camp. His surroundings were very different from what the word suggests here in America. The camp was located in a temple grove, and the part of the temple where the priests lived was given over to the officials and their high-rank prisoner; and although Father was alone among enemies, he was treated as an honoured guest.

"His faithful attendant was separated from him, but instead, were youthful samurai, who with respectful attention cared for every want. For recreation they had trials in art defencing and various samurai sports; and sometimes, as was the social custom among samurai, they would spend hours together in poem competition or in singing classic songs of Old Japan. He had every physical comfort and mental recreation, but he was outside the world. Even his books were poems and prose of fine old literature which held no word of present life. At the close of each monotonous day he would lay his head upon his pillow and his restless mind would wonder—wonder: Had the Imperialist army reached Echigo? Who was in charge of Nagaoka Castle? What was the unknown fate of his retainers? of his son? of his wife and daughters?

"There was a beautiful garden where he walked daily. Perhaps there were guards outside the gate. He did not know. He saw nothing to tell him that he was not free, and probably there was nothing, for his guardians knew that he was held by chains stronger than any that could be forged—the spirit of samurai honour.

"During this lonely time Father's dearest hours were those he spent with his writing brushes and in games of *go* with the commander-general—a man of superior culture, who often came to talk with him. The two men had similar tastes and an equal sense of honour—differing only in that they were loyal to different masters—and those months together formed and sealed the friendship of a lifetime. Both were fond of playing *go* and both played well and earnestly. Neither spoke his secret thought, but, long afterward, Father confided to Mother that he was conscious that in every game they played each in his own heart was fighting for his own cause. Sometimes one would win, sometimes the other; oftener still there was a draw; but always the vanquished gravely congratulated the victor, and as gravely received his formal thanks in reply.

"So passed the days, and weeks, and months, and more months and more, until he dreaded to think back and count. And not a word or look or hint had come to him of any world outside the temple walls.

"Late one beautiful spring afternoon he was sitting quietly in his room overlooking the garden. A priestly chanting was faintly heard from distant rooms. There was a breeze, and falling cherry blossoms were drifting across the garden, their fragrant petals slipping and catching in tinted drifts against the uneven stepping-stones. A young moon was chasing shadows in the pine branches. It was a picture Father never forgot.

"A young attendant approached, and in his usual deferential manner, but with grave face, announced, 'Honourable Guest, the evening meal is served.'

"Father bowed his head and the little lacquer table was brought and placed before him on the mat.

"At last the expected message had come. The rice bowl was on the right, the soup was on the left; the chop-sticks were standing upright as if to place before a shrine, and the browned fish in the oval dish was without a head. It was the silent command from a samurai to a samurai.

"Father ate his dinner as usual. When the time came for his bath, the attendant was ready. His hair was washed, and the queue, no longer needed to bear the helmet's weight, was left unoiled and loose, to be tied with a paper cord. He donned his white linen death-robe and over it placed the soft-tinted *kamishimo* of the samurai who goes to death. Then quietly he waited for the midnight hour.

"The commander-general entered, and greeted him with the soldierly stiffness that hides deep feeling.

"'I come not as an official of the State,' he said ,'but as a friend, to ask you to honour me with a message.'

"'I thank you deeply,' Father replied, 'for this and other kindness. I left my home to return no more. I gave instructions then. I have no message.'

"But he asked that the Commander would care for his attendant who, by Father's death, would become a masterless man. The General assured him that this should be done; and also told him that his own highest retainer would be Father's attendant at the last. Thanks were bowed and formal courtesies exchanged, then these two men, who had grown to know and respect each other deeply, parted with no other word. It seems cold to an American; but it was the samurai way, and each knew the other's heart.

"The hour came. Father held the highest rank of the seven who waited for the midnight hour; so, first and alone, clothed in his death-robe and with the pride of centuries in his bearing, he walked toward the temple yard. As he entered the enclosure, the others on the opposite side, white-robed and silent, were waiting. One was a child with an attendant close behind. Father saw—saw without looking—the gray face and strained eyes of Minoto, his own little son's guardian.

"The child made a motion, so slight it was scarcely more than a quiver. Minoto clutched the boy's sleeves. Father strode on. The quiver passed, the boy sat erect, his eyes looking straight forward. It was my brother. Oh, whatever he has been since, in this new world so unfamiliar to him, there, in his own world—the world which by inheritance and environment he understood—he was a samurai! My father took his place with calm and dignified bearing with his head upright and his eyes looking straight forward—unseeing. But in his heart—— Oh, why could not the God he did not know pity him?" And I clutched the big collar of the old army coat and buried my coward face within its folds—for I had lost my samurai spirit. America had been too good to me, and part of me had died. I felt Mother's hand upon my shoulder but I dared not lift my head and shame my father, for moisture was on the face of his un-brave daughter.

"Oh, my little girl! My dear little girl! But he did not die! He did not die!"

I lifted my head, but I did not wipe my eyes.

"The war had ended, and the new Government had pardoned all political prisoners," I said, calm again. "The decision was already known to the officials, and the messengers were on the way; but, until they came, the forms had to be carried out to the very end."

"Yes, I have known of things like that in the days when messages were carried by galloping horses and running men," said Mother sadly. "And no one was to blame. If laws could be changed by unproved knowledge, the country would soon be guided by guesswork. And that would never do! That would never do!"

I looked at Mother in surprise, for with red cheeks and misty eyes she was clutching tight the army coat on her lap and looking straight at me.

"How close together are the countries of the world," she went on. "Your old nurse was right, Etsu, when she said that the earth is flat and you are on the other side of the plate, not far away, but out of sight."

Then we both smiled, but Mother's lips were trembling. She put her arm around me gently, and—I've loved Mother ever since!

Another "memory stone" in my life was the day that I entertained the club. Mother belonged to a literary society the members of which studied about different countries and wrote essays. The meetings were held at the homes of the members, and early on the morning of the very day that it was Mother's turn to entertain she received a message calling her to the city for a "between trains" visit with a dear friend who was passing through the city on her way to a distant land. Mother would be back before the meeting was over, but I was dismayed to be left with the responsibility of arranging the rooms and receiving the guests.

"There is nothing for you to be worried about," said Matsuo who was just starting to his business. "I heard Mother tell William to bring more chairs from upstairs and you have only to see that he places them like in a church. Clara knows how."

"But Mother meant to have flowers, and she said something about a little table for the president and—Oh, the piano has to be pushed back! Mother said so. I do wish she were here!" I cried, in real anxiety and distress.

"Don't make a mountain out of a mole-hill! Clara is equal to anything"; and Matsuo ran across the lawn in response to the waving hand of a neighbour who was waiting in his buggy at the iron gates.

I knew he was right, for Clara had cleaned the rooms the day before, and everything really necessary had been done; but, nevertheless, I felt lost and helpless.

In the midst of my hour of woe I saw walking up the path around the lawn an old lady of the neighbourhood who sometimes came in for an informal chat with Mother. I ran out and welcomed her most cordially, eager to ask her advice.

"The piano is not in the way," she said. "These rooms are large enough as they are, even if everyone comes. You won't have to do a thing except put in more chairs. "But"—and she looked around the big double parlours with the lace-curtained windows and the long mirror with gilded frame—"the rooms do look empty with the centre table taken out. Why don't you scatter about some of those Japanese trinkets that you have upstairs? They would add wonderfully to the general effect."

As soon as she was gone I brought down several Japanese things and placed them here and there about the room. Then I arranged a few iris blossoms in a vase according to the graceful, but rigid, rules of Japanese flower arrangement, and stepped back to view the effect.

From the flowers my eyes went slowly around the room. I was disappointed. What was wrong? The Japanese articles were each one of rare workmanship, and the vase of blossoms was beautiful; but for some mysterious reason Mother's parlours never before had looked so unattractive. Suddenly my eye fell on a little bronze incense burner, which had been given me in my childhood, by one of the Toda children, for my doll festival set. It looked oddly out of place on top of the American bookcase; and when, lifting my eyes, I saw above it an etching of a dancing faun, I almost hysterically snatched it away. With lightning swiftness my mind flew to the cool, light rooms of my Nagaoka home—to the few ornaments, each in the place designed for it—and I began to understand. My Japanese treasures would be beautiful in their proper surroundings, but here they were neither beautiful themselves, nor did they add to the attractiveness of our stately rooms. They were only odd, grotesque curios. Hurriedly putting them away and removing my carefully arranged vase of iris to the kitchen, I ran to a field back of our carriage house and gathered an armful of daisies and feathery grasses. Soon I had all the vases in the house, regardless of shape or hue, loosely filled with the fresh, wild blossoms. The rooms looked beautiful, and they were in perfect harmony with the broad lawn outside, stretching in rolling waves of green down to the gray stone wall.

"West is West, and East is East," I said, as I sank on a sofa with a sigh of relief. "I think while I'm here I'll forget the conventional standard of beauty; for only the charm of naturalness is suited to these big, free, homelike rooms of Mother's."

CHAPTER-18
Strange Customs

WE HAD a large stone church in our suburb which was not quite paid for, and a society of church-women called "The Ladies' Aid" occasionally gave a fair or concert and sometimes a play with local talent, in order to obtain money to add to the fund.

One evening Mother, Matsuo, and I attended one of these concerts. On the programme was a vocal solo of some classic selection. The singer was the gifted daughter of a wealthy citizen and had received her musical education in Europe. I knew her as a rather quiet young woman with a gentle voice and dignified manner; therefore I was surprised, when the music began, to see her step forward briskly and informally, bow smilingly to the audience, right and left, and then, with much facial expression, give a vocal exhibition of high, clear trills and echoes that to my untrained ears was a strange and marvellous discord, but the most wonderful thing that I had ever heard in my life.

The effect left on my mind was of brightness, quick motion, and high-pitched sound. In strong contrast is our classic music, which always suggests subdued colours, slow movement, and deep, mellow tones. Also, like most Japanese art, our music requires listening eyes as well as ears. Otherwise its appeal is lost.

Our classic stage is always the same. The entire back is one solid board of natural cedar wood, on which is painted a gigantic dwarf pine. The floor is of camphor wood and is bare. On this the singers, who, of course, are always men, sit as motionless as dolls. Their dress is the old-fashioned, soft-hued garment of ceremony. Each one, before beginning to sing, makes a slow, deep bow, and, with studied deliberation, places his fan horizontally before him on the floor. Then, with his hands on his knees, palms down, and sitting very erect and motionless, he tells in song, and with incredible elocutionary power, some wonderful tale of war and romance; but wholly without movement of body or change of facial expression.

At the close the singer's face is often flushed with feel ing, but, with no change of expression, he bows, then gently takes up his fan and resumes his former impassive attitude. The audience sits in profound silence. The listeners may be touched to tears or raised to the highest pitch of excitement, but this can be detected only by the sound of subdued sniffling or the catch of a quick sigh. For centuries repression has been the keynote of everything of a high character, and the greatest tribute that can be paid to a singer or an actor of classic drama is to be received in deep silence.

One thing in America, to which I could not grow accustomed, was the joking attitude in regard to women and money. From men and women of all classes, from newspapers, novels, lecturers, and once even from the pulpit, I heard allusions to amusing stories of women secreting money in odd places, coaxing it from their husbands, borrowing it from a friend, or saving it secretly for some private purpose. There was never anything dishonourable implied in this. Perhaps the money was saved to get new curtains for the parlour, or even a birthday present for the husband. These jokes were a puzzle to me—and a constantly growing one; for as time passed on, I myself saw things which made me realize that probably a foundation of serious truth might lie beneath some of the amusing stories.

Our suburb was small and we were all interested in each other's affairs, so I was acquainted with almost everybody. I knew the ladies to be women of education and culture, yet there seemed to be among them a universal and openly confessed lack of responsibility about money. They all dressed, well and seemed to have money for specific purposes, but no open purse to use with free and responsible judgment. Once, at a church fair, where I had a table, several ladies, after walking around the hall and examining the various booths, had bought some small, cheap articles, but left the expensive ones, saying, "My husband will be here later on and I'll get him to buy it," or "When the gentlemen come those high-priced things will sell." I had never known a Japanese man to buy any thing for his home, or be expected to.

Once, when I was shopping with a friend, she stopped at her husband's office to ask him for money. I thought that was strange enough, but a still more curious thing happened when I went with Mother to a meeting of the church ladies where they were raising a certain amount for some unusual purpose. The Ladies' Aid had recently made a great many calls on the husbands' purses, and so this time each member had pledged herself to bring five dollars which she must obtain without asking her husband for it. The meeting I attended was the one where the money was handed in, each lady telling, as she gave it, how she had succeeded in getting her five dollars. Most had saved it in various ways, a little at a time. One said that she had made a real sacrifice and returned to her milliner a new hat—paid for, but not worn—receiving in exchange one that was five dollars less in price. Another had sold two theatre tickets which had been given her. Still another told, in very witty rhyme, how she, a poor Ladies' Aid lady, had spent most of her leisure time for a week, and had pledged herself for a week longer, in darning stockings for the children of her neighbour, a rich non-Ladies' Aid lady.

The meeting was intensely interesting. It reminded me of our poem-making parties, only of course this was gayer and these stories were on an undignified subject. I enjoyed it all until a pretty, bright, and beautifully dressed woman rose and said that she didn't know how to save money and she didn't know how to earn it. She had promised not to cheat in her charge account at the store, and she had promised not to ask her husband for the five dollars, so she had done the only thing that was left for her to do: she had stolen it from her husband's pocket when he was asleep.

This report caused a great deal of merriment, but I was saddened. All the reports seemed tragic after she said, "That was the only thing left to do." It seemed incredible, here in America, where women are free and commanding, that a woman of dignity and culture, the mistress of a home, the mother of children, should be forced either to ask her husband for money, or be placed in a humiliating position.

When I left home, Japan, at large, was still following the old custom of educating a girl to be responsible for the well-being of her entire family—husband included. The husband was the lord of the family; but the wife was mistress of the home and, according to her own judgment, controlled all its expenses—the house, the food, the children's clothing and education; all social and charitable responsibilities, and her own dress, the material and style of which were expected to conform to her husband's position.

Where did she get the money? The husband's income was for his family, and his wife was the banker. When he wanted money for himself he asked her for it, and it was her pride to manage so that she could allow him the amount suitable for a man of his standing. As to what the requirements of his position might be, there was little question, for to know this was part of the wife's education. The husband might shrug his shoulders and say, "It's very inconvenient," but the entire house and its standing were his pride, and any disarrangement that would mar the whole was his loss. Therefore the needs of the home came first. A man married, primarily, as a duty to the gods and to his ancestors; secondarily, to obtain a mistress for his home who would guide it in such a manner that it and his family might be a credit to him. If she managed well, he was complimented by his friends. If she failed, he was pitied.

This was true of all classes except lords of large estates or financial kings of business. In these cases there was a home treasurer, but he was at the call of the mistress, and her judgment as to her needs was supreme. The treasurer's only power of protest lay in the right to say, with many apologies, "The Honourable Mistress is about to overdraw her account." The hint was generally sufficient, for a Japanese woman, like everyone in a responsible position, desired to do her duty creditably.

Conventional forms are losing in rigidity year by year, but even yet the people are considerably influenced by rules which in the past were uniform and recognized by all. Any marked deviation from these is still considered bad form.

The standards of my own and my adopted country differed so widely in some ways, and my love for both lands was so sincere, that sometimes I had an odd feeling of standing upon a cloud in space, and gazing with measuring eyes upon two separate worlds. At first I was continually trying to explain, by Japanese standards, all the queer things that came every day before my surprised eyes; for no one seemed to know the origin or significance of even the most familiar customs, nor why they existed and were followed. To me, coming from a land where there is an unforgotten reason for every fashion of dress, for every motion in etiquette—indeed, for almost every trivial act of life—this indifference of Americans seemed very singular.

Mother was a wonderful source of information, but I felt a hesitation about asking too many questions, for my curiosity was so frequently about odd, trifling, unimportant things, such as why ladies kept on their hats in church while men took theirs off; what was the use of the china plates which I saw hanging on the walls of some beautiful houses; why guests are taken to the privacy of a bedroom and asked to put their hats and cloaks on the *bed*—a place that suggested sleep or sickness; why people make social calls in the *evening*—the time of leisure in Japan; what originated the merriment and nonsense of Hallowe'en and April Fool's days, and why such a curious custom exists as the putting of gifts in stockings—*stockings*, the very humblest of all the garments that are worn.

It seemed strange to me that there should never be any hint or allusion to these customs in conversation, in books, or in newspapers. In Japan, tradition, folklore, and symbolism are before one all the time. The dress of the people on the streets; the trade-mark on the swinging curtains of the shops; the decorations on chinaware; the call of the street vender; the cap of the soldier; the pleated skirt of the schoolgirl: each points back to some well known tale of how or why. Even the narrow blue-and white towel of the jinrikisha man and the layer lunch-box of the workman bear designs suggesting an ancient poem or a bit of folklore, as familiar to every Japanese child as are the melodies of Mother Goose to the children of America.

One afternoon, at a small reception, a lady spoke pleasantly to me of the healthfulness to the foot of a shoe like my sandal and then referred with disapproval to the high heels and pointed toes then in vogue.

"Why are these shapes worn?" I asked. "What started them?"

"Oh, for no reason," she replied. "Just a fashion; like—well, like your folding your dress over left-handed."

"But there is a reason for that," I said. "It is only on a corpse that the kimono is folded over from the right."

That interested her, and we had a short talk on the peculiarity of Japanese always honouring the left above the right in everything, from the Imperial throne to the tying of a knot. Then, lightly touching the back of my sash, she asked, "Would you mind telling me what this bundle is for? Is it to carry the babies on?"

"Oh, no," I replied, "it is my sash, and is only an ornament. A baby is carried in a hammock-like scarf swung from the nurse's shoulders."

"This material of your sash is very beautiful," she said. "May I ask why you arrange it in that flat pad instead of spreading it out, so that the design can be seen?"

Since she seemed really interested, I willingly explained the various styles of tying a sash for persons differing in rank, age, and occupation; and for different occasions. Then came the final question, "Why do you have so much goods in it?"

That pleased me, for to a Japanese the material beauty of an article is always secondary to its symbolism. I told her of the original meaning of the twelve-inch width and twelve-foot length, and explained how it represented much of the mythology and astrology of ancient Oriental belief.

"This is very interesting," she said as she turned to go, "especially about the signs of the zodiac and all that; but it's a shame to hide so much of that magnificent brocade by folding it in. And don't you think, yourself, little lady," and she gave me a merry smile, "that it's positively wicked to buy so many yards of lovely goods just to be wasted and useless?"

And she walked away with a long train of expensive velvet trailing behind her on the floor.

Mother's furniture, which was of beautiful wood and some of it carved, at first made me feel as if I were in a museum; but when I went into other homes, I found that none were simple and plain. Many reminded me of godowns, so crowded were they with, not only chairs, tables, and pictures, but numbers of little things—small statues, empty vases, shells, and framed photographs, as well as really rare and costly ornaments; all scattered about with utter disregard, according to Japanese standards, of order or appropriateness. It was several months before I could overcome the impression that the disarranged profusion of articles was a temporary convenience, and that very soon they would be returned to the godown. Most of these objects were beautiful, but some of them were the shape of a shoe or of the sole of the foot. This seemed to be a favourite design, or else my unwilling eyes always spied it out, for in almost every house I entered I would see it in a paper-weight, a vase, or some other small article. Once I even saw a little wooden shoe used as a holder for toothpicks.

Generations of prejudice made this very objectionable to me, for in Japan the feet are the least honoured part of the body; and the most beautiful or costly gift would lose all value if it had the shape of footwear.

And Japanese curios! They were everywhere, and in the most astonishingly inappropriate surroundings. Lunch boxes and rice-bowls on parlour tables, cheap roll pictures hanging on elegant walls; shrine gongs used for dining-room table bells; sword-guards for paper-weights; ink-boxes for handkerchiefs and letter-boxes for gloves; marriage-cups for pin-trays, and even little bamboo spittoons I have seen used to hold flowers.

In time my stubborn mind learned, to some extent, to separate an article from its surroundings; and then I began to see its artistic worth with the eyes of an American. Also I acquired the habit, whenever I saw absurd things here which evidently arose from little knowledge of Japan, of trying to recall a similar absurdity in Japan regarding foreign things. And I never failed to find more than one to offset each single instance here. One time a recollection was forced upon me by an innocent question from a young lady who told me, in a tone of disbelief, that she had heard in a lecture on Japan that elegantly dressed Japanese ladies sometimes wore ordinary, cheap chenille table covers around their shoulders in place of scarfs. I could only laugh and acknowledge that, a few years before, that had been a popular fashion. Imported articles were rare and expensive, and since we never used table covers ourselves, we had no thought of their being anything but beautiful shawls. I had not the courage to tell her that I had worn one myself, but I did tell her, however, of something that occurred at my home in Nagaoka when I was a child.

On my father's return from one of his visits to the capital he brought Ishi and Kin each a large turkish towel with a coloured border and a deep fringe. The maids, their hearts swelling with pride, went to temple service wearing the towels around their shoulders. I can see them yet as they walked proudly out of the gateway, the white lengths spread evenly over their best dresses and the fringe dangling in its stiff newness above their long Japanese sleeves. It would be a funny sight to me now, but then I was lost in admiration; and it seemed perfectly natural that they should be, as they were, the envy of all beholders.

Of all my experiences in trying to see Japanese things with American eyes, one particularly inharmonious combination was a foolishly annoying trial to me for many months. The first time I called on Mrs. Hoyt, the hostess of an especially beautiful home, my eyes were drawn to a lovely carved *magonote*—"hand of grandchild," it is called in Japan, but in America it has the practical name, "scratch-my-back"—which was hanging by its silk cord on the cover of an ebony cabinet. Beside it, thrown carelessly over the same cord, was a rosary of crystal and coral beads. The little ivory finger-rake was exquisitely carved, and the rosary was of rare pink coral and flawless crystal; but to the eye of an Oriental all beauty was ruined by the strange arrangement. It was like putting the Bible and a toothbrush side by side on a parlour table.

I did not criticize the judgment of the hostess. Her superior taste in all things artistic was beyond question, and in America the *magonote* was an object of art only. From that viewpoint it was properly placed. I realized this, and yet, whenever afterward I entered that room, I persistently kept my eyes turned away from the ebony cabinet. It was only after two years of close friendship with the hostess that I had the courage to tell her of my shocked first visit to her home. She laughs at me even yet, and I laugh too; but there is a warm feeling of satisfaction in my heart this moment as I remember that the rosary and the *magonote* no longer hang side by side.

There was another thing in Mrs. Hoyt's home which was removed at the same time the rosary and the "hand of grandchild" parted company. It was a large coloured photograph of a scene in Japan—not an ancient print, but a modern photograph. It was an attractive picture in graceful arrangement and delicate colouring, and my hostess had placed it in a conspicuous place. Her ignorant eyes beheld only its artistic beauty, but my heart turned sick with shame. That picture would never have been allowed in any respectable house in Japan, for it was the photograph of a well-known courtesan of Tokyo taken at the door of her professional home. "Oh, why do Japanese sell those things?" I shudderingly asked myself; but immediately came the puzzling response, "Why do Americans want to buy?"

One day I went into the city with a friend to do some shopping. We were on a street car when my attention was attracted by a little girl sitting opposite us who was eating something. Children in Japan do not eat on the street or in a public place, and I did not know then that it is not the custom in America as it is with us never to eat except at a table.

My friend and I were busy talking, so for a while I did not notice the child, but when I chanced to glance at her again, I was surprised to see that she was still eating. Two or three times afterward I looked at her, and finally I turned to my friend.

"I wonder what that child is eating," I said.

"She is not eating anything," my friend replied. "She is chewing gum."

Again I looked at the child. She was sitting, drooped and weary, her loose hands lying in her lap, and her feet spread around her bundle in a very awkward and difficult position. As I watched her tired face, suddenly I remembered something that had happened on the train on my trip across the continent.

"Is she sick?" I asked,

"No, I think not. Why do you ask?"

"I think I took that medicine on the train," I replied.

"Oh, no!" my friend said, laughing. "Chewing gum is not medicine. It's a sort of wax, just to chew."

"Why does she do it?" I asked.

"Oh, most children of her class chew gum, more or less. It's not an elegant thing to do. I don't allow my children to touch it."

I said nothing more, but a partial light began to dawn upon my experience on the train. I had been uncomfortably car-sick, and Mrs. Holmes had given me a small, flat block of fragrant medicine which she said would cure nausea. I put it in my mouth and chewed a long time, but I could not swallow it. After a while I got tired, but Mrs. Holmes was still eating hers, so, concluding that it must be a medicine possessing wonderful merit, as it would not dissolve, I wrapped it carefully in a piece of white tissue paper and put it in the little mirror case that I wore in my sash.

I never heard what originated this peculiar custom, but I think I never found anything odd in America for which I could not find an equivalent in Japan. Gum-chewing reminded me of *hodzuki*-blowing, a habit common among some Japanese children; and also much practised by tea house girls and women of humble class. The *hodzuki* is made from a little red berry having a smooth, tough peeling. The core is very soft and with proper care can be squeezed out leaving the unbroken peeling in the shape of a tiny round lantern. This little ball is elastic and though it has no special taste, children love to hold it in the mouth and by gently blowing the hollow shell make what they call "mouth music." It sounds somewhat like the soft, distant croaking of a pond frog. *Hodzuki*-blowing is not beautiful music, nor is it a pretty custom, but it is neither harmful nor unclean. The worst that can be said of it is what many a nurse calls to her charge:

"Take that squeaky thing out of your mouth. It will make your lips pouty and ugly."

CHAPTER-19
Thinking

AT THE broad corner where our front and side porches joined was where my hammock swung. It was shaded by a big apple tree, and I used to put in a big cushion and sit Japanese fashion while I read. I could never get used to lying in it, as Mother sometimes did, but I liked to imagine that I was in an open *kago*—a quiet, not a swaying one—and watch for glimpses between the trees of carriages and country teams that passed occasionally on the road beyond the big evergreens and the stone wall.

From there, too, I could look across a little stretch of green, and on, through the break made in the lilac hedge by the drawbridge, to the home of our nearest neighbour. We did not have many close neighbours, for our suburb was a wide-spreading one with the houses far apart, each set in the midst of its own stretch of lawn and shrubbery. Many of these lawns were separated from each other by only a narrow gravelled path or a carriage road.

I loved these fenceless homes. In Japan I had never known of a home not inclosed by walls of stone or plaster. Even humble village huts had hedges of brushwood or bamboo. One of the odd fancies of my childhood was to imagine how wonderful it would be if, without warning, all hedges should fall and the hidden gardens be suddenly revealed to every passerby. In my American home I felt that my childhood wish had come true. The fences were all down and the flowers and grass free for all to see and enjoy. Then my mind drifted to the gardens of Japan where was shut-in beauty for the few.

I was thinking all this one pleasant afternoon as I sat in the hammock, sewing, while Mother was tying up the crimson rambler that covered part of the porch with a curtain of green.

"Mother," I said suddenly, as a new thought came to me, "did you ever think of a Japanese woman as being in prison with the key to her cell in her pocket; and not unlocking the door because it would not be a polite thing to do?"

"Why—no!" said Mother, surprised. "What are you thinking, Etsu?"

"That idea came to me the day I went to my first afternoon tea. Do you remember?"

"Yes, indeed," said Mother, smiling. "You looked like a drooping blossom as you came up the path with Miss Helen. She said that everyone was there and that you were the 'belle of the ball'; and then you sat down on the porch step and quietly remarked that people here were just like their lawns. I never quite understood what you meant."

"I shall never forget that day," I said. "All the time I was dressing to go, I pictured how the ladies would look, sitting in Mrs. Anderson's parlour in their pretty dresses and wavy hair, talking pleasantly the way they do when we make calls. But they did not sit at all. It was like being in the street, for they all kept on their hats and gloves, and stood in groups or walked around the crowded rooms, all talking at once. I was so confused by the buzz of voices that my head was really dizzy, but it was all intensely interesting, and not exactly undignified. People asked me queer questions, but everyone was kind and everyone was happy."

"Was it the noise and the excitement that tired you so?" asked Mother.

"Oh, no, I liked it. It was a happy noise. I liked everything. But on the way home, Miss Helen asked me to tell her about our ladies' receptions in Japan. I could see in my mind just how everyone used to look at an anniversary celebration in my home at Nagaoka; Mother sitting so gentle and stately, and all the ladies in their ceremonial dresses, having a quietly nice time and expressing every emotion, in a kind of suppressed way, by smiles and bows and a few gestures; for at a formal gathering in Japan it is rude to laugh aloud or to move too much."

"It is beautiful and restful," said Mother.

"But it is not nature!" I cried, sitting upright in my excitement. "I've been thinking about it ever since. Our conventionality is too extreme. It is narrowing to the soul. I hate to be so happy here—and all those patient, subdued women sitting hushed in their quiet homes. Our lives in Japan—a man's as well as a woman's—are like our tied-down trees, our shut-in gardens, our——"

I stopped abruptly; then added slowly, "I am growing too outspoken and American-like. It does not suit my training."

"You want to pull the fences down too suddenly, dear," said Mother gently. "The flowers of Japan have blossomed in a shadowy garden, and a sudden, bright sunlight might kill their beauty and develop them into strong, coarse weeds. It is only morning there, now. The blossoms will grow with the light, and by noon the fences will have fallen. Don't pull them down too suddenly."

Mother leaned over the hammock and, for the first time, kissed me softly on the brow.

One time I went with some lady friends to see Ellen Terry in "The Merchant of Venice." It was an afternoon performance, and after the play we went to some place and had tea. The ladies were all enthusiastic in their praise of the great actress, but I could say nothing, for that afternoon was one of the great disappointments of my life. I had been quite excited over seeing for the first time a Western actress of world-wide fame, and had formed a picture in my mind of a modest young doctor of laws, who would walk across the stage with slow-moving ceremony and with grave dignity deliver the wonderful monologue. Of course, I unconsciously pictured the Japanese ideal.

Instead, a tall figure in scarlet gown and cap, which reminded me of the dress of a Japanese clown, swept on to the stage with the freedom and naturalness that belong only to common-class people in Japan. Portia talked too loud and fast for a lady of elegance and culture, even in disguise. And the gestures—oh, most of all, the vigorous, manlike gestures! I had no impression but one of shocked surprise.

The beautiful moonlight scene where Jessica meets her lover, and also the last act, where the two husbands recognize their wives, were full of too many kisses and seemed to be most indelicate. I wished I was not there to see.

In the midst of the conversation, one of the ladies, who had watched me rather curiously during the last scene, turned to me.

"Do you have love scenes on the Japanese stage?" she asked.

"Oh, yes," I answered. "Our stage shows life as it is, and Japanese are just like other people."

"But your face got crimson, little lady, and you looked as if you had never seen a lover before," she said smilingly.

I explained as well as I could that for generations we have been taught that strong emotional expression is not consistent with elegance and dignity. That does not mean that we try to repress our feelings; only that public expression of them is bad form. Therefore on our stage the love scenes are generally so demure and quiet that an American audience would not be thrilled at all. But the dignified bearing of our actors has a strong effect on Japanese people, for they understand the feeling that is not shown."

"What do lovers do when they are—well—very enthusiastic?" asked a young lady.

"They gently turn their backs to each other," I replied.

"Turn their backs to each other! My stars!" was the very peculiar exclamation of the young lady.

In a moment she turned to me again.

"Is it really true," she asked, "that in Japan there is no kissing—even between husband and wife?"

"There is bowing, you know," I replied. "That is our mode of heart expression."

"But you don't mean that your mother never kissed you!" exclaimed the young lady. "What did she do when you came to America?"

"Only bowed," I replied, "and then she said very gently, 'A safe journey for you, my daughter.'"

I had not been here long enough then to understand the odd expression that came over the faces of the ladies, nor the moment's silence that followed before the conversation drifted into other channels.

Bowing is not only bending the body; it has a spiritual side also. One does not bow exactly the same to father, younger sister, friend, servant, and child. My mother's long, dignified bow and gentle-voiced farewell held no lack of deep love. I felt keenly each heart-throb, and every other person present also recognized the depth of hidden emotion.

Japanese people are not demonstrative. Until late years the repression of strong emotion was carefully drilled into the mind and life of every Japanese child of the better class. There is much more freedom now than formerly, but the influence of past training is seen everywhere—in art, in literature, and in the customs of daily life. With all the cheerful friendliness of everyday intercourse there is a certain stiffness of etiquette which holds in check all exuberance of expression. It dictates the ceremonies of birth and the ceremonies of death, and guides everything between—working, playing, eating, sleeping, walking, running, laughing, crying. Every motion is chained—and by one's own wish—with the shackles of politeness. A merry girl will laugh softly behind her sleeve. A hurt child chokes back his tears and sobs out, "I am not crying!" A stricken mother will smile as she tells you that her child is dying. A distressed servant will giggle as she confesses having broken your treasured piece of china. This is most mystifying to a foreigner, but it means only an effort to keep in the background. A display of one's own feelings would be rudeness.

When American people judge the degree of affection between Japanese husband and wife by their conduct to each other, they make a great mistake. It would be as bad form for a man to express approval of his wife or children as it would be for him to praise any other part of himself; and every wife takes pride in conducting herself according to the rigid rules of etiquette, which recognize dignity and humility as the virtues that reflect greatest glory on the home of which she is mistress.

One other thing may explain some seeming peculiarities. The Japanese language has no pronouns, their place being taken by adjectives. A humble or derogatory adjective means "my" and a complimentary one means "your." A husband will introduce his wife with some such words as these: "Pray bestow honourable glance upon foolish wife." By this he simply means, "I want you to meet my wife." A father will speak of his children as "ignorant son" or "untrained daughter" when his heart is overflowing with pride and tenderness.

I shall never forget my first experience in sees kissing between man and woman. It was on my trip across the continent when I came from Japan. A seat near me was occupied by a young lady, very prettily dressed and with gentle, almost timid, manners. She was a young married woman returning from her first visit to her parents. I was much attracted by her free, yet modest, actions and planned how I would try to imitate her. One morning I noticed that she was dressed with unusual care, and it was evident that she was nearing the end of her journey. Finally the train began to slow down and she watched out of the window with eager interest. The train had barely come to a stand when in rushed a young man, who threw his arms around that modest, sweet girl and kissed her several times. And she did not mind it, but blushed and laughed, and they went off together. I cannot express my feelings, but I could not help recalling what my mother said to me just before I started for America: "I have heard, my daughter, that it is the custom for foreign people to lick each other as dogs do."

There was no criticism in my mother's heart—nothing but wonder. I repeat her words only as an illustration of how an unfamiliar custom may appear to the eyes of a stranger. Years of residence in this country have taught me that the American mode of heart expression has its spiritual side, just as bowing has. I now understand that a kiss expresses kindness or gratitude, friendship or love; each of which is a sacred whisper from heart to heart.

Matsuo was very fond of Mother, and often, when he had received a new assignment of goods from Japan, he would select something especially pretty or appropriate and bring to her. Once he gave her a small lacquer box which looked something like an old-fashioned medicine case hung from the sash by people of ancient time. The outside was marked with lines corresponding to the partitions in a medicine case, but when I opened it, I saw that instead of being a succession of layers, it was an open box divided into two upright partitions to hold playing cards. The lacquer was poor and the work roughly done, but it was an ingenious idea to make a box to hold a means of pleasure in imitation of a case to hold a cure for pain.

"What original people Americans are!" I said. "But I didn't know that lacquer was made here."

Matsuo turned the little box over, and, on the bottom, I saw a label, "Made in Japan."

A few days after, I went down to Matsuo's store and he showed me whole shelves of articles called Japanese, the sight of which would have filled any inhabitant of Japan with a puzzled wonder as to what the strange European articles could be. They were all marked, "Made in Japan." Matsuo said that they had been designed by Americans, in shapes suitable for use in this country, then made to order in Japanese factories and shipped direct to America, without having been seen in Japan outside the factory. That troubled me, but Matsuo shrugged his shoulders.

"As long as Americans want them, design them, order them, and are satisfied, there will be merchants to supply," he said.

"But they are not Japanese things."

"No," he replied. "But genuine things do not sell. People think they are too frail and not gay enough." Then he added slowly, "The only remedy is in education; and that will have to begin here."

That night I lay awake a long time, thinking. Of course, artistic, appreciative persons are few in comparison to the masses who like heavy vases of green and gold, boxes of cheap lacquer, and gay fans with pictures of a laughing girl with flower hairpins. "But if Japan lowers her artistic standards," I sighed, "what can she hope for from the world? All that she has, or is, comes from her art ideals and her pride. Ambition, workmanship, courtesy—all are folded within those two words."

I once knew a workman—one who was paid by the job, not the hour—to voluntarily undo half a day's work, at the cost of much heavy lifting, just to alter, by a few inches, the position of a stepping-stone in a garden. After it was placed to his satisfaction, he wiped the perspiration from his face, then took out his tiny pipe and squatted down, near by, to waste still more unpaid-for-time in gazing at the re-set stone, with pleasure and satisfaction in every line of his kindly old face.

As I thought of the old man, I wondered if it was worth while to exchange the delight of heart-pride in one's work for—*anything*. My mind mounted from the gardener to workman, teacher, statesman. It is the same with all. To degrade one's pride—to loose one's hold on the best, after having had it—is death to the soul growth of man or nation.

CHAPTER-20
Neighbours

WHEN I came to America I expected to learn many things, but I had no thought that I was going to learn anything about Japan. Yet our neighbours, by their questions and remarks, were teaching me every day new ways of looking at my own country.

My closest friend was the daughter of a retired statesman, the General, we called him, who lived just across the steep little ravine which divided our grounds from his. Our side was bordered by a hedge of purple lilacs, broken, opposite the path to the well, by a rustic drawbridge. One autumn afternoon I was sitting on the shady step of the bridge with a many-stamped package in my lap, watching for the postman. Just about that hour his funny little wagon, looking, with its open side-doors, like a high, stiff *kago*, would be passing on its return trip down the hill, and I was anxious to hurry off my package of white cotton brocade and ribbons of various patterns and colours—the most prized gifts I could send to Japan.

Suddenly I heard a gay voice behind me reciting in a high sing-song:

"Open your mouth and shut your eyes
And I'll give you something to make you wise."

I looked up at a charming picture. My bright-eyed friend, in a white dress and big lacy hat, was standing on the bridge, holding in her cupped hands three or four grape leaves pinned together with thorns. On this rustic plate were piled some bunches of luscious purple grapes.

"Oh, how pretty!" I exclaimed. "That is just the way Japanese serve fruit."

"And this is the way they carry flowers," she said, putting down the grapes on the step and releasing a big bunch of long-stemmed tiger lilies from under her arm. "Why do Japanese always carry flowers upside-down?"

I laughed and said, "It looked very odd to me, when I first came, to see everybody carrying flowers with the tops up. Why do you?"

"Why—why—they look prettier so; and that's the way they grow."

That was true, and yet I had never before thought of any one's caring for the appearance of flowers that were being carried. We Japanese have a way of considering a thing invisible until it is settled in its proper place.

"Japanese seldom carry flowers," I said, "except to the temple or to graves. We get flowers for the house from flower-venders who go from door to door with baskets swung from shoulder poles, but we do not send flowers as gifts; and we *never* wear them."

"Why?" asked Miss Helen.

"Because they wither and fade. And so, to send flowers to a sick friend would be the worst omen in the world."

"Oh, what a lot of pleasure your poor invalids in hospitals are losing!" said Miss Helen. "And Japan is the land of flowers!"

Surprised and thoughtful, I sat silent; but in a moment was aroused by a question. "What were you thinking of when I came—sitting here so quietly with that big bundle on your lap? You looked like a lovely, dainty, picturesque little peddler."

"My thoughts were very unlike those of a peddler," I replied. "As I sat here watching the dangling end of the bridge chain I was thinking of a Japanese lover of long ago who crossed a drawbridge ninety-nine times to win his ladylove, and the one hundredth time, in a blinding snow-storm, he failed to see that it was lifted, and so fell to his death in the moat below."

"How tragic!" exclaimed Miss Helen. "What did the poor lady do?"

"It was her fault," I said. "She was vain and ambitious, and when she saw a chance to win the love of a high official at court, she changed her mind about her lover and commanded her attendants not to lower the bridge the day he expected to come triumphant."

"You don't mean that the cold-blooded creature actually planned his death?"

"It was the storm that caused his death," I said. "She was fickle, but not wicked. She thought that when he found the bridge lifted he would know her answer and go away."

"Well, sometimes our girls over here are fickle enough, dear knows," said Miss Helen, "but no American woman would ever do a thing like that. She was actually a murderess."

I was shocked at such a practical way of looking at my romantic tale, and hastened to add that remorseful Lady Komachi became a nun and spent her life in making pilgrimages to various temples to pray for the dead. At last she partially lost her mind, and, as a wandering beggar, lived and died among the humble villagers on the slopes of Mount Fuji. "Her fate is held up by priests," I concluded, "as a warning to all fickle-minded maidens."

"Well," said Miss Helen, drawing a deep breath, "I think she paid pretty dearly for her foolishness, don't you?"

"Why—well, perhaps," I replied, rather surprised at the question, "but we are taught that if a woman so loses her gentle modesty that she can treat with scorn and disrespect the plea of a loyal lover, she is no longer a worthy woman."

"Suppose a man jilts a maid, what then?" quickly asked Miss Helen. "Is he no longer considered a worthy man?"

I did not know how to reply. Instinctively I upheld to myself the teachings of my childhood that man is the protector and guide and woman the helper—the self-respecting, but nevertheless, uncritical, dutiful helper. Often afterward Miss Helen and I had heart-to-heart talks in which her questions and remarks surprised and some times disturbed me. Many of our customs I had taken for granted, accepting the ways of our ancestors without any thought except that thus they had been and still were. When I began to question myself about things which had always seemed simple and right because they were in accordance with laws made by our wise rulers, sometimes I was puzzled and sometimes I was frightened.

"I am afraid that I am growing very bold and man like," I would think to myself, "but God gave me a brain to use, else why do I have it?" All my childhood I had hidden my deepest feelings. Now again it was the same. My American mother would have understood, but I did not know; and so, repressing all outward signs, I puzzled my way alone, in search of higher ideals—not for myself, but for Japan.

Miss Helen's father was ninety years old when I knew him. He was a wonderful man, tall, with broad shoulders just a trifle stooped and with thick iron-gray hair and bushy eyebrows. A strong face he had, but gentle and humorous when he talked. I looked upon him as an encyclopedia of American history. I had always loved the study of history, in childhood and at school, but I had learned little of the details of America's part in the world; and would sit with the General and his invalid wife listening by the hour while he told stories of early American life. Knowing that incidents of personal history especially appealed to me, he once told me that his own large estate was bought by his father from an Indian chief in exchange for one chair, a gun, and a pouch of tobacco; and that Mother's large home was once an Indian village of bark tents and was purchased for half-a-dozen split-seated kitchen chairs. These incidents seemed to me almost pre-historic; for I had never known any one whose home did not date back into a far past.

When America was a still youthful nation the General had represented his country as a diplomat in Europe, and, with his beautiful young wife, had taken part in the foreign social life in Paris and later in Washington. My first glimpse of American life abroad, I received through the word pictures of this gracious lady, and through her experiences I began to understand, with sympathy, something of the problem in Japan of Americans trying to understand the Japanese, which heretofore I had looked upon only as the problem of Japanese trying to understand Americans.

From childhood until I met the General the word "ancient" had commanded my reverence. I had been conscious that the Inagaki family tree was rooted in a history centuries old, and that our plots in the cemetery were the oldest in Nagaoka. It had seemed an unquestioned necessity that we should follow the same customs that our ancestors had observed for hundreds of years, and it was my pride that they were the customs of a dynasty which was among the very oldest in the world.

After I became acquainted with the General and heard him talk of the wonderful development of a nation much younger than my own family tree, the word "ancient" lost some of its value. Even the General's own lifetime—the years of only one man's life—represented such a marvellous advance in national growth that sometimes I looked upon him almost with awe, wondering how much real value should be attached to antiquity. "Perhaps," I sometimes said to myself, "it would be better not to look back with such pride to a glorious past; but instead, to look forward to a glorious future. One means quiet satisfaction; the other, ambitious work."

One evening, after Matsuo and I had been over to call on the General, Miss Helen walked back with us across the drawbridge. Matsuo went on to join Mother on the porch, and Miss Helen and I sat down on the step of the bridge, as we often did, to talk.

"When Father told that story about Molly Pitcher," said Miss Helen, "I wondered if you were thinking about Japanese women."

"Why?" I asked.

"Well," she replied hesitatingly, "several times I've heard you say that American women are like Japanese. I don't see that Molly Pitcher is much of a Japanese specimen."

"Oh, you don't know Japanese history," I exclaimed. "We have many women heroes in Japan."

"Yes, of course," said Miss Helen quickly. "In every country there are heroic women who rise to noble sacrifice on occasion. But they are exceptions. Books and travellers all speak of Japanese women as being quiet, soft-spoken, gentle, and meek. That picture doesn't apply to the American type of women."

"The training is different," I said, "but I think that at heart they are much the same."

"Well," said Miss Helen, "when it becomes the fashion for us to wear our hearts on our sleeves, perhaps we will appear gentle and meek. But," she added as she rose to go, "I don't believe that Japanese men think as you do. To-night, when I spoke of the book on Japan that I have been reading, and said that I believed the author was right when he declared that 'for modesty and gentle worth, Japanese women lead the world,' your husband smiled and said, 'Thank you,' as if he thought so too."

"Miss Helen," I said earnestly, "although our women are pictured as gentle and meek, and although Japanese men will not contradict it, nevertheless it is true that, beneath all the gentle meekness, Japanese women are like—like—volcanoes."

Miss Helen laughed.

"You are the only Japanese woman that I ever saw—except at the Exposition," she said, "and I cannot imagine your being like a volcano. However, I'll give in to your superior knowledge. You have had Molly Pitchers among your women, and flirts—that Lady What's-her-name whom you told me about the other day: she *was* a flirt, with a vengeance!—and now you say that you have volcanoes. Your demure-appearing countrywomen sees to have surprising possibilities. The next time I come over I'm going to challenge you to give me a specimen of a Japanese genuine woman's-rights woman."

"That is easy," I said, laughing in my turn. "A genuine woman's-rights woman is not one who *wants* her rights, but one who *has* them. And if that means the right to do men's work, I can easily give you a specimen. We have a whole island of women who do men's work from planting rice to making laws."

"What do the men do?"

"Cook, keep house, take care of the children, and do the family washing."

"You don't mean it!" exclaimed Miss Helen, and she sat down again.

But I did mean it, and I told her of Hachijo, a little island about a hundred miles off the coast of Japan, where the women, tall, handsome, and straight, with their splendid hair coiled in an odd knot on top of the head, and wearing long, loose gowns bound by a narrow sash tied in front, work in the ricefields, make oil from camellia seeds, spin and weave a peculiar yellow silk which they carry in bundles on their heads over the mountains, at the same time driving tiny oxen, not much larger than dogs, also laden with rolls of silk to be sent to the mainland to be sold. And in addition to all this they make some of the best laws we have and see that they are properly carried out. In the meantime, the older men of the community, with babies strapped to their backs, go on errands or stand on the street gossiping and swaying to a sing-song lullaby; and the younger ones wash sweet potatoes, cut vegetables, and cook dinner; or, in big aprons and with sleeves looped back, splash, rub, and wring out clothes at the edge of a stream.

The beginning of this unusual state of things dates back several centuries, to a time when the husbands and sons were forced to go to another island about forty miles away, for fishing, very little of which could be done near Hachijo. When silk proved more profitable than fish, the men returned to the island, but the Government was in capable hands which have never given up their hold.

I told all this to Miss Helen, and closed by saying, "A subject for your meditation is the fact that with these women rulers, both men and women are healthy and happy; and the social life there is more strictly moral than it is in any other community of equal intelligence in Japan."

"You had better join the Equal Suffrage party," said Miss Helen, "and go on the lecture platform with that story. It has a list toward moral uplift and might win voters for the cause. Well," and again she rose to go, "your women are such unexpected creatures that I am more than ever convinced that American women are not like Japanese. We talk so much and are so noisily interested in public affairs that we are expected to do almost anything. Whatever happens, we cannot surprise the world. But for one of your timid, shrinking kind suddenly to burst out into a bold, strong act, like lifting drawbridges and that sort of thing, completely upsets our preconceived ideas. And then to hear of its being quietly but effectively done *en masse*, like those island women, is rather—disconcerting."

She ran over the bridge, calling back, "Anyway, although you are the sweetest little lady that ever walked on sandals, you haven't convinced me. American women are *not* like Japanese women—more's the pity!"

With this absurd compliment from my extravagantly partial friend ringing in my ears, I started to walk toward the porch, when suddenly a voice called from the dusky shadows across the bridge, "Oh, I didn't think of Mrs. Newton! I'll give up. *She* is like a Japanese woman. Good-night."

I smiled as I walked on toward the porch, for I was thinking of something Mother had told me that very morning about Mrs. Newton. She was our nearest neighbour on the opposite side of our place from Miss Helen's home, and I knew her very well. She was a gentle woman, soft-voiced and shy, who loved birds and had little box-houses for them in her trees. I understood why Miss Helen should say that she was like a Japanese woman, but I had never thought that she was. Her ideas were so very sensible and practical; and she allowed her husband to be too attentive to her. He carried her cloak and umbrella for her; and once, in the carriage, I saw him lean over and fasten her slipper strap.

What Mother had told me was that, a few days before, Mrs. Newton was sitting by the window sewing, when she heard a frightened chirping and saw a large snake reaching up the trunk of a tree to one of her bird-boxes on a low branch. She dropped her sewing, and running to a drawer where her husband kept a gun, she shot through the open window, right into the snake's head, and her little bird family was saved.

"How could she do it?" I said to Mother. "I never would have believed that frail, delicate Mrs. Newton would dare even *touch* a gun. She is afraid of every dog on the street, and she starts and flushes if you speak to her unexpectedly. And then, anyway, how could she ever *hit* it?"

Mother smiled.

"Mrs. Newton can do many things that you don't know about," she said. "When she was first married she lived for several years on a lonely ranch out West. One stormy night, when her husband was gone, she strapped that same gun around her waist and walked six miles through darkness and danger to bring help to an injured workman."

I recalled Mrs. Newton's soft voice and gentle, almost timid manner. "After all," I said to myself, "she *is* like a Japanese woman!"

CHAPTER-21
New Experiences

AS THE weeks and the months had drifted by, unconsciously in my mind the present had been linking itself more and more closely with the past; for I had been learning more clearly each day that America was very like Japan. Thus, as time passed, the new surroundings melted into old memories and I began to feel that my life had been almost an unbroken continuation from childhood until now.

Beneath the chimes of the church bells calling: "Do not—forget—to thank—for gifts—you ev—ery day—enjoy," I could hear the mellow boom of the temple gong: "Protection for all—is offered here—safety is within."

The children who, with their burden of books, filled the streets with laughter and shouts at 8:30 A.M. made the same picture to me as our crowds of boys in uniform and girls in pleated skirts and shining black hair, who, at 7:30 A.M., clattered along on wooden clogs, carrying their books neatly wrapped in squares of patterned challie.

Valentine's Day with its lacy scenes of bowing knights and burning hearts, all twined about with ropes of rosebuds, and with sweet thoughts expressed in glowing, endearing words, was our Weaving Festival, when swaying bamboos were decorated with festoons of gay sashes and scarfs, and hung with glittering poem prayers for sunshine, that the herdsman and his weaver wife might meet that day on the misty banks of the Heavenly River which Americans call the Milky Way.

Decoration Day, with its soldiers of two wars, with its patriotic speeches and its graves with tiny flags and scattered blossoms, was our Shokonsha memorial to our soldier dead, when, all day long, hundreds march through the great stone arch to bow with softly clapping hands; then march away to make room for hundreds more.

The Fourth of July with its fluttering flags, with snapping crackers, with beating drums and its whirling, shooting rockets in the sky, was our holiday on which the flag of Japan waved beneath crossed cherry branches in honour of the coming to the throne, twenty-five centuries ago, of our first Emperor—a large bearded man in loose garments, tied at wrist and ankle with twisted vines, and wearing a long, swinging necklace of sickle-shaped gems which is to-day one of the three treasures of the throne.

Hallowe'en, with its grotesque lanterns, its witches and many jokes, was the Harvest Festival of Japan, when pumpkins were skilfully scraped into lovely pictures of shady gardens with lanterns and flowers; when ghost games were played and pumpkins piled at the gate of round-faced maidens; and when orchards of the stingy man were raided and their trophies laid on graves for the poor to find.

Thanksgiving, the home-coming day, with its turkey and pie, and jolly good cheer, was our anniversary when married sons and daughters with their children gathered for a feast of red rice and whole fish, gossiping happily while they ate, with the shrine doors open wide and the spirits of kindly ancestors watching over all.

Christmas, with its gay streets and merry, hurrying, bundle-laden crowds, with its sparkling tree and many gifts, with its holy memories of a shining star and a Mother with her Babe, was something like our seven days of New Year rejoicing, but with a difference—the difference between the soft organ tones of an old melody and the careless, lilting song of a happy child.

At New Year's time, above every doorway in our crowded streets was stretched a rope of ragged rice-straw with pine trees growing on either side, and the air resounded with children's laughter and the tinkle of tiny hidden bells in running shoes; with the gay tap-tap of flying shuttlecocks and the cheerful greetings of bowing friends. In every home were thick rounded cakes of *mochi;* every babe had another birthday, every maiden had a new sash, and poetry cards were played by boys and girls together. Oh, it was gay in Japan at New Year's time! There was no thought of solemnity anywhere, for the chrysalis of the past was broken, the butterfly had burst forth, and the world had begun again.

My first Christmas Day in America was a disappointment. We were all invited by a lady friend to attend Christmas services and afterward to go home with her to dinner and to see her tree. She had children, and I had pictured the scene as being gay, pretty, and pleasant, but with an undercurrent of dignity and reverence. I had idealized too much the wide influence of the symbolism of the day; and everything seemed such a strange combination of the spiritual and the material that I was lost. The star on the tree and the thought of unselfish giving were beautiful, but little was said of either—except in church; and just beneath the star were festoons of pop corn and cranberries—things we eat. Indeed, except for the gaiety of giving and receiving gifts, most things especially belonging to the day seemed to be only the serving of certain kinds of food and the very inartistic and peculiar custom of hanging in a prominent place the garments of the lowest part of the body for the purpose of holding gifts of toys and jewellery—even candy and fruit. That was a custom difficult for a Japanese to understand.

That evening, Mother and I went over to call on Miss Helen. And there, in her big quiet parlour, spreading over a large snowy cloth on the floor, stood her tree—large and pine-scented, sparkling with lights and coloured, swinging ornaments. It was wonderful! The tree, though so big and beautiful, reminded me, as an American skyscraper may remind one of a tiny temple pagoda, of the fairy-like branch of our Cocoon Festival from which swing and float, swaying with the lightest breath, myriads of fairy-like, sugar-blown replicas of every delicate symbol of the day. Miss Helen's father and mother were there, and we talked of the holidays of America and of Japan. Then a little niece and a neighbour's child sang Christmas carols, and my heart was full of joy, for I felt that my ideal Christmas had really come.

The morning after Christmas we had our first snow—a flying mist of dry, feathery flakes that was no more like the heavy fall of Echigo's damp, solid clots than fluffy silk-floss is like weighty cotton-batting. All day long it fell, growing thicker toward nightfall, and when we wakened the next morning the world was white.

Just at the curve where our driveway turned into the broad public road stood the coachman's cottage. He had three children and they asked Mother if they might make a snow man on our back lawn. Mother gave her consent, and then the most interesting things happened! The children rolled a big ball, then piled on it another, and on the top of that, a small one. Then with much pushing and patting of red-mittened hands, they formed rude features and, with shiny bits of hard coal, gave the image a pair of bright eyes and a row of buttons down the front. An old hat of their father's and a pipe from somewhere completed their work, and there stood a clumsy, shapeless image that reminded me of Daruma Sama—the Indian saint whose devotion cost him his feet.

I had never expected to see a Buddhist saint in America, but I greeted the likeness with merriment and entertained the children by telling them the story of the cheerful rice-pounder who threw away his pestle to become the founder of a new religion; and who asked that his image be not honoured with reverential bows, but be made into amusing toys that children's hands would use and children's hearts enjoy. Later on I saw a Damura Sama at other places than on our snowy lawn. To my surprise, the little squatting figure muffled in a scarlet cloak seemed to be a familiar object, but no one knew his story or his name. All my life I had been accustomed to sees Daruma Sama in the shape of every toy that can be made for careless baby fingers; but I was really shocked one evening at a card party to find the little red, rolling figure used as a booby prize.

"It is such an odd selection for a card-game prize," I said to Matsuo. "Why should a Daruma Sama be chosen?"

"Not odd at all," replied Matsuo. "Very appropriate. A man so well balanced that, however he may fall, the next moment he is again right side up, makes an excellent booby prize. It means, 'Down only for a moment.' Don't you see?"

In Japan we always treat a Daruma Sama rather disrespectfully, but it is a kind of affectionate disrespect; and my sensations, as I walked home with Matsuo from the party, were rather mixed. Finally, just as I reached the iron gate, I drew in a long breath, and with a ridiculous feeling of loyalty and protection tugging at my heart, I surprised Matsuo by saying, "I wish that either you or I had won the booby prize!"

It was an unusual thing for snow to remain on the ground longer than a few days, but Mother laughingly declared that the American gods of the weather had evidently planned a special season in order to keep me from being homesick. At any rate, more snow fell and still more, and we began to see sleighs go by—light, carriage-like vehicles, filled with laughing ladies in furs and with gay scarfs floating behind them as they flew by. It was like a scene from the theatre. How different from the deep snows of Echigo, over which snow-booted men pulled heavy sledges—built for work, not fun—chanting, as they pulled, a steady, rhythmic "*En yara-ya! En yara-ya!*" I missed the purity of Echigo's clear skies and snowy mountain-sides, for it was only a few days until the coal-tainted air had stolen the fresh whiteness from our snow, but the happiness of the children was not spoiled. Daruma Samas stood on every lawn, and the streets were filled with boys throwing snowballs. One day from my window I saw a lively snow-fight in which a group of besiegers pressed hard a heroic few, bravely dodging behind two barrels and a board with snow piled beneath. When the besiegers called a truce and ran around the corner for reinforcements, I pushed up my window and clapped as hard as I could.

The boys had a good time, but as I watched their soiled tracks in the snow and the smoky colour of the balls, my mind went to Ishi's stories of the snow-battles held in the courtyard of the old mansion at Nagaoka during the first years of Mother's life there. In those days life in the daimio households of even small castle towns was based on the customs of the lords and ladies in the court of the shogun, and, in a less degree, it was as luxurious and as frivolous.

Occasionally, when the winter season was late, the first snows that fell were light and dry. On the morning after such a snow had fallen, when the air was full of the cool sunshine of Echigo, and the ground white and sparkling, the men would lay aside their swords, and with their pleated skirts gracefully caught up at the sides, run out into the big open court. Soon they would be joined by the women, their gay trains looped over their scarlet skirts and their long, bright sleeves held back with gay cords. No one wore wooden shoes or even sandals, for that would mar the purity of the snow, but with only the white foot-mitten on the feet, with bare heads and tinkling hairpins, all joined in the battle of snowballs. There was running, with laughter, and merriment, and the air filled with flying and breaking balls through which could be seen the tossing of bright sleeves and dodging black heads powdered with snow. Our old servants often told me of those gay scenes, and Baya, the oldest of them all, would solemnly shake her head from side to side and sigh over the fact that Etsu-bo's enjoyment must consist only of climbing the snow hills piled in the street, and of racing with Sister on snow-shoes as we went to and from school.

The children of my American neighbours had no snow shoe races, but there was great excitement over coasting. Ours was a hilly suburb and almost every lawn had at least one curving slope; but the snow was thin and no one wanted the grass worn off or beaten down. Of course the sidewalks were cleaned and the streets were forbidden. The older boys had discovered a few long slopes and monopolized them, but the smaller children could only stand around and watch, unless some big brother or kind friend would occasionally take pity and give a ride.

One day I saw a group of four or five little girls with two red sleds standing by our iron gates and looking wistfully up at the long slope of our side lawn.

"It would ruin the appearance of the whole place for them to be allowed to make a brown track there," I said to Mother.

"It is not the appearance, Etsu," Mother replied. "Probably all the track those little folks would make would not kill the grass; but it is too dangerous.

They would have to bump over two gravel paths and end abruptly at the top of the stone wall. The battlements are not high, and the sleds might leap over on to the outside walk, four feet below. I should be afraid to risk it."

That afternoon as Mother and I were walking to a meeting of the Ladies' Club we passed the home of Doctor Miller. His lawn was small but it was one of the prettiest and best kept in our neighbourhood. The hill began at the roadway and swept in a straight, rather steep slope ending in a level stretch. At least a dozen children were gathered there, among them the forlorn little group with the two red sleds that I had seen in the morning. A long, smooth track had already been worn on which every moment a sled went down laden with a squealing, shrieking mass of hunched-up little figures. And on an uphill path beside the track a line of rosy-cheeked, rosy-nosed, panting coasters were pulling their sleds and shouting—not for any reason at all, except that they were having the best time of any coasters in the world.

Day after day, as long as the snow lasted, that hill was reserved for the little folks, and every child that went gliding down the smooth slide, and every one that came struggling up the broken path, had laughter in the eyes, happiness in the heart, and, hidden somewhere within, a growing germ of unselfishness, kindness, and godliness that had been planted there by the kind act of a man who could see from the viewpoint of a child.

It was like my father to have done that kind deed. Afterward I never saw Doctor Miller, even to pass him on the street, that I did not look to see if behind his fine, grave, intellectual face I could not see the heart of my father. I have not seen it, but I know it is there, and that some day, on the other side of the Sandzu River, those two beautiful souls will be friends.

January brought to Matsuo and me a quiet celebration of our own. For weeks before, the letters from Japan had been coming more frequently, and occasionally the postman would hand in a package wrapped in oil-paper and sealed with the oval stamp of Uncle Otani's house, or the big square one of Inagaki.

One of these packages contained a thin sash of soft white cotton, each end of which had been dipped in rouge, and also two emblems of congratulation—baby storks of rice-dough, one white and one red.

These were Mother's gifts for the "Five-month ceremony," a special celebration observed by expectant parents on that date. My thoughtful, loving, far-away mother! The tears came to my eyes as I explained it all to my dear American mother, who in sweet under standing of the sacred ceremony asked how to prepare everything according to Japanese custom.

At this celebration, besides the husband and wife, only women members of the two families are present. The young father-to-be sits beside his wife and the sash is passed through the sleeves of his garment from left to right. Then it is properly adjusted around the wife. From then on, she is called "a lady of retirement," and her food, exercise, amusements, and reading are all of a character called "education for the Coming." The gay, light balls of many-coloured silk thread which are seen in American shops belong to this time.

In the package with the sash was a charm-card from my good Ishi. To obtain it she had made a pilgrimage of two days to the temple of Kishibo-jin—"Demon of the Mother-heart"—believing sincerely that the bit of paper with its mysterious symbols would protect me from every evil.

According to an ancient legend there lived in the time of the Buddha a mother of many children, who was so poor that she could not obtain food for them, and in helpless misery saw them starving. At last her agony became so great that it changed her loving mother heart into that of a demon. Every night she roamed the country stealing little babes, so that, in some uncanny way belonging to demon lore, their nourishment might be transferred to her own children. Her name became a horror to the world. The wise Buddha, knowing that however many children a woman may have she always loves the youngest with special tenderness, took her babe and hid it in his begging bowl. Hearing the child's voice, but not being able to trace it, the mother was wild with distress and grief.

"Listen," said the merciful Buddha, restoring the infant to her arms: "You have a thousand children, while most women have but ten; yet you mourn bitterly for the loss of one. Think of other aching hearts with the sympathy you feel for your own."

The mother, thankfully clasping the babe to her breast, saw within the tiny arms a pomegranate, and recognized it as the miracle-fruit whose never-withering freshness can nourish the world. Remorse and gratitude healed her heart, and she vowed to become for ever a loving guardian to little children. This is why in all Kishibo temples the goddess of the altar is a demon-faced woman surrounded by children and standing in the midst of draperies and decorations of pomegranate.

These recollections flooded my mind as I sat stitching on dainty, wee garments into every one of which I breathed a prayer that my baby might be a boy. I wanted a son, not only because every Japanese family believes it most desirable that the name should be carried on without adoption, but also for the selfish reason that both Matsuo's family and my own would look upon me with more pride were I the mother of a son. Neither Matsuo nor I had, to any great extent, the feeling that woman is inferior to man, which has been so common a belief among all classes in Japan; but law and custom being what they were, it was such a serious inconvenience—yes, calamity—to have *no* son, that congratulations always fell more readily from the lips when the first-born was a boy.

Little girls were always welcome in Japanese homes. Indeed, it was a great sorrow to have all sons and no daughter—a calamity second only to having all daughters and no son.

The laws of our family system were planned in consideration for customs which themselves were based on ancient beliefs, all of which were wise and good—for their time. But as the world moves on, and the ages overlap each other, there come intervals when we climb haltingly; and this means martyrdom to the advanced. Nevertheless, perhaps it is wiser and kinder to the puzzled many for the advanced few to accommodate themselves somewhat to fading beliefs, instead of opposing them too bitterly, unless it should be a matter of principle, for we are climbing; slowly, but—climbing. Nature does not hasten, and Japanese are Nature's pupils.

Mother had a magic touch with flowers, and when spring came the crimson rambler that formed a heavy brocade curtain on one side of our veranda was thick with tiny buds. One morning I had gone to the door to see Matsuo off, and was wondering how soon the tiny roses would bloom, when I was joined by Mother.

"There are hundreds of buds here," I said. "This will be a bower of rich beauty some day. How much joy we Japanese miss because of superstition! Roses do not look beautiful to us because they have harmful thorns."

"And how much joy you have because of traditions," said Mother, smiling. "In the poem you taught me last night,

> "The sacred lotus that bravely lifts its snowy head in purity and beauty,
> Although its roots are buried in earthly mire,
> Holds a lesson of pride and inspiration.

"Have you another blossom that is 'a teacher'?"

"And the modest plum," I answered quickly, "that blossoms on snow-laden branches, is a bridal flower, because it teaches courage and endurance."

"And how about the cherry?" asked Mother.

"Oh, that has an important meaning," I quickly replied.

> "The quick-falling cherry, that lives but a day
> And dies with destiny unfulfilled,
> Is the brave spirit of samurai youth,
> Always ready, his fresh young strength
> To offer to his lord."

"Bravo!" Mother cried, clapping her hands. "This is a real, albeit a second-rate, poetry contest that you and I are having. Do you know any more flower poems?"

"Oh, yes-Morning glories!" And I rapidly recited in Japanese:

> "In the dewy freshness of the morning, they smile respectful greetings to the goddess of the Sun."

Oh, Mother, this is just like Japan—the way you and I are doing now! Japanese people often gather—a group of friends—and write poems. They meet at a Flower Viewing festival and hang poems on the flowery branches; or at a moon-gazing party where they sit in the light of the moon and make poems. There is one place where the moonlight falls on a plain of ricefields and from the mountain-side the silvery reflection can be seen in every separate field. It is wonderful! And then everybody goes home feeling quiet and peaceful—and with new thoughts."

"Ah!" exclaimed Mother, starting quickly toward the door, adding, as she looked back over her shoulder, "Our poetry contest has given *me* a new thought!" And she disappeared within the house.

Our conversation had reminded her of a package of morning-glory seeds that a friend had sent when she learned that a Japanese lady was living with her.

"I had almost forgotten about them," said Mother, returning with a trowel in her hand. "These were gathered from the vines which my friend had grown from seeds that came from Japan. She says the blossoms are wonderful—four and five inches across. Where shall we plant them? We must choose some appropriate spot for the little grandseeds of a Japanese ancestor."

"I know exactly the place!" I cried, delighted, and leading Mother to our old-fashioned well I told her the legend of the maiden who went to a well to draw water and, finding a morning-glory tendril twined about the handle of the bucket, went away rather than break the tender vine.

Mother was pleased, and she planted the seeds around the well curb while I softly hummed, over and over, the old poem:

"The morning-glory tendril has chained my heart.
Let it be:
I'll beg water of my neighbour."

We watched the vines eagerly as they reached out strong arms and climbed steadily upward. Mother often said, "The coming of the blossoms and of the baby will not be far apart."

One morning I saw from my window Mother and Clara standing by the well. They were looking at the vines and talking excitedly. I hurried downstairs and across the lawn. The blossoms were open, but were pale, half sized weaklings—not resembling at all the royal blossoms we treasure so dearly in Japan. Then I remembered having read that Japanese flowers do not like other lands and, after the first year, gradually fade away. With a superstitious clutch at my heart, I thought of my selfish prayer for a son and vowed to be gratefully content with either boy or girl if only the little one bore no pitiful trace of the transplanting.

And then the baby came—well and sweet and strong—upholding in her perfect babyhood the traditions of both America and Japan. I forgot that I had ever wanted a son, and Matsuo, after his first glimpse of his little daughter, remembered that he had always liked girls better than boys.

Whether the paper charm of Kishibo-jin was of value or not, my good Ishi's loving thought for me was a boon to my heart during those first weeks when I so longed for her wisdom and her love. And yet it was well that she was not with me, for she could never have fitted into our American life. The gentle, time-taking ways of a Japanese nurse crooning to a little bundle of crêpe and brocade swinging in its silken hammock on her back would never have done for my active baby, who so soon learned to crow with delight and clutch disrespectfully at her father's head as he tossed her aloft in his strong arms.

We decided to bring the baby up with all the healthful freedom given to an American child, but we wanted her to have a Japanese name.

The meaning of Matsuo's name was "pine"—he emblem of strength; mine was "ricefield"—the emblem of usefulness. "Therefore," said Matsuo, "the baby is already a combination of strength and usefulness, but she must have beauty also. So let us give her the name of our kind American mother, which, translated, means 'flower.'"

"And if we use the old-fashioned termination," I cried with delight, "it will mean 'foreign fields' or 'strange land.'"

"Hanano—Flower in a Strange Land!" cried Matsuo, clapping his hands. "Nothing could be better."

Mother consented, and thus it was decided.

CHAPTER-22

Flower in a Strange Land

FOR months after the baby came my entire life centred around that one small bit of humanity. Wherever I went, and no matter who came to see me, the conversation was sure to drift to her; and my letters to my mother held little else than the information that a few ounces had been added to the baby's weight, or a new accent to the little cooings and gurglings, or that she had developed a dimple when she smiled. My mother must have seen the germ of a too-selfish love in my devotion; for one day I received from her a set of Buddhist picture-books which had belonged to Father's library. How familiar and dear they looked! There were no stories—only pictures—but as I turned the pages, I could hear again the gentle voice of Honourable Grandmother and see the old tales acted before my mind as plainly as in the days of my childhood. Mother had marked some of the pages with a dot of vermilion. On one of these was a scene from "The Mount of Spears." The story is of a favourite disciple of Buddha who grieved so bitterly over the loss of his beloved mother that the pitying Master exerted his holy power and took the sorrowing son to a place from which the mother could be seen. The disciple was horrified to behold his precious mother climbing painfully over a hilly path made of sharp spears.

"Oh, good Master," he cried, "you have brought me to the 'Hell of Seven Hills.' Why is my mother here? She never, throughout her life, did a wicked deed."

"But she had a wicked thought," sadly the Buddha replied. "When you were a baby, her only care was for you, and one day when she saw a little field-mouse happily playing, she so longed to have its gray, silky tail for a cord to tie your holiday coat, that her wish was thought murder."

I closed the book with a half-smile, for I understood at once the wordless warning of my gentle, anxious mother; but my heart was full of loving gratitude as I bowed respectfully in the direction of Japan and resolved that my love for my baby should make me more thoughtful and tender toward all the world.

One of the first callers the baby had was our faithful black laundress, Minty. She had been washing for Mother for years, and, when I came, she accepted the additional burden of my queer clothes with kind good nature. She had never spoken of them as being different from others, but several times I noticed her examining them with interest, especially my white foot mittens. These were made of cotton or silk, with the great toe separated, as is the thumb of a hand mitten. When she came upstairs to see the baby, the nurse was holding the little one on her lap, and Minty squatted down by her side and began talking baby talk, cooing and clucking in the most motherly fashion.

Presently she looked up.

"Can I see her feet?" she asked.

"Certainly," said the nurse, turning up the baby's long dress and cuddling the little pink feet in her hand. "My lawsy me!" cried Minty in a tone of the greatest astonishment. "If they ain't jus' like ourn!"

"Of course," said the surprised nurse. "What did you think?"

"Why, the stockin's is double," said Minty, almost in a tone of awe, "and I s'posed they wuz two-toed folks."

When the nurse told my husband he shouted with merriment and finally said, "Well, Minty has struck back for the whole European race and got even with Japan."

The nurse was puzzled, but I knew very well what he meant. When I was a child it was a general belief among the common people of Japan that Europeans had feet like horses' hoofs, because they wore leather bags on their feet instead of sandals. That is why one of our old-fashioned names for foreigners was "one-toed fellows."

Neither Mother nor I knew much about the latest theories of taking care of babies; so I rocked Hanano to sleep with a lullaby. Whether or not it was the influence of the foreign atmosphere which so entirely surrounded me I do not know, but it seemed more natural for me to sing "Hush-a-bye, baby!" than the old Japanese lullaby that Ishi used to croon as she swayed back and forth with me snuggled comfortably against her back.

"Baby, sleep! Baby, sleep!
Where has thy nurse gone?
She went far away to Grandmother's home

Over the hills and valleys.
Soon she will bring to thee
Fish and red rice,
Fish and red rice."

It was not the foreign atmosphere, however, that was responsible for the prayer with which, as soon as she was old enough to lisp it, Hanano was tucked into her little bed at night. That dates back to the memory-stone day when my wonderful "Tales of the Western Seas" came to me. In one of the thin volumes of tough paper tied with silk cord was a musical little poem that I committed to memory, all unknowing that years after I would teach it, clothed in strange, foreign words, to my own little child. It was—

Ware ima inentosu.
Waga Kami waga tamashii wo mamoritamae.
Moshi ware mesamezushite shinaba,
Shu yo! waga tamashii wo sukuetamae.
Kore, ware Shu no nani yorite negotokoro nari.

Now I lay me down to sleep.
I pray the Lord my soul to keep.
If I should die before I wake,
I pray the Lord my soul to take.
This I ask for Jesus' sake.

There is a saying in Japan, "Only the fingers of a babe can tie a uniting knot that will pull two families together." As the Japanese marriage is not an affair of individuals I had never applied the saying to Matsuo and myself, but one day some Mysterious Power twisted this bit of truth into an incident that played an unsuspected and important part in my life and in that of my husband.

Matsuo was a man who had always been vitally interested in his business. I think that, before the baby came, there had been nothing in his life to which it was second. He and I were very good friends, but we seldom talked freely to each other except in the presence of others. Indeed, we had no common topic of conversation; for he was interested in his own plans, and my mind was taken up with my home and my new friends. But from the day the baby came, everything was changed. Now we had many things to talk about, and for the first time I began to feel acquainted with my husband.

But always, deep in my heart, was the feeling that the baby was *mine*. I did not trace any likeness to Matsuo; nor did I want to. I do not mean that

I objected to her resembling him, but that I never thought of her as really *belonging* to any one but myself and my own family.

One day when I was in the city I stopped for a few moments at my husband's store. He happened to be busy and I waited in the office. His desk looked to me in great disorder, and right in front, in a wide pigeon-hole, was an odd thing to be in a cluttered-up office. It was a little lacquer box of exquisite workmanship and bearing a crest that is rarely seen outside a museum. I lifted the lid, and there, before my startled eyes, were three strange objects—a green paper whirligig, some little pieces of clay the baby's fingers had pressed into crude shapes, and a collapsed balloon.

I stood still, my heart beating quickly; then I turned away, feeling as if I had taken an unbidden glance into the heart of a stranger. In that moment came the realization that there was another claim on my baby as tender and as strong as my own, and with a throb of remorse my heart turned toward my husband with a strange new feeling.

Among the strong influences in Hanano's life were the frequent calls and unfailing kindness of our good friend Mrs. Wilson. She seldom came that she did not bring flowers for Mother, and on Easter and family anniversaries our parlours were bowers of bloom from her generous conservatory.

One day, when Hanano was about a year old, she was sitting on Mother's lap by the window when she saw the familiar carriage coming up the driveway. It stopped and Mrs. Wilson stepped out. Glancing up and sees the baby she waved a white-gloved hand and smiled. The sun was shining on her stately figure in its gown of soft heliotrope shade, with flowers in her arms.

"Oh, oh!" cried the baby, joyfully clapping her hands. "Pretty Flower Lady! Pretty Flower Lady!"

Thus was she christened in the baby's heart, and "Flower Lady" she has been to us all ever since. May the many blossoms which her generous hands have scattered far and wide bloom anew for her in all their symbolism of happiness and peace when she reaches the beautiful gardens across the river.

From the time when Hanano first recognized her father as a separate individual, he brought her toys, and she was no sooner toddling about and beginning to prattle than he spent most his leisure time in playing with her, carrying her about or even taking her to call on the neighbours.

One Sunday afternoon just after Matsuo had started off somewhere with her, Mother said: "I have never known a more devoted father than Matsuo. Are all Japanese men as unselfish with their children?"

"Why, I—don't—know," I replied slowly. "Aren't American men fond of their children?"

"Oh, yes," she answered quickly, "but Matsuo comes home early every evening to play with Hanano, and the other day he closed his store for the entire afternoon just to take her to the zoo."

My mind went back to my father—and Mr. Toda—and other fathers; and suddenly I saw Japanese men in a new light. "They have no chance!" I thought, a little bitterly. "An American man can show his feelings without shame, but convention chains a Japanese man. It pulls a mask over his face, closes his lips, and numbs his actions. However a husband many feel toward his wife, he cannot in public show her affection, or even respect; nor does she wish him to. It is not good form. The only time a man of dignity dares betray his heart is when he is with a little child—either his own or another's. Then he has the only outlet that etiquette allows; and even then he must guide his actions by rule. A father becomes his little son's comrade. He wrestles with him, races with him, and acts with him scenes of samurai daring, but he love his little daughter with a great tenderness and accepts her gentle caresses with a heart hunger that is such pathos it is tragedy.

Matsuo was more demonstrative to me than would have been polite had we been living in Japan, but we both respected formality, and it was years before I realized how deep were his feelings for his family.

After that remark of Mother's and the thoughts that it aroused I delayed Hanano's bedtime, and she had many a romp with her father after the hour when children are supposed to be asleep. One moonlight evening I came down and found them running around the lawn, chasing each other and dodging this way and that, while Mother sat on the porch laughing and applauding. They were playing, "Shadow catch Shadow."

"I used to play that on moonlight nights when I was a little girl," I said

"Why, is there a moon in Japan?" asked Hanano in great surprise.

"This very same one," her father replied. "Wherever you go, all your life, you will see it above you in the sky."

"Then it walks with me," said Hanano with satisfaction, "and when I go to Japan, God can see my Japanese grandma."

Matsuo and I glanced at each other, a little puzzled. Hanano had always associated the Man in the Moon with the face of God, but I did not know until afterward that she had heard a lady who was calling on Mother that afternoon express regret that "beautiful Japan is a country without God."

Hanano's odd idea was somewhat startling, but it was a pleasant one to her and I did not correct it. "She will learn soon enough in this practical country," I thought with a sigh. In Japan children are saved many a puzzling heartache, for most of our people retain sympathy for childish illusions even to old age; thus poetic fancies are less apt to be too suddenly shattered. Daily life over there is full of mystic thought. To the masses of people, nothing in the active life about us is more real than the unseen forces which people the earth and air; and no day passes that does not bring to almost everyone some suggestion of the presence of kindly spirits. Most of the gods we look upon as friendly comrades, and the simple duties we owe them we perform with calm and pleasant feelings of gratitude and courtesy. There is little fear of penalty for neglect other than humiliation for a lack of politeness, which weighs a good deal with a Japanese. The house shrines remind us that relatives are watching over us, and we show our appreciation with incense and prayer. The fire goddess is the helpful ruler of the kitchen, whose thanks are the slender ends of a weave of cloth hung beside the kitchen fire-box. The goodly god of rice asks that we keep the fire beneath the rice-kettle free from rubbish. The water goddess, who blesses the streams and rivers, demands that the wells be clean. The seven gods of fortune—Industry, Wealth, Wisdom, Strength, Beauty, Happiness, and Long Life—are seen everywhere and always greeted with a smiling welcome; and the two especially honoured by tradesmen, Industry and Wealth, are perched on a prominent shelf in every store, from which their faces look down, giving to the master the comfortable assurance that friends are near. The hideous gods beside temple doors are not hideous to us, for they are the fierce watch-dogs who protect us from danger, and the gods of the air—Thunder, Wind, and Rain—are guardians for our good. Above all these lesser gods the Sun goddess, ancestress of our Imperial line, watches over the entire land with kindly, helpful light.

These various gods are a confused mixture of Shinto and Buddhist; for the religion of the masses vaguely combines both beliefs. As a rule this is not a religion of fear, although the evil spirits of the hells, if seriously accepted as pictured in ancient Buddhist books, are fearful indeed; but even they allow two days in each year when the repentant may climb to a higher plane. Thus, to the Japanese, even the sad and puzzling path of transmigration, into which unconscious footsteps so often wander, leads at last, after the long period of helplessness and gloom, to a final hope.

Buddhism, on its ages-long journey from India to Japan, seems to have dropped many of its original elements of terror; or else they were softened and lost in the goodly company of our jolly and helpful Shinto gods. Not one of these do we dread, for, in Shintoism, even Death is only a floating cloud through which we pass on our journey in the sunshine of Nature's eternal life.

Our man-made laws of convention have had more power in moulding the lives of the people and have left a more lasting stamp on their souls than have our gods. Our complex religion arouses the interest of the intellectual, and it teaches genuine resignation; but it does not guide the ignorant with a comprehending wisdom, nor does it give to the brooding and the sorrowful the immediate comfort of cheerfulness and hope that comes with a belief in the peasant priest of Nazareth.

CHAPTER-23
Chiyo

AFTER Hanano had learned that the moon was a friend she could depend upon wherever she might travel, she became intensely interested in moon stories. I postponed telling her the legend of the white rabbit who is fated for all time to pound rice dough in a great wooden bowl, for it is his shadow which Japanese children see in every full moon; and I thought I would allow her to drift gradually from her idealization of the American legend. But I told her of our moon-gazing parties where families or groups of friends gather in some beautiful open spot and write poems praising the brilliant leaves of the moon vine which causes the glow of autumn that in America is called Indian summer.

We were sitting on the doorstep of the back parlour one evening, looking out across the porch at the moon sailing round and clear in a cloudless sky, and I told her how in Japan, on that very night, every house, from the palace of the Emperor to the hut of his humblest subject, would have on the porch or in the garden where it could catch the glow of the full moon a small table with fruits and vegetables—everything round—arranged in a certain manner, in honour of the goddess of the moon.

"Oh, how pretty!" cried Hanano. "I wish I could be there to see!"

There was the rustling of a newspaper behind us.

"Etsu," called Matsuo, "there is some kind of a child's story about that celebration. I remember once when my elder sister and I had been teasing our little sister, who was a timid child, that my aunt told us a story of gentle Lady Moon and naughty Rain and Wind who tried to spoil her pleasure on an August full-moon night."

"Oh, tell me!" cried Hanano, clapping her hands and running to her father.

"I'm not much on stories," said Matsuo, taking up his paper again, "but your mother will know it. Etsu, you tell it to her."

So Hanano came back to the doorstep, and I tried to recall the half-forgotten story of

LADY MOON AND HER ENEMIES

One pleasant evening in August the beautiful Lady Moon was sitting in front of her toilet stand. As she lifted the powder puff to clear and soften her bright colouring she said to herself:

"I must not disappoint the Earth people to-night. Of all the nights of the year they look forward to the 'Honourable Fifteenth,' for this is the time when my beauty is at the crown of its glory."

Turning the mirror a trifle, she carefully arranged her fluffy collar.

"It seems a poor sort of life—to do just nothing but smile and look happy! But that is my only way to gladden the world, so to-night I will shine my brightest and best. And," she added, as she peeped over the edge of her balcony and saw the Earth beneath, "after all, it is a pleasant duty—especially to-night!"

It was no wonder she smiled with pleasure, for the whole world was decorated in her honour. Every city and town, every little village, every lonely hut on the mountain-side, and every humble fisher cot on the shore had upon its porch or placed in front where it could be seen by the eye of the Lady Moon a tiny table laden with treasure balls. There were rice dumplings, chestnuts, potatoes, persimmons, peas, and plums, and, standing in their midst, two circular *sake* vases, holding, stiff and upright, their folded white papers. Everything had been carefully selected as being the nearest a perfect round in shape that could be obtained, for "round" is the symbol of perfection, and on this night only the very best of everything was considered worthy to be shown to the pure and perfect "Lady of the Sky."

Mistress Rain, who lived near Lady Moon, peered through her misty windows with envious eyes. She saw the Earth houses decorated in honour of her neighbour, and caught the breath of the messages floating upward from the lips of young girls: "Great Mysterious! Make my heart as pure as the moonbeams and my life as perfect as the bright and round Lady Moon above!"

As Mistress Rain listened she swished her skirts so viciously that all the umbrellas which decorated them suddenly flew open, and she had to clutch them quickly to keep the water with which they were filled from spilling over the Earth. Even as it was, a shower of drops fell sparkling through the moonlight, and the Earth people looked up in surprise.

"I haven't seen the like since last August," continued the angry Mistress Rain. "Every flower vase on the earth appears to be filled with August moon-flowers, and all the porches are newly polished and spread with finest cushions, so the honourable aged ones may be seated where they can behold the glory of Lady Moon. It is not fair!"

There was another swish, and again a shower of rain drops went sparkling through the moonlight.

Just then the Wind god sailed by, holding tight in his hands the ends of his bag of breezes. Mistress Rain noticed the dark scowl on his brow, and called:

"Good evening, Kase no kami San! I am glad to see you passing this way. You look as if you are searching for unexpected work."

The Wind god stopped and seated himself upon a cloud, still holding tight to the ends of the bag.

"Earth beings are the queerest of creatures!" he complained. "Lady Moon lives in the world of Sky, and so do we; yet they think only of her! She has an honourable title given to her, and not a single month of the year passes that the fifteenth day is not observed in her honour. Even on the third day, when she climbs out of her cellar, they welcome her face as she peeps over the wall with such joy that one would think they had never expected to see her again!"

"Yes, yes!" excitedly cried Mistress Rain, "and especially this August night! They always look with anxious eyes for fear that you or I may appear, although uninvited and unwelcome."

"This August night!" exclaimed the Wind god with great scorn. "Yes, this very night I'd like to show those Earth creatures what I could do!"

"It would be such fun," said sly Mistress Rain, "to go with a rush and upset all the things displayed in honour of Lady Moon."

"Ho! Ho! Ho!" laughed the Wind god, so pleased with the idea that he loosened his hold on one end of the bag, and a sudden gust of wind swept through the sky, causing consternation among the Earth people.

Lady Moon was quietly and calmly smiling upon the world, her mind busy with gentle and unselfish thoughts, when the Wind god and Mistress Rain silently slipped behind the mountains and journeyed a long way so that they could come unexpectedly from the side of the sea. But Lady Moon saw them, and, sad and disappointed, she hid behind a curtain while her triumphant enemies swept on over the world.

Oh, it was a terrific whirl of angry Wind and Rain! On rushed the god, pushing his big bag before him with loosened ends, and close behind whirled Mistress Rain with a loud "swish!—swish!" as torrents of water poured from the hundreds of wide-open umbrellas on her skirts.

But, ah, what disappointment was theirs! The rollicking laugh of the Wind god, which had loosened for an instant his hold on the end of the bag, had been warning enough, even if the sharp-eyed Earth people had not seen the clouds of mist sweeping around the mountains. Every house was prepared for the storm. The beautiful little tables had disappeared, and the wild rushes of Wind and Rain were met by closed wooden doors. They howled and shrieked and darted and whirled until both were exhausted; then, with the god muttering and Mistress Rain weeping, they hurried across the valley to their homes.

When all was once more quiet the sorrowful Lady Moon lifted her head.

"My pleasure is spoiled!" she sighed. "The beautiful decorations of the Earth houses are now hidden, and the people have closed their eyes in sleep."

Suddenly a brilliant smile spread over her face, and she said bravely:

"But I will do my duty! Even though no one sees me, I will smile my brightest and best!"

She pushed aside her curtain and looked down upon the world. Her gentle, unselfish sweetness received its reward, for all the doors of the Earth houses were open wide, and the people were gathered on the porches watching for her face. When it appeared songs of welcome floated upward.

"Oh, see the beautiful Lady Moon!" the voices cried. "Again she smiles upon us! After a storm she is always doubly beautiful, and all the world is doubly glad!"

"That's a very moral story," said Hanano thoughtfully. "I feel kind of sorry for Mr. Wind and Mrs. Rain, but I love Lady Moon. Let us fix a table like they have in Japan. Clara will give us the things and the moonshine is beautiful on our porch edge."

"I have something just as good," said Matsuo, starting for the stairway. "Wait a moment."

He brought a small wooden box and put it on the table. It was a phonograph with records on spools of wax and with a little horn attached, into which we could talk and make records of our own voices. Matsuo was to start to Japan in a few days on a business trip and he had selected the phonograph as a gift for my mother, that it might carry to her the voice of her little granddaughter. We called Mother, and all of us had quite an exciting time watching Matsuo arrange the machine. Then he took his seat before it, with Hanano on his lap, and they had a rehearsal. Not until she began to prattle away in her sweet, childish English did it dawn upon us that her puzzled grandmother would not be able to understand a word that she said.

This made us realize what a little American we had in our Japanese nest, and brought directly before us one of the great problems of Japan.

"If our daughter were a boy," Matsuo said that night, "we might have reason to look serious. I should not want to prepare my son to live in a country where, if capable, he would not be welcome to occupy the highest position his country has to offer its citizens."

"Even for our daughter," I replied, "there is no permanent place in this country; nor in Japan either, with only an American education."

The result of this conversation was that when Matsuo returned from Japan he brought an entire set of school readers, from kindergarten to high school; also the five steps of articles for the Doll Festival. This festival is ages old and educational in character. Any one who understands it thoroughly has a nearly complete knowledge of Japanese folklore, history, customs, and ideals. Every girl has a doll festival set, and when she marries, takes it with her to her new home. The set Matsuo brought to Hanano was mine—the one which Brother objected to my bringing with me to America.

When the set came we all went out to the big, light carriage house, and after William had opened the rough board box, Matsuo and he carefully lifted out the smooth, various-sized whitewood boxes, each holding a doll. My eyes fell on a long, flat package wrapped in purple crêpe bearing the Inagaki crest.

"Why, Mother has sent the Komoro *kamibina!*" I cried in astonishment, lifting the package respectfully to my forehead.

"I thought all the Komoro dolls were gone except the two that you used to play with," said Mother.

"The *kamibina* are different," said Matsuo.

"Yes," I said slowly, "the *kamibina* are different. They belong to the family. They can never be sold, or given away, or disposed of in any way. My mother must have had these put away for years—and now she has sent them to me."

I was touched, for it brought forcibly before me the truth that I was the last of the "honourable inside" of the house of Inagaki. A doll festival set belonged to the daughter; the master of the house having no control over the home department.

No doll festival set, however elaborate, is complete without these two long, odd-shaped dolls. In olden time they were always of paper. Later, extravagant families sometimes made them of brocade or crêpe, but however rich the material, they were *called* paper dolls and were always folded in the same crude shape of the primitive originals. When the set is arranged for the celebration, these dolls have no fixed place, as all the others have, but may be put anywhere, except on the top shelf reserved for the Emperor and Empress.

The origin of the Doll Festival reaches back to the crude days of Shintoism. At that time a sinful person would seek purification by bathing in a stream. As time passed, and power or riches brought independent thought, it became customary for the lazy and the luxurious to send a substitute. Still later, an inanimate sacrifice in human form was considered satisfactory, and from anything near and dear as a part of one's own self the two images were made. There were tiny wooden spools, two cocoons or simply shaped bunches of floss, the most valued possession of weaving villages; even crudely cut vegetables in farming districts. There were always two, supposed to be male and female, thus representing the entire family—both men and women members. Gradually, dolls rudely cut from paper—a precious material in those days—came to be universally used and were called *kamibina* which means "paper dolls."

In time one fixed date was decided upon for universal atonement, and the "First Serpent Day of Spring" was chosen, because the time of the dragon's change of skin is symbolic of the slipping from winter's darkness of sin into the light and hope of spring. That date is the one still observed.

In the days of shogun power, when the Emperor was considered too sacred to be seen, this festival represented an annual visit from the invisible ruler to show his personal interest in his people; thus it encouraged loyalty to the loved and unseen Emperor. In feudal times, when, in the samurai class, a wife's duties became those of her absent husband, and children were necessarily left to the care of high-bred attendants, this festival became, in those families, the only opportunity for girls to be trained in the domestic duties which were such an essential part of every Japanese girl's education.

The lunar calendar advanced "First Serpent Day" to March 3d, and after Hanano's set came, we celebrated that day each year just as it is done in

Japan. Five steps were put up in the parlour and covered with red cloth. On these we arranged the miniature Emperor and Empress with court ladies, musicians, and various attendants. There were also doll furniture and household implements. On the lowest steps were tiny tables with food prepared by Hanano herself, with some help from me, and served by her to the playmates who were always invited to join her. And so "Third Day of Third Month" came to be looked forward to by Hanano's little American friends just as it has been by little Japanese girls for almost a thousand years.

One of these celebrations, when Hanano was almost five years old, was an especially busy day for her, as, in addition to her duties as hostess, she received several telephone messages of congratulation, to which, with a feeling of great importance, she replied in person. Her happy day was made more so because her best friend, Susan, brought her little sister, a delicate-faced, golden-haired child who was just learning to walk. Hanano was a gracious hostess to all, but she was especially attentive to the dainty little toddler. That night when she was ready for her usual evening prayer she looked up at me very seriously.

"Mamma, may I say to God just what I please?" she asked.

"Yes, dear," I replied, but I was startled when, from the little bowed figure with clasped hands, came a sudden, "Hello, God!"

I reached out my hand to check her. Then I remembered that I had always taught her to respect her father next to God, and that was the greeting she used to him when he was too far away to be seen. I softly withdrew my hand. Then again I was startled by the solemn little voice, whispering, "Please give me a little sister like Susan's."

I was too much surprised to speak, and she went on with "Now I lay me" to the end.

As I tucked her into bed I said, "How did you happen to ask God for a little sister, Hanano?"

"That's how Susan got her sister," she replied. "She prayed for her a long time, and now she's here."

I went away a little awed, for I knew her prayer would be answered.

The March festival was long past, and May almost gone, when one morning Hanano's father told her that she had a little sister and led her into the room where the baby was. Hanano gazed with wide-open, astonished eyes upon black-haired, pink-faced little Chiyo. She said not a word but walked straight down the stairs to Grandma.

"I didn't pray for *that*," she told Mother, with a troubled look. "I wanted a baby with yellow hair like Susan's little sister."

Clara happened to be in the room, and with the freedom of an American servant, said, "Yellow hair on a Japanese baby would be a funny sight!" and burst out laughing.

"It's *not* a Japanese baby!" Hanano indignantly cried. "I didn't *ask* for a Japanese baby! I don't *want* a Japanese baby!"

Mother took the child on her lap and told her how proud we all were to have two little Japanese girls in our home, and so brought a slow comfort to the disappointed little heart.

That afternoon Mother saw Hanano sitting a long time very quietly in front of the big mirror that stood between the two front windows of the parlour.

"What is it you see, dear?" Mother asked.

"I s'pose I'm a Japanese girl, too," Hanano answered slowly. "I don't look like Susan or Alice."

She winked several times very fast, then, with a choking gulp, her loyalty to blue eyes and yellow hair succumbed to loyalty to love, and she added, "But Mamma is pretty! I'm going to be like her!" and climbed down from the chair.

No one can sound the depths of a child's thoughts, but from that day Hanano developed an interest in Japanese things. Matsuo was fond of listening to her prattle and of playing with her, but she depended upon me for stories; and so, night after night, I would talk of our heroes and repeat to her the songs and fairy lore which had been part of my child life. Best of all she liked to have me talk of the pretty black-haired children—I always said they were pretty—who made chains of cherry blossoms or played games in a garden with a stone lantern and a curving bridge that spanned a pond set in the midst of flowers and tiny trees. I almost grew homesick as I painted these word pictures for her, or sat in the twilight singing a plaintive Japanese lullaby to the baby, while Hanano stood beside me, humming softly beneath her breath.

Was this sudden love for the land she had never seen an inheritance, or—for children sometimes seem to be uncannily endowed with insight—was it premonition?

One day the old familiar world ended for me, leaving me with memories—comforting ones and regretful ones—all closely wrapped in a whirl of anxious, frightened questioning, for no longer had I a husband or my children a father. Matsuo, with a last merry word and a sleepy smile, had quickly and painlessly slipped over the border into the old-new country beyond our ken.

And now, for my children and myself, nothing was left but farewells and a long, lonely journey. The country that had reached out so pleasant a welcome to me, that had so willingly pardoned my ignorance and my mistakes, the country where my children were born and where I had received kindness greater than words can express—this wonderful, busy, practical country had no need of, nor did it want, anything that I could give. It had been a broad, kindly, loving home for me and mine, but a place for the present only. It held no promise of usefulness for my growing children and had no need of my old age. And what is life if one can only learn, and of what one learns give nothing?

The past years were like a dream. From a land of misty, poetic ideas I had drifted through a puzzling tangle of practical deeds, gathering valuable thoughts as I floated easily along, and now—back to the land of mist and poesy. What was ahead of me? I wondered.

CHAPTER-24

In Japan Again

WHEN the weary sight of tumbling and tossing waves was past and I was once again in Japan, I found myself in th emidst of surroundings almost as strange as those I had met when I landed in America.

The provinces and classes in Japan had for so many centuries held steadfast, each to its own customs, that even yet there were only occasional evidences to be seen of their slow yielding to the equalizing influences of modern life; and I had gone at once to Matsuo's home in western Japan, where standards of dress and etiquette, ideals, and even idioms of speech were entirely different from those of either Nagaoka or Tokyo.

We were met on our arrival by a crowd of Matsuo's relatives, all in ceremonial dress, for we had brought the sacred ashes with us; and from then until the forty-nine days of ceremonies for the dead were over, I was treated as an honoured messenger-guest. After that my position was very humble, for a son's widow is an unimportant person in Japan, and, virtually, that is what I was, Matsuo having been, until he decided to remain in America, the adopted son of Uncle Otani.

I was very anxious about my little girls; for in Japan children belong to the family—not to the parents. Hanano, on the death of her father, had become the head of our little family, but we were only a branch of the main family of which Uncle Otani was the head. So it had been taken for granted by all relatives, my own as well as Matsuo's, that the children and I would make our home with Uncle Otani. He would have made room for me in his handsome house and would have supplied me with beautiful clothes, but I should have had no authority, even over my own children. This might not have been so bad under some circumstances; for Uncle Otani would have been generous in giving the children every advantage that he considered proper for them to have. But with all his kindness—and a kinder man never lived—I could not forget that he belonged to the old-fashioned merchant class that considered education beyond the grammar school undesirable for girls.

The situation was difficult; for, from my humble position, I could not say a word. But I had one hope. Hanano, although legal head of our family, was a minor; and her mother, as present regent, held a certain power. Exerting this, I asked for a consultation with Uncle Otani. I explained to him that Matsuo had expressed in his will a desire that, since he had no son, his daughters should receive the liberal education that had been planned for them in America. Then I boldly asked, in Hanano's name and by the power of her father's request, that I should be allowed the privilege of guiding their studies.

Uncle Otani was astonished at such an unheard-of request, but the situation was unusual and a family council was summoned at once. In the case of a consultation concerning a widow, it is customary for her family to be represented; and Brother being unable to be present, Mother sent in his place my progressive Tokyo uncle—the one who had taken so vigorous a part in our council meetings before my marriage. It was necessary for Hanano, as official head of her family, to be present, but of course she was to speak only through me.

Since she had not yet learned to wear Japanese dress properly, I put on her best white dress, trimmed with lace and ruffles. I arranged everything so that it would be very loose; for it is difficult to sit quietly in Japanese fashion while wearing American clothing, and yet it is inexcusably rude at a ceremonial gathering to move—however slightly—the lower part of the body. I explained this to Hanano, and told her how her grandfather, when two years younger than she, had held the seat seat of state in the formidable political meetings before the Restoration. "Honourable Grandmother told me he always sat very straight and was dignified," I said, "and you must be like him." Then we went in to the meeting.

I could not help being uneasy about the way my bold request might be received. To most of the council I was nothing but a widowed dependant of my daughter—a woman with advanced and peculiar notions—and they had the power, if three voices of the council disapproved of me and my ideas, not only to refuse my request, but to separate me from my children entirely. I should be well provided for, in my present home, if I chose, or elsewhere, but the children would remain with their father's people; and no law of Heaven or earth was powerful enough in Japan to prevent it. Matsuo's family had no desire to do any unjust thing; nor did I suspect that they had, but—they held the power.

The conference, which was long, consisted of a series of polite suggestions and earnest, but never excited, arguments. I listened with my head bowed, occasionally—but not too often—glancing toward my little anxious-eyed daughter, sitting erect and motionless in the midst of the dignified row of elders. For two hours she did not move. Then one poor, cramped little leg jerked, her fluffy dress spread out, and with a quick catching at her knee, she gasped, "Oh!"

Not a face turned toward her, but with an anguished clutch in my throat I bowed to the floor, saying, "I humbly pray the honourable council to pardon the rudeness of my foreign-trained child, and permit her to retire with me from the august assembly."

Uncle Otani, without moving, gave a grunt of assent.

As I made my last bow at the sliding door and slipped it back in place, my Tokyo uncle tapped his pipe carefully against the rim of the tobacco box by his side.

"It is fortunate that O Etsu San seems a reliable woman," he said slowly; "for surely it would be a puzzling venture for any of us to take into our family two rough American children with their untrained feet, their flouncing garments, and their abrupt speech."

Whether that remark was intended to be kind or cruel, I never knew; and whether or not it had influence, I never knew; but after another hour of slow, careful, earnest, and perfectly fair discussion, the council decided that on account of Matsuo's request, combined with the fact that his widow appeared to be a trustworthy person, consent was given to a temporary trial of the experiment.

That night I pulled my cushions in between my children's beds—close, close—and crept beneath the covers, faint with relief and gratitude.

CHAPTER-25
Our Tokyo Home

A FEW weeks later the children and I, with capable little Sudzu in the kitchen, were settled in a pretty home in Tokyo. The arrangement with Matsuo's family was that some one of the relatives would visit us at intervals to see that everything was satisfactory; and that I was to consult the council about every new, even trifling, problem which might arise.

I was chained—but I was content.

My relatives in Nagaoka were much concerned over my peculiar position; and Mother, because it would be undignified for a young widow to be alone, decided to come and live with us. Not being able, however, to make immediate arrangements, she sent Taki, who was now a widow, and who, because her father and her grandfather had served in our family, had claimed the right to return to Mother and calmly settle herself as a member of the household. When she came to Tokyo she at once assumed the combined responsibilities of chaperon, housekeeper, cook, seamstress, and commander-general of us all—including Sudzu.

In less than three days Taki had discovered the best fish-shop in the neighbourhood; and in less than a week all second-rate vegetable venders and fruit peddlers went trotting by our kitchen door, holding their swinging baskets away from the keen eyes of our countrywoman who knew so well when the first blush of freshness was gone.

From the first I relied entirely upon Taki's judgment. Nevertheless, I had some annoying experiences, for to her heart I was still little Etsu-bo Sama, although her lips acknowledged that I had reached the dignified position of "Oku Sama"—Honourable Mistress—and although I had acquired some wonderful ideas and possessed two astonishingly active children, who dressed queerly and talked too loud.

My troubles began the very first night. After Taki had closed the outside gates and fastened the front and kitchen doors I heard her sliding the wooden panels which ran along the outer edge of the porch overlooking the garden. These were for protection in stormy weather and to keep us safe at night, but when closed they shut out the air completely.

"Don't close the *amadoes* tight, Taki," I called. "Leave a little space between them. We need fresh air for the rooms."

"*Maa! Maa!*" cried Taki, with profound astonishment in her voice. "You left your home when you had but little learning, Oku Sama. Air without the smile of the august Sun goddess has poison in it."

"But, Taki," I protested, "this is like a foreign house. It has gas for the heaters, and we need outside air, even at night."

She hesitated, evidently much distressed.

"It may be that air in the honourable foreign house is different," she muttered, "but it seems peculiar—peculiar. And besides, it is not safe in a great city where burglars live."

She walked away shaking her head and grumbling to herself. Feeling that I had established my authority, I went to bed, only to be awakened by a stealthy, intermittent rumbling, which presently ended in a muffled snap as Taki pushed in the wooden bolt of the last panel.

"Well," I said to myself, half provoked, half amused, "Taki always had her own way, even with the jailer of Nagaoka prison. So what could *I* expect!"

Like many Japanese women of the working class, Taki had been obliged to take a large share of the burden of livelihood on her own shoulders. Her husband was a kind man and a good workman, but he drank too much *sake*, and that meant not only a mysterious slipping away of wages, but frequent imprisonment for debt.

Whenever this happened Taki came to our home, and Mother would give her employment until she had saved enough to set her husband free. One day while she was working for us, my older sister went out with her on an errand. Just beyond the gate they saw two men approaching. One was a well-dressed man, his head covered with the basket mask worn by all prisoners outside the walls. Sister said that Taki stood still, watching the men suspiciously, and did not seem surprised when they stopped.

The officer bowed and said pleasantly: "Only three *yen* is due now. Pay that and he is free."

"Oh, please, Mr. Officer," exclaimed Taki in great distress, "*please* keep him just a few weeks longer. Then I shall have all the debts paid and a little start for the next time. *Please* keep him just a little longer. Please!"

The husband, poor man, stood meekly by while his wife and the officer argued, but Taki stubbornly refused to pay the three *yen*, and the officer walked away with his basket-headed prisoner. Taki stood looking after them, triumphant. But a few moments later she pulled a fold of paper from her sash and, wiping her eyes, sniffed a few times and said: "Come, little Mistress; we have wasted much time. We must hurry!"

I said nothing more about not closing the *amadoes*, but several days later I had a carpenter put up a wide, open-work strip of carved iris—the flower of health—between the eaves and the top of the panels. At intervals were inserted iron bars run through the hollow tubes of bamboo. Thus we were safe in every way; for not enough poison air could filter through the health-giving blossoms of the carving to injure us, even in the opinion of our good, fanatical Taki.

The children surprised me by the readiness with which they accepted conditions in this strange land. Hanano, from babyhood, had been attracted by new things, and I concluded that our life of constant change had kept her from homesickness. And three-year-old Chiyo—who had always been a contented little thing—seemed so happy in the unbroken companionship of her sister that I did not realize the possibility of her having opinions and desires of her own. While we were visiting she expected strange things, but when we reached a place that I called "home" and she found her clothing arranged in drawers and her playthings put where she could get them, she began to miss many things.

"Mamma," she said one day, coming up and leaning against my shoulder as I sat sewing, "Chiyo wants——"

"What does Chiyo want?" I asked.

She took my hand and led me slowly through our six tiny rooms. White mats were on all the floors except the kitchen. In the parlour alcove hung a roll picture with a flower arrangement on the polished platform beneath. A small upright piano stood in one corner. Sliding doors of silk separated the parlour from my own and the children's rooms, side by side, just beyond. In both, standing against the tan-coloured plaster wall, were whitewood chests of drawers with ornamental iron handles. My desk and Hanano's, both low white tables with books and pen-stands on top, were so placed that, when the paper sliding doors were pushed back, we could see across the narrow porch into our pretty little garden with its well-trimmed shrubbery, its curved path of stepping-stones, and its small lake with nine darting gold-fish.

The dining room, at right angles to our rooms, overlooked the garden, too. It was the sunniest room in the house. The closets were hidden by sliding doors covered with tan-coloured tapestry, and the long, square-cornered fire-box with drawers—the invariable adjunct of every dining room in Japan—was a handsome one of white birch. On one side was always a cushion, ready any moment for the mistress when she came to talk over house matters with the maid, called from the kitchen just behind another tan-coloured door which looked a part of the wall. The bathroom, Taki's and Sudzu's room, and the servants' entrance, were just beyond. Our own "shoe-off place" and entrance hall were in front, opening toward the big wooden gates with the "camel's-eye door" in one of them.

From room to room Chiyo led me, stopping in each and pointing aimlessly here and there. "Chiyo wants——" she repeated, but her wants were so many that she had no words. The emptiness, which I loved, oppressed her. She longed for the big canopy beds of Mother's home, for the deep-cushioned chairs, the large mirrors, the big square piano, the flowered carpets and the windows curtained with lace, the high ceilings, the wide rooms, the spaciousness! I looked at the wistful little face and my heart smote me. But when she pulled my sleeve and, burying her face in the folds of my dress, said piteously, "Oh, Mamma, take me home to Grandma and Papa's picture! Please! Please!" I caught her in my arms and, sinking to the floor, hugged her close and, for the first time since I could remember, I sobbed aloud.

But this could not last. Where was my samurai blood? Where my childhood training? Had my years of unrestrained freedom in America weakened my character and taken away my courage? My honourable father would be shamed.

"Come, Little Daughter," I said, choking and laughing together, "Chiyo has shown Mamma what we have not in our new house; now Mamma will show Chiyo what we have."

So, gaily we went over the same road. In the parlour I pushed back the low silk doors beneath the moon window, and we saw two deep shelves in which were neatly arranged all of Hanano's and Chiyo's pretty books from America. I pointed to the wonderful panel over the doors—a broad, thin slab of wood, strangely delicate and beautiful—carved by unknown years of dashing waves into its odd, inimitable pattern. I showed her the post of the alcove: only the scaled and twisted trunk of a forest pine, yet so polished that it looked as if it were enclosed in crystal. We looked at the rich, dark wood of the alcove floor, "as smooth and shining as Grandma's mirrors in the big parlour at home," I told her, and she bent over to see the reflection of a grave little face, changing, as she looked, into one with a twisty smile. In another room I opened the tiny door of our unused shrine. Within the dainty carved interior stood her father's picture, framed in America, which was to hang over the piano when the carpenter could come to put it up. I showed her the big closets where our bed cushions slept in the daytime, gathering, in their silken flowers, talk, music, and laughter to weave into pleasant dreams for her to find hidden in her pillow at night. I gently opened the wee mountain of ashes in the dining-room fire-box so that she could see the softly glowing charcoal, always waiting with warmth and comfort for any one who wanted a sip of tea. I had her peep into the tiny drawers—one for small rice-cakes of pink and white, in case a child should come to visit, one for extra chopsticks, and one for a tiny can of tea with its broad wooden spoon near by. But the big, broad drawer at the bottom—Oh, dear! Oh, dear!—we didn't need at all. That was made for some old-fashioned grandmother who sometimes, after she had told a fairy story to her little grandchild, would reach in for a long, slender pipe with a silver thimble for a bowl. After three whiffs she would tap it on the edge of the box—just here—three times, tap-tap-tap, and then put it away with its fragrant silken bag (sniff, sniff!—poof, poof! Mamma doesn't like!) to wait for another time of meditation or loneliness, or perhaps for an hour when another dear old grandmother might chance to call. Then there would be three more whiffs, or perhaps double three, while the two grandmothers sipped their tea and talked in gentle voices of olden time.

"And here is where Sudzu keeps the boats of the food fairies," I said, "all waiting for their burden of good things to eat."

I pushed back one of the panels which didn't look at all like a door, and we peeped into a closet of many shallow shelves, on which, in piles of five, were wooden bowls for soup, china bowls for rice, oval plates for fish, deep ones for pickles, and many plates and cups and dishes, each shaped for a special purpose and each decoration telling a story of old Japan. Below were our lacquer tables, each a foot square and a foot high; and piled up, a little distance away, were our cushions,

"Just One and Two and Three,
For She and Her and Me!"

as Hanano sang when Sudzu brought them out for meals.

"And now the kitchen," I went on. "This door doesn't slide, but opens by turning a little bronze pine-cone. Step into these sandals, Chiyo; for no one goes into the kitchen with only foot mittens on—or stockings. Here we are! One half the floor is of smooth, dark boards, you see, and the other half—step down!—of cement. There is the gas range, and close beside it a pottery fire-box for the big swelling rice-kettle with its heavy wooden top. No bit of waste-paper or scrap of any kind must be thrown on *that* fire; only straw to start it and charcoal to continue it, for it is used just to cook rice—the staff of life for Japan—and we must treat it with respect. Here comes Taki; and now she will show us something, little Chiyo, that will make you want to run to the big box that smells all camphory, like the forest near Uncle Otani's house, and get out the fur collar that Grandma gave you last Christmas Day. See!"

Taki stuck two fingers in two little holes in one of the narrow boards of the floor and lifted it; then other, and another. Next, up came a light, broad square of whitewood, and there, within easy reach of Taki's hand, was a small cellar where was a block of ice, roughly cut in shelves, on which were set wooden plates of fish and vegetables, eggs and fruit.

"That is what becomes of the cold, cold bundle the man brings every morning in the straw saddle on his back," I said. "And there is Taki's wooden sink, standing high up from the cement part of the floor, just like a table with legs made of water-pipes.

"Now, turn to the right. Down the narrow little hall we go—five steps of mine and eight of yours—and here we are in the bathroom. The oval whitewood tub, with its two faucets above and little row of gaslights below, is so deep that even Mamma can kneel with the water up to her chin. Here are the three little shelves for our bran bag, cup, and toothbrush, each with a carved towel-hanger below; and over in the corner is a big bamboo basket for laundry and a coil of hose to water the garden. Oh, it's a very interesting little house, Chiyo; just like a big play-house, with Mamma at home all the time to play with you when Hanano has gone to school."

CHAPTER-26

Tragic Trifles

MY FINDING a suitable school for Chiyo almost at once was a piece of good fortune. Not far from our house there lived a gifted educator who was interested in modern methods of teaching young children. He and his wife had in their home a small model kindergarten, to which I was given the privilege of sending my little girl. Chiyo could not speak Japanese, but fortunately there were in the class two children of an American missionary, who spoke the language well, so the little Japanese-born Americans became kind interpreters to the little American-born Japanese; thus forming an international combination that resulted, on one side at least, in a lifetime remembrance of grateful friendliness.

But Hanano's education was a problem. In selecting a school for her the remembrance of my own happy school life in Tokyo naturally influenced me in favour of a mission school; but, after careful examination, I concluded that, although the atmosphere of the mission schools was unquestionably superior, they could not compete with the government schools in scholarship. Therefore I decided upon a public school, the principal of which was reputed to be one of the best in Tokyo, and which, fortunately, was not far from our home. Of this I knew Matsuo's relatives would approve.

Hanano's knowledge of the Japanese language was meagre, but of the history, literature, and traditions of Japan, she knew almost as much as other children her age, and so was too advanced for the primary class.

It was a puzzle for the authorities to know what to do with her; for rules in Japan are not flexible. Official life still moves in grooves, and in a minor officer, the old feudal pride in rigid faithfulness is frequently so extreme that to be jostled out of the established line is hopelessly disconcerting. Time and again I heard with a sinking heart that no place could be found for Hanano in any class, but—I did not *dare* fail! Patiently I persisted, arguing that, since Japan claims her foreign-born children, and also has the rule of compulsory education, surely something could be done.

Well, I had a world of trouble and felt as if the child were being wound closer each day in a red-tape cocoon, but at last she was admitted into the third grade and I given permission to sit in the rear of the room, a silent spectator with a notebook.

I shall never forget those first days. Hanano was naturally quick and observing and already familiar with third-grade stories; but the ideographs were wholly unknown to her, and she could understand very little of the teacher's explanations. Again and again I would see her face light up with an expression of alert attention, which the next moment would change to a puzzled look and then gradually settle into one of blank hopelessness. Every evening our home was turned into a schoolroom, where I went over each lesson of the day, translating and explaining in English. At odd hours, even during meal-time, we played games in which words were limited to those in common use, and whenever Hanano heard Taki bargaining with vendors at the kitchen door, she was immediately at her elbow. But I think her greatest help from any one thing came from the playground at school. There she was a delightful curiosity. She took part in all games, running, gesticulating, and chattering in English, while the others ran, gesticulated, and chattered in Japanese, all having a good time, and Hanano piling up, by the dozen, unforgettable words which carried their own definitions too clearly to need interpretation.

I was faithful in my reports to Uncle Otani, and, on the whole, rather enjoyed the "investigation visits" of the relatives; but my being required to ask council advice before making a change, however slight, in my programme, was often very trying and useless. Formally to request an opinion regarding which of two studies to select for Hanano, when not a member of the council knew or cared to learn anything of her former school work, and every single member considered both of the suggested studies entirely unnecessary for a girl to waste her time over, was absurd. But I was conscientious to the minutest degree, and as time passed the visits from relatives became less frequent and more friendly; and my requests were mostly returned with orders to use my own judgment.

When Hanano reached the stage where she began to recognize characters on the street signs and to listen intelligently to conversation going on about her, I gave up my visits to the school and turned my attention to home duties. Here I found many problems. Some were seemingly too small to be noticed, and yet, like stinging gnat bites, extremely annoying. I had thought it would be well to keep the children in American clothing. They had a goodly supply, and progressive families were beginning to advocate it for children, except for formal use. As the weather grew colder I put heavy underclothes and woollen stockings on them; for the schoolrooms were heated only with two charcoal fire-boxes in each large room. But, notwithstanding my care, one day Chiyo came home with a cold. The next morning was chilly and damp. I had no heart to keep her from her greatest enjoyment; yet to risk her taking more cold was out of the question. What could I do? Suddenly I had a wicked inspiration. She had a coat of soft woollen goods which covered her dress completely. I put it on, buttoned it up close and, telling her not to take it off, sent her on her way.

Then I sat down to have it out with my conscience. In Japan, when one enters a house, the shoes, wrap, and hat are removed. It was as unpardonable for Chiyo to keep on her wrap in school as if it had been her hat; but I knew that, in the eyes of the teacher, the pretty red coat with its lace collar and cuffs would be only a foreign dress, no more suggesting a wrap than did her usual clothing. And to think that I had taken advantage of the ignorance of the teacher and done this deceitful thing! I thought of Kishibo-jin and wondered if in every mother's heart is hidden an unborn demon.

Presently, with a sigh, I rose to my feet and prepared to go out. As I approached the mirror to arrange my hair I stopped with a half-ashamed laugh. For one instant a superstitious hesitation had held me back, as if I might see in the reflected face a hint of the deceit in my heart.

I went direct to the nearest shop and purchased material for a *hifu*—a loose but proper and elegant house-garment, which in winter is padded with the cobwebby cut silk taken from empty cocoons. It is the lightest and warmest garment in Japan. Taki, Sudzu, and I sewed all day, and the next morning Chiyo went happily to school with her *hifu* over her American dress.

It was this incident that decided me to change the children from American to Japanese clothing.

There is another link, less tragic, in the chain of my memories of growing adaptability. When riding in jinnikishas it is the custom for the honoured person to go first. Therefore a child should follow a parent. But I never felt sure that some unexpected thing might not happen to my active little ones; so I always put them together in one jinrikisha just ahead of me. One day, as we were passing through a busy street, I saw Hanano looking back and waving frantically; almost standing up in her eagerness to have me see a small table and two chairs of bamboo in a shop window. Both children pleaded for me to buy them. It was nonsense to take them to our pretty home; for chair legs ruin the soft mats, and foreign furniture is wholly inartistic in a Japanese room. But the children looked at them so longingly that I made the purchase, ordering thin strips of wood to be fastened on the feet to make a flat foundation that would not injure our floor. They were to be delivered the next day.

Early the following morning I went shopping, returning home about noon. What was my astonishment when I entered the house to see the bamboo table in the centre of the parlour and on each side of it a chair, with Hanano seated on one and Chiyo on the other! They had no books, no toys. Sudzu said they had been there for an hour, occasionally changing places, but otherwise sitting still or talking in low voices.

"What are you doing, children," I asked, "sitting here so quiet?"

"Oh, just enjoying!" replied Hanano.

After a moment Chiyo said: "Grandma's chairs are soft, but this one has knobs on the edge. Let's swap gain, Hanano."

Then there was the affair of the bedclothes. The pride of a Japanese housewife is to have not only dainty and pretty, but also appropriate, bed cushions. Mother had sent with Taki enough silk and linen for both children's beds. The pattern for Hanano's was, for her flower-name, the "Flowers of the Four Seasons," in which bunches of many-coloured blossoms were scattered loosely over a background of shadowy pink. Chiyo's—for her name, which means "Long Life"—was a flock of white storks flying across a blue sky with floating clouds. Taki and Sudzu had sewed steadily for several days making the cushions, so, on the night they were finished, and when Sudzu had made up the beds side by side, I told the girls that I would put the children to bed and they could go out to a street fair held on the temple grounds, not far away. In the midst of the undressing some friends came to call and I left the children to finish alone.

My friends stayed late. I heard Taki and Sudzu come in, and a short time later there was a disturbance in the children's room. Hanano's voice sounded clear and loud in English, "It isn't fair! Stop! It isn't fair!' Then came a low murmuring in Japanese—sleepy complaints—a soft scrambling—a gentle, "Pardon my disturbing you. Honourable good-night!"—a sliding door, whisperings, and presently—silence.

As soon as the guests had gone I hurried into the children's room. Both were sleeping quietly. I waited for Sudzu to come in after locking the gate, and then I learned what had happened. Faithful Taki, on her return, had peeped into the children's room to see that all was safe, and behold! the "Flower in a Strange Land" was asleep beneath the flying storks and the long-life lassie was peacefully reposing beneath the scattered blossoms of the four seasons. Taki's orderly habits of a lifetime had sprung to the rescue of an upset world. Pulling off the covers with a jerk, she had lifted Hanano in her strong arms, and then, standing the startled child upright, had caught Chiyo and plumped her into Hanano's bed, muttering constantly, "Ignorant children! Ignorant children!" Paying no attention to Hanano's indignant protests that they had changed purposely, "just to swap," she had tossed her back into bed, whirled up the covers, and then, politely bowing good-night, had softly pushed the doors together and retired as gently as if she feared to awake a sleeping child.

"Taki is just like she used to be," I thought as I lay down on my own bed with a laugh. "People who think Japanese women are always gentle ought to widen their acquaintance."

But one thing about which I have never laughed was a peep I had into a hidden part of my children's lives. Hanano always had been brave about bearing silently little troubles that could not be helped, and she seemed so busy and interested in her new life that I did not realize that deep in her heart was a longing for the old home. Our garden had two entrances, one through the house and one through a little brushwood wicket on the path that led from a wooden gate to the kitchen door. One day, just as I reached home, a sudden shower threatened to drench me. So, instead of going around to the big gateway, I slipped through the wooden gate, and ran across the stones of the garden to the porch. Leaving my shoes on the step I was hurrying to my room when I heard the voices of the children.

"This shady place," said Hanano, "is where Grandma's chair always was, on the porch. And under this tree is where the hammock was where you took your nap and where Papa almost sat down on you that time. And this is the big stone steps where we always had firecrackers on Fourth of July. And this is the well. And this is the drawbridge. And this is the place where Clara went to feed the chickens. It's all exactly right, Chiyo, for I drew it myself, and you must not forget again. Don't tell Mamma, for she would be sorry, and she is our only treasure that we have left. All the rest are gone, Chiyo, and we can never have them again. So it can't be helped, and we just have to stand it. But you mustn't forget that all this—for ever—is where our love is. And now, let us sing."

They stood up, holding hands, and the childish voices rose in a clear, steady "My Country, 'tis of Thee!"

I cried softly as I moved about in the next room and thought of the transplanted morning glories. "Is it right," I wondered, "to plant a little unasked flower in a garden of love and happiness, from which it must soon be wrenched away, only for another, and a dwarfed, start in strange, new surroundings? The garden had much to give of strength and inspiration, but is it worth the cost? Oh, is it worth the cost?"

CHAPTER-27
Honourable Grandmother

"Honourable Grandmother is coming—coming!
Honourable Grandmother is coming to-day!"

happily sang Chiyo as her little foot mittens came pattering over the white mats, following me as I went through the rooms giving touches here and there to complete arrangements for our expected guest.

Foot mittens took the place of stockings now, and the free American dress had given way to a gay-flowered kimono with scarlet lining and graceful swinging sleeves.

"Japanese fashions are the prettiest for Japanese people," I thought as I looked at Chiyo's black hair, short in the back and cut square across the forehead. She had not been a pretty child in American dress. Japanese clothes were much more becoming, but oh, the opportunities for comfortable and healthful bodies the untrammelled children of America have! I sighed, yet I was so bound by outside influences that I could not regret having changed the children into Japanese dress before their grandmother saw them.

We had been very busy after the arrival of Mother's letter saying that she was ready to come. The children and I moved in together, and I arranged a cosy little room for her, which I knew she would find more convenient and comfortable than any other in the house. I wanted everything to look homelike to her; so I had the swinging electric lights changed to three-foot-high floor lamps shaded by black lacquer frames with paper panels, like the candle-stands at the Nagaoka home. Our gas heaters were already in bronze braziers so ingeniously set up that they looked like charcoal burners. Mother would have accepted everything new with the smiling philosophy of a lifetime, but I did not want her to "accept" things; I wanted everything to look homelike so she could fit in happily without effort.

The empty shrine I had been using for books and the children's hats. Even Taki had not objected to "high objects," as she called them, being placed there; for Japanese people are taught to respect books as "intellectual results," and hats as pertaining to the revered "crown of the body." But, nevertheless, she was unreservedly pleased when I removed the things and began to prepare the carved wooden alcove for the small belongings that Mother would bring with her from the large shrine at home.

"Where shall we put the shrine that Honourable Grandmother will bring?" asked Hanano, thinking of the elaborate gilded and lacquered cabinet in Uncle Otani's home.

"It's as easy for Honourable Grandmother to wrap up all the really necessary things for her shrine as it would be for a Christian to carry a Bible and a prayer book," I answered; "and we will have this little alcove all fresh and clean for them. Honourable Grandmother loves the things that have been sacred to her through all the sorrows and joys of her life."

"Do Honourable Grandmother's God and our God know each other up in heaven?" asked Chiyo.

I was leaning in the alcove to brush a bit of dust off the carving, and Hanano replied.

"Of course they do, Chiyo," she said. "Jesus had just as hard a time as the August Buddha did to teach people that God wants them to be good and kind and splendid. Mamma always says that Honourable Grandmother and our dear American Grandma are good, just alike."

While we were talking, there had been sounding a constant pata-pata-pata from the next room, where Sudzu, with her sleeves looped back and a blue-and-white towel folded over her freshly dressed hair, was vigorously cleaning the paper doors with a *shoji* duster—a bunch of cut papers tied on the end of a short stick. The sound stopped abruptly and Sudzu appeared in the doorway.

Quickly removing the towel and pulling off the cord that held back her sleeves, she bowed to the floor.

"Taki San thinks that the bath water heated by gas will be too harsh for the delicate body of Honourable Retired Mistress," she said. "Shall I go for a carpenter?"

I had forgotten the belief of country people that only charred wood must be used for bath fuel when one is frail or old. I hurried Sudzu out on her errand, and within two hours the gas coil had been exchanged for a small charcoal furnace, and our arrangements were complete.

That evening was a memorable one for the children. We all went to the station to meet Mother, except Taki. She remained behind so that the welcoming red rice and the fish, baked head and all, would be in hot readiness; and after we reached home, even before the bustle of welcome was over, she had the shrine belongings in place and the candles lighted. Then, with the gilded doors wide open and the pungent odour of incense filling the air, she brought in the little shrine table laden with food. Our own tables came next, and once again I was sitting down to a meal with my mother beside me and the kindly spirits of the ancestors welcoming me and mine into cheerful companionship. Afterward we retired to the parlour and spent an hour in what Hanano called "getting-acquainted talk," before Mother would confess to the weariness which her pale face already betrayed. Then we all gathered before the shrine, Taki and Sudzu sitting just within the doorway.

How familiar, and yet how strange! The chanting, the soft sound of the little bronze gong, Mother's voice reading the sacred Buddhist scriptures that so often I had heard from the lips of the dear one who long ago had passed away—oh, how quiet and safe it all seemed! The anxious loneliness of months was gone, and there crept into my heart a peace that had not been mine since the protected days when my little family were all together in the dear, dear home of our kind, beloved American mother.

"How alike are the two sides of the world!" I thought. "Both have many gods of little worth, but with one wise, loving, understanding Power over all, the time must surely come when we shall *all* understand."

The weeks following were filled with new and unexpected lessons. I had had no thought but that family loyalty and natural affection were the only requisites necessary to draw together my mother and my children. But I soon discovered that, though neither loyalty nor affection was lacking, mutual interests were only possibilities of the future.

My attempts to combine the old and the new frequently resulted in my having to give up the combination and decide wholly in favour of one or the other. With material things this was only an inconvenience; but a puzzling problem, indeed, when it came to Mother's old-fashioned ideas clashing with the advanced training of modern schools. Mother never criticized. She met all situations with a smile or some pleasant remark about the "new ways of the world"; but it was evident that she greatly distrusted the wisdom of spending so much time on boys' studies and so little on flower-arranging, tea-serving, *koto* music, and other womanly accomplishments. And the gymnastic exercises which the children enthusiastically described, where whole classes of girls drilled on the school grounds, marching and singing with vigorous energy, were wholly contrary to her ideas of dignity.

I tried to explain that these exercises were believed to be good for health and growth. I told her it was no longer considered bold and mannish for girls to sit straight and to carry the head upright when they walked; and that even Hanano's habit of chatting happily about school matters while we were eating, which seemed to Mother the manners of a coolie, was in accordance with her training at school.

Chiyo's gentle ways had appealed to Mother at once, but her sister's quick, busy, energetic manner was a constant surprise and puzzle. Hanano was so active, so apt to speak without being spoken to, and so constantly doing what, according to strict etiquette, were abrupt and discourteous things, that I was continually on the alert to watch for and check her unexpected acts. It was not long before I became unhappily conscious that my only hours of freedom from anxiety lay between the time when Hanano tied up her school books and, jumping into her clogs at the door, ran off, gaily waving a good-bye, and the afternoon hour when the door would slide open and a cheery, "I have come back!" come echoing through the hall.

But this did not last. Gradually, I scarcely know when or how, the silent strain lessened. Hanano was growing more quiet in her talk, more gentle in her manners. Frequently I would see her settle herself beside Chiyo at Mother's fire-box to listen to stories or to receive help as she read aloud, and one day I found both children snuggled up close, one on each side, while Mother showed Hanano how to write the characters for "American Grandma."

Chiyo had loved Mother from the beginning. The child's affectionate advances were somewhat of a shock at first, but very soon the two were congenial companions. It was odd that religion should be one of the binding cords. The kindergarten was just beyond the temple, so Chiyo was familiar with the road, and as I did not like to have Mother go alone, Chiyo often went with her when Sudzu was busy. The child liked to sit in the great solemn place and listen to the chanting, and she liked to be given rice-cakes by the mild-faced priestess who served tea to Mother after the service. One day Mother said: "Chiyo, you are very kind to come with me to the temple. Next time I will go with you to your church." So Chiyo took her to hear our minister, a good man who preached in Japanese. After that they often went together, sometimes to the temple, where Chiyo stood with bowed head while her grandmother softly rubbed her rosary between her hands and murmured, "*Namu Amida Butsu!*" and sometimes to the Christian church, where Mother listened attentively to the sermon and bowed in reverence when the Minister prayed. Then hand in hand they would come home together, talking of what they had heard at one place or the other.

One day as they entered the gate, I heard Mother say gently: "It may be that he said true things, Chiyo, but I must not go to a better place than where my honourable husband is. Even if he is in the dreadful Hell of Cold, it is my duty to be with him. The Christian faith is for the new generation, like you, little Chiyo, but I must follow the path of my ancestors."

One afternoon, when I was sewing in my room, I heard Chiyo's voice beyond the closed doors.

"Honourable Grandmother," she said, "when are you going to die?"

I pushed back the sliding door. There was Mother with Chiyo snuggled up beside her on the same cushion. I was astonished, for in my day no child would have dared to be so familiar with an elder, but there she was, and both were looking down gravely at an array of tiny lacquer boxes spread out on the floor. A large box, into which the smaller ones fitted closely, was near by. How well I remembered that box! All through my childhood it was kept in a drawer of my mother's toilet cabinet, and every once in a while she would take out the little boxes and sprinkle powdered incense into each one. This was what she was doing now.

"I wish I had those pretty boxes for my dolly," said Chiyo.

"Oh, no, little Granddaughter," Mother said, lifting one of the tiny boxes and shaking gently the curved bits that looked like shavings of pale shell. "These are my nail clippings that have been saved all my life."

"Your finger-nails—and your toe-nails!" cried the child. "Oh, my! How funny!"

"Hush, little Granddaughter. I am afraid you have not been trained to respect the traditions of your ancestors. We have to save our nails and cut-off baby hair so that our bodies may be perfect when we start on the long journey. The time cannot be far away," she said, gazing thoughtfully out into the garden.

Chiyo had been peering curiously into the boxes, but now her face suddenly sobered and she drew a little closer to her grandmother.

"My heart is troubled, Honourable Grandmother," she said. "I thought it would be a long, long time. You said you had always, even when you were a little girl, put perfume in the boxes to keep them nice and all ready for your death."

Mother lovingly stroked the little black head with her wrinkled hand.

"Yes, but it will not be long now. I have finished my life work, and the merciful Buddha is preparing my platform of lotus blossoms, I am very sure."

"Does the merciful Buddha want you to take your old clipped nails with you when you go to the lotus platform?"

"No; he does not care about my body. He cares only for me."

"Then why did you save your nails so carefully?"

Mother glanced toward the closed shrine.

"The holy shrine, little Chiyo, is only a box when it is empty," she said, "and my body is only a borrowed shrine in which I live. But it is proper courtesy to leave a borrowed article in the best condition."

Chiyo's eyes looked very deep and solemn for a moment.

"That's why we have to take a bath every day and always keep our teeth clean. Dear me! I never thought of that as being polite to God."

I had been so anxious over the children's shortcomings in etiquette and so happy over the slow but satisfactory outcome that I had never given a thought to the changes which my years in America must have made in myself. One afternoon, coming back from a hurried errand, I was walking rapidly up the road toward home when I saw Mother standing in the gateway watching me. I knew that she disapproved of my undignified haste, as indeed she should, for nothing is more ungraceful than a hurrying woman in Japanese dress.

She met me with her usual bow, then said with a gentle smile, "Etsu-bo, you are growing to be very like your honourable father."

I laughed, but my cheeks were hot as I walked up the path beside her, accepting silently the needed reproof, for no Japanese woman likes to be told that her walk suggests that of a man. Occasional hints like this kept my manners from marching with my mind on the road to progress; and under the same quiet influence my two active American children gradually changed into two dignified Japanese girls. Within two years' time both spoke Japanese without accent and both wore Japanese dress so well that to strangers they appeared to have lived always in Japan.

"Just to be in the same house with Mother is excellent training for a girl," I thought, congratulating myself that Hanano had adapted herself so well to her grandmother's standards. Selfishly busy with my daily duties, and content that our home was so harmonious, I had forgotten that, when duty lies between the old and the young, Nature's law points direct to youth. I was counting the gain only—but what of the loss?

One day in the cherry-blossom season, Hanano was sitting at her desk near mine when a light breeze touched the branches of a cherry tree near the porch and some pale pink petals drifted across her desk. She picked one up and after holding it a moment, pressed it gently between her fingers, then threw it aside, and sat looking at the damp spot on her finger.

"What are you thinking, Hanano?" I asked.

She looked up startled, then slowly turned away.

"One time in America," she said after a moment, "when many people were at our house—I think it must have been an afternoon tea—I got tired and went out on the lawn. I climbed to my castle, you remember, the seventh limb of the big apple tree. The blossoms were just falling and a petal fell right into my hand. It left a wet spot, just like this cherry petal did. Oh, Mamma, wouldn't you give just *everything* to see Grandma again—and the porch, and the trees, and——"

The little black head went down on the desk, but before I could reach her it was up again, held high.

"It's all right," she said; "I love Japan—now. But there used to be times when my breast was just full of red-hot fire, and I had to run fast—fast. And once, when you were all away, I climbed the prickly pine by the porch—just once. But I don't want to any more. It's all right. I love it here."

I remembered, then, how sometimes she had scampered around and around the garden, her sleeves flying in the wind and her clogs clattering over the stepping-stones; and I, ignorant and unsympathetic mother that I was, had taken her to my room and talked to her about being gentle and quiet.

But that was a long time before. Gradually she had learned to talk a little lower, to laugh a little less, to walk a bit more noiselessly on the matting, and to sit silent and attentive with bowed head when her elders were speaking. Only the other day Mother had said: "Granddaughter shows great promise. She is growing gentle and graceful."

As I sat and thought, I wondered if Hanano was ever really happy any more. She never seemed sorrowful, but she had changed. Her eyes were soft, not bright; her mouth drooped slightly and her bright, cheery way of speaking had slowed and softened. Gentle and graceful? Yes. But where was her quick readiness to spring up at my first word? Where her joyous eagerness to see, to learn, to do? My little American girl, so full of vivid interest in life, was gone.

With a feeling of helplessness I looked over at her desk and was comforted; for the touch of homesickness had passed away and she was studying busily.

An hour later, when I went unexpectedly to her room, I saw her kneeling beside an open drawer where her American clothes were kept. She had pulled out her old serge suit, and her face was buried in its folds. I crept away to the garden. I could not see, and I stumbled over a flower pot. It was a dwarf pine. The pushing roots had burst the pot, and my touch had caused it to fall apart, disclosing the roots cramped together in a twisted knot.

"It is just like poor Hanano!" I moaned. "They will bind it again to-morrow, and neither it, nor she, will *ever* be free!"

CHAPTER-28
Sister's Visit

THAT summer Mother was far from well. Lately her occasional attacks of asthma had become more frequent and trying. Thinking that a visit from my elder sister, who had always lived near our old home, would give Mother the happiness, not only of seeing her daughter, but also of hearing the pleasant gossip of old neighbours and friends, I wrote asking her to come to Tokyo. In a few weeks she was with us and proved a veritable blessing to us all. She was a comfort to Mother, a wise adviser to me, and an encyclopedia of interesting family history to the children; for there was nothing Sister liked better than telling stories of our old home as it was when she was a child.

Almost every day that summer, about the time the sun was sinking behind the tiled roof of our neighbour's tall house and the cool shadows were creeping across our garden, we would gather in the big room opening on the porch. One at a time we came, each fresh from a hot. bath and clothed in the coolest of linen. Mother sat on her silk cushion, straight and dignified; but Sister, more informal, usually discarded a cushion, preferring, instead, the cool, clean mats. She was a beautiful woman. I can see her now, slipping quietly into her place, the suggestion of a wave in her shining widow-cut hair, and her sweet face seeming to be only waiting for an excuse to break into one of her gentle smiles. Between Sister and Mother were the children: Hanano's fingers, always busy, shaping bits of gay silk into a set of bean-bags or cutting out a paper doll for Chiyo, who, gazing with loving admiration at her sister, sat with her own dear, lazy little hands folded on her lap.

This was our hour to spend in talking of the small happenings of the day: school successes and trials, incidents connected with home affairs and stray items of neighbourhood gossip. But almost inevitably the conversation would eventually drift into a channel that called forth from someone the familiar, "Oh, isn't that interesting! Tell us about it!" or "Yes, I remember. Do tell that to the children."

One afternoon Mother mentioned that the priest had called that day to make arrangements for a certain temple service called "For the Nameless" that was held by our family every year.

"Why is it called 'For the Nameless'?" asked Hanano. "It has such a lonesome sound."

"It is a sad story," replied Mother. "A story that began almost three hundred years ago and has not yet ended."

"How could Kikuno's story have anything to do with the little room at the end of the hall?" I asked abruptly, my mind going back to the half-forgotten memory of a door that was never opened. "It didn't happen in that house."

"No; but the hall room was built right over the haunted spot," replied Sister. "Is it true, Honourable Mother, that after the mansion was burned someone planted chrysanthemum in the garden, and soft, mysterious lights were seen floating among the flowers?"

Hanano had dropped her sewing into her lap, and both children were gazing at Sister with eager, wide-open eyes.

"Your fate until dinner time is decided, Sister," I laughed. "The children scent a story. Now you can tell them why you wouldn't use the cushion decorated with chrysanthemums at the restaurant the other day."

"I must seem foolish-minded to you, Etsu-bo, with your progressive ideas," said Sister, with a half-ashamed smile, "but I have never outgrown the feeling that chrysanthemums are an omen of misfortune to our family."

"I know," I said, sympathetically. "I used to feel so, too. I didn't really get over it until I went to America. The name Mary is as common there as Kiku is here, but I had associated it only with sacredness and dignity; for it is the holiest name for a woman in the world. Some people even pray to it. And when, one time, just after I went to America, I heard a shopwoman call roughly, 'Mary, come here!' and out ran a ragged child with a dirty face, I was astounded. And a neighbour of ours had an ignorant servant girl by that name. It was a shock at first; but I finally learned that association is a narrow thing. When we apply it broadly the original feeling does not fit."

"People learn to forget when they travel," said Sister quietly; "but as far back as I can remember, no chrysanthemum flower was ever brought into our house, no chrysanthemum decoration was ever used on our screens, our dishes, our dresses, or our fans; and, with all the pretty flower names in our family, that of Kiku—chrysanthemum—has never been borne by an Inagaki. Even a servant with that name was never allowed to work for us unless she was willing to be called something else while she lived in our house."

"Why? Oh, do tell us about it!" pleaded both children.

So again I heard the story, familiar from childhood, but changing continually in its significance as I grew older, until it became fixed in my mind as the hero tale of a brave old samurai who represented the double virtue of a great and tender love combined with the hard, cold strength of loyalty to duty.

This ancestor of mine was lord of our family during the period when it was a government requirement that men of his class should have two handmaids. This was to guard against the possibility of there being no heir, that being an unspeakable calamity to people who believed that a childless family meant heavenly annihilation. Handmaids were always selected by the wife, from families of her own rank; and their position, although inferior in influence, was considered as honoured and lofty as that of the wife.

The second of my ancestor's handmaids was named Kikuno. Her lord was old enough to be her father, but it must be true that he loved her, for our family records show that he loaded her relatives with gifts and with honours. Of course, we Japanese never say anything not nice about our ancestors, and it may be that family traditions are not always reliable, but they all praise this man, and I like to believe them true.

Every house of noble class, in those days, was divided into the home department, ruled by the mistress, where there were only women attendants, and the lord's department, where every branch of work was done by men. For delicate and artistic duties, such as tea-serving and flower-arranging, graceful youths were chosen who dressed in gay garments with swinging sleeves like girls, and wore their hair in an artistic crown-queue with fluffy sides.

Among these attendants of my ancestor was a youth who was an especial favourite. He must have possessed both rank and culture, for he was the son of his lord's highest retainer. Although the departments of the lord and the mistress were entirely separate, there was daily passing back and forth on formal errands, and also many gatherings for duty or for entertainment, in which both men and women took part. On these occasions the gentle Kikuno and the handsome youth were frequently thrown together. She was only seventeen. Her lord was twice her age, and his thoughts were of war and its grim duties. The gentle, soft-voiced youth, whose talk was of poetry and flowers, won her heart; and it was the old story of Launcelot and Guinevere.

We have no reason to believe that any real wrong was in the heart of either; but a Japanese girl was taught from childhood to subdue self, and when she married—and to become a handmaid was one type of marriage—she was expected to live with no thought of self at all.

Rumours reached the ears of the master, but he waved them aside as absurd. One day, however, he walked into the great room adjoining the court and found the two talking in low voices, and—an unpardonable breach of etiquette—alone. This was, of course, a stain on the family name, which, according to the code of honour of that day, could be wiped out only with blood, or—a disgrace a thousand times worse than death—the exile of the culprits through the water gate, thus making them outcasts.

The old lord was merciful and allowed them honourable death by the sword. Both recognized the justice of their fate. Kikuno went away to prepare for death, and the young man, with slow and ceremonious dignity, removed this two swords and slipped his right arm from his outer dress, leaving only the white silk undergarment. Then he gave the sash a quick, loosening jerk, and with his short sword in his hand, quietly seated himself on the mat. I often pity the wronged lord as I think of him sitting there, erect and silent. I know his heart was full of grief as well as bitterness and indignation, but whatever the struggle within, he had to be true to the duty plainly marked out by the inexorable usage of the day.

Poor Kikuno went to her baby boy for a few last loving touches as he lay sleeping in his nurse's arms, but she said good-bye to no one else. She washed the rouge from her lips, loosened her hair, tied it with the paper death-bow, and put on her white death-robe. Then she went back to the room where her lover and her lord were silently waiting.

Without the slightest deviation, the unchanging ceremony of Japanese etiquette was carried out. She kneeled and bowed deeply, first to her wronged lord and then to the beautiful girl-dressed youth beside him. Seating herself with her face to the west, she took her long sash of soft crêpe and tightly bound her folded knees. For one moment she placed together her hands, clasping a crystal rosary; then slipping the rosary over one wrist, she lifted her dagger to press the point to her throat. Her lord was a stern and a just man, but he must have loved the woman very tenderly, for he did a wonderful thing. Leaning quickly forward, he took away her dagger and placed in her hand his own short sword. It was a Masamune, a precious family heirloom, and sacred because a gift to his grandfather from the great Ieyasu.

Well, they both died: the youth, bravely, like a samurai; but poor Kikuno threw out one hand as she fell, which struck the plaster wall and left a lasting stain.

The man's body was sent to his family with the polite message that his death had taken place suddenly. Everyone understood, and, like the youth himself, recognized the justice of his fate. He was buried at midnight, and ever afterward both the temple and his family gave him only silent death anniversaries. But the woman was buried with great honour—suitable to the mother of the young lord—and a large sum was given to charity in her name. Then the lord forbade any of his descendants ever to cultivate the chrysanthemum flower or to allow the name, Kiku, in the household. The baby, whose frail mother had robbed him of his birthright, was sent away—for no stain must descend to the next generation—and a later-born little one carried on the family name.

The blood-stained room was closed, and until the burning of the mansion about two hundred years later was never opened. When my father rebuilt his ruined home many of the relatives urged him to leave an open space above the site of that room, but he refused, saying that the kindly spirit of living friends had taught him to believe in the kindly spirit of the dead. My father was a very progressive man for that day.

But the servants never forgot. They said the new room had on its plaster wall the same faint, dark stain of a wide-open hand that was on the wall of the old; and so many ghostly stories were told, that finally, for purely practical reasons, my mother was obliged to close this room also.

The little son of Kikuno became a priest who, in later life, built a small temple on Cedar Mountain. It was so placed that its shadow falls over a lonely nameless grave guarded by a statue of the goddess of Mercy.

But the memory of love and pity cannot die. For almost three hundred years my stern old ancestor has lain among his people in his extravagant bed of vermilion and charcoal; and for almost three hundred years the descendants of the name whose honour he upheld have, in respect for his unexpressed heart wish, held each year a sacred service in memory of "The Nameless."

CHAPTER-29

A Lady of Old Japan

ONE afternoon Sister and I were sewing in my room when Hanano came in. It was warm weather and the paper doors had been lifted off so that the entire fronts of the rooms facing the garden were open. We could look across and see Mother sitting beside the dining-room fire-box, holding her long, slender pipe in her hand and gazing out into the garden as if her thoughts were far away.

"Mother is happy in this home," said Sister. "Her face has the calm, peaceful look of the August Buddha."

"I wonder," said Hanano thoughtfully, "if Honourable Grandmother was ever really, strongly, *terribly* excited in all her life."

Sister looked at Hanano with a strange smile.

"I never saw her *seem* excited," she said slowly. "It was a terrible time when we left the old home, but Mother was calm and steady. She commanded like a general on the battlefield."

"Oh, tell me!" cried Hanano, sitting up very straight. "Tell me all about it."

Perhaps it would be well, Sister," I said. "Hanano is old enough to know. Tell her all of Mother's life that you can remember."

So she told how Mother, when only thirteen years of age, was lifted into her wedding palanquin and, accompanied by a long procession of attendants, headed by spearmen and followed by her father's guards, journeyed to her new home. Father was First Counsellor of the daimiate, and his bride came to a mansion so spacious that in all the years she lived in it there were rooms in which she never set her foot. She saw little of her husband, for his duties as ruler obliged him to make frequent journeys to the capital, and the young wife filled her time in writing poems on slender cards of gold and silver, or playing dolls with her attendants; for, after all, she was only a child.

In time, a son and two daughters were born; but the little girls, with nurses to take every care from their mother, were a good deal like beautiful playthings to her; and her son, the heir who was to carry on the family name, had so many attendants with various duties that she saw him only at stated intervals. He was like a precious jewel for which she had strong affection, but still stronger was the feeling of pride. So in the big, peaceful mansion the girl-wife passed the pleasant, uneventful years.

Then changes came, for clouds of war were gathering slowly over the land. Her husband gradually told her of many important things, and one day he left home on a mission that filled her heart with dread. She was not far out of her teens, but she knew the duties of a samurai's wife, and with suddenly awakened womanhood she called her son's tutor and they disguised in shabby clothing her small son, whose life as heir would be forfeit if his father came to harm, and sent him, in the care of faithful Minoto, to the protection of our ancestral temple on the mountain. Then she waited, while every day the clouds grew more threatening. One dark, rainy night there came a warrior to her home bearing the tidings that Father was a prisoner and on his way to the capital. Near the midnight toll of the temple bell he would pass the road at the foot of the mountain, and she would be permitted an interview.

She looked at the messenger steadily. If there should be treachery what would become of her son?

"Are you a samurai?" she asked.

Solemnly the man put his hand to the hilt of his sword.

"I am a samurai," he answered.

"Whether friend or enemy," she said, "if you are a samurai, I will trust you."

Though she believed him, those were dangerous days, and so she washed her hair and put on her death-robe, covering it with an ordinary dress. Then, slipping her dagger into her sash and bidding her faithful servant Yoshita to be loyal to his young master, whatever happened, she told the messenger she was ready.

Through the rain and darkness they went—the warrior, his wet armour shining in the lantern-light, followed by Mother in her hidden death-robe. They passed through empty streets and along narrow paths of lonely ricefields until finally they came to the road which curved around the foot of the mountain. There they waited.

Presently lights came swaying through the darkness and they could hear the dull, soft thuds of trotting carriers, coming nearer and nearer, then to a stop. A palanquin covered with a rope net was rested on the ground, a warrior on each side. The carriers stood back. Mother looked up and saw Father's pale face gazing at her through the small square window. The crossed spears of the warriors were between them. There was a moment's silence, then Father spoke.

"My wife, I trust you with my sword."

That was all. Both knew that listening ears were eager for word of the son. Mother only bowed, but Father knew that she understood.

The reed screen was dropped before the face of the prisoner, the warriors shouldered their spears, the carriers lifted the poles of the palanquin to their shoulders, and the little procession passed on into the darkness. The guide she had trusted raised his bowed head and turned toward the ricefields, and poor Mother followed, carrying with her the knowledge of a sacred trust; for those few words from Father's lips meant: "Death is before me. I trust to you the son who will continue the name of Inagaki and thus insure the heavenly salvation of hundreds of ancestors."

Again poor Mother bore the heavy burden of anxious uncertainty, until one autumn night when a messenger brought word that the plain was full of soldiers marching toward Nagaoka. For that she had been waiting; so, calm and fearless, she commanded that the entire house be arranged as for honoured guests. The most treasured roll pictures were hung, the rarest ornaments placed on *tokonomas*, then the retainers and servants were ordered to leave by a rear gateway and to scatter in various directions.

Sister was only a child of seven, but she remembered every detail of that awful night. She and little Sister were awakened by frightened nurses and hurried into dress and sash—for even in their haste and horror the sash, emblem of virtue to every Japanese girl, could not be forgotten by the trusted servant of a samurai family—and taken part way up the mountain to wait in the darkness for Mother, coming more slowly with Honourable Grand-Mother and two menservants.

Sister smiled faintly as she told how Honourable Grandmother and Mother looked as they came up the narrow path, disguised as farmers. Honourable Grandmother's straw coat kept pulling apart and showing her purple dress, which was of a kind worn only by a retired mistress of her rank, and which she had stubbornly refused to have removed. And she would *not* walk with her toes turned out as peasants do.

Leaving Honourable Grandmother with them on the mountain-side, Mother went back to the mansion with Yoshita. They could see the two, carrying torches of twisted paper, as they passed from point to point, Yoshita piling straw and Mother lighting with her own hands the fires to destroy her home. Honourable Grandmother sat perfectly quiet, gazing straight before her, but the servants knelt on the ground swaying back and forth, sobbing and wailing, as servants will. Then Mother, with dishevelled hair and smoke-stained face, came toiling up the path, and by the pale light of early dawn the two little girls were dressed in servants' clothes from the bundle on Yoshita's back, and the nurses were told to take them in different directions to places of safety. Servants were trustworthy in those days. To each was given a dagger with orders to use it in case capture was inevitable. Those crested daggers are still held as treasures in the families of the faithful nurses.

Sister said it was a long time before she saw Mother again. Her nurse took her to a farmer's family where she dressed and lived as they did, and her nurse worked in the ricefield with the farmer's wife. Every night, after her bath, she was rubbed with a brown juice squeezed from wild persimmons—for castle people are lighter than peasants—and was told to talk like the children she played with. She was treated like the others in every way except that always she was served first. "I know now," explained Sister, "that the farmer suspected who I was, but we were in one of the districts where Father had bestowed upon the headman the privilege of owning two swords, and so we were not betrayed. Little Sister was in a similar place of safety."

In the meantime, Honourable Grandmother and Mother, in the care of Yoshita, all wearing the dress and wide, drooping hats of peasants, had been wandering from place to place, sometimes living in the mountains, sometimes in a farmer's family, and sometimes for a few weeks finding refuge in a temple. More than two years this dreadful time lasted; always hiding, always hunted; for though Father was a prisoner and his cause lost, conquest was not complete until the enemy had extinguished for ever the family and name.

"At last," Sister went on, "Mother came to the farmhouse where I was. She looked so thin, so brown, and so wild that I didn't know her, and cried out. That night Minoto brought Brother. He told us that the priest, in order to save the child's life, had given him up, and for several months he had been a prisoner with Father. Both had been very near the honourable death, but a message that the war was ended and all political prisoners were pardoned had saved them. Brother seemed to have almost forgotten me and would not talk much, but I heard him tell Mother that, one day, when soldiers were seen coming up the mountain, the priest had put him in a book chest and, covering him with rolls of sacred writings, had left the cover off and seated himself beside it as if arranging papers. Brother said that he heard rough footsteps and falling furniture, and when all was quiet and he was lifted out, he saw that spears had been thrust through the closed chests standing in the row with the one where he was hidden.

The next day Mother had gathered her family together and Yoshita found a place where they could live. Then Father came, and in a modest way life began all over again.

"So you see, Hanano," said Sister, "your grandmother's life has not always been full of peace."

"It was a wonderful life," said Hanano in a tone of awe, "wonderful—and terrible. But Honourable Grandmother *did* things! Oh, she *did* things!"

I looked at the lithe young body, held so straight, at the uplifted head and the tightly clasped hands. She was very like Mother. One generation removed from the ancient pride and rigid training; one generation ahead of the coming freedom; living, alas! in the sad present—puzzled, misunderstood, and alone!

Sister remained with us throughout the autumn and into the winter. I shall always be doubly thankful for her visit, for those weeks were Mother's last with us, and they were happy ones. The long talks when she and Sister lived over the old days were like those of friends rather than mother and daughter; for there was only fourteen years between them and Sister was as old-fashioned in many ways as Mother. And when the sorrowful time came, Sister's presence was an especial comfort to me, for she was familiar with all the old customs and could direct with a tenderness that no other could have shown.

On our sad journey to the temple, as we followed the death *kago* swaying on the shoulders of the white-robed coolies, my thoughts went back to another day long before, when I, a child of eleven, walked in a procession of mourning friends, my little hands clasped tight about the tablet bearing my father's name. Over the narrow paths of the ricefields we wound after the chanting priests, while from the high, tossing baskets carried on long poles by their attendants showered hundreds of tiny pieces of the five-coloured sacred paper. They filled the air with clouds of soft colours, floating and mingling as they drifted downward to settle gently on the straw hats and white robes of the mourners.

Now, everything was different. Even the honours we show our dead must bow to the world's changes, and the services for Mother were the simplest possible to be in accord with her former rank. But she had requested that, in addition to the rites for herself, there should be held the ceremony for "The Nameless."

My noble, loyal mother! True to her wifehood and to her husband's family, even as she was entering the door of death she had remembered poor Kikuno, for whom no prayer was ever offered except in this lonely service. And since Brother, the head of the family, was a Christian, she knew it would never again be observed.

All through the calm and peaceful intoning, beneath which sounded the rhythmic throb of the wooden drum, my mind was on my gentle mother's life of unswerving duty to her highest belief, and I wondered what power had kept her so strong and true. Then, dully, I became aware that the soft music was melting into a weird and mournful chanting that carried my thought to the hopeless soul who had lost the way to Heaven because of her great sin. And so, once more, the descendants of the name she had dishonoured, sat, lowly bowed, while the priests chanted the prayer that help be given to guide the wanderer on her lonely path.

When we came to the pause in the music where the high priest chants the arrival of the dead at the gates of Heaven to present the plea for mercy, the priests raised their cymbals above their heads, and, bringing them slowly together, clashed a long, quivering accompaniment to the soft, muffled beat of the wooden drum. Before my misty eyes the swinging sleeves made a blur of purple, scarlet, and gold, and, listening to the wailing and pleading prayer that had for almost three hundred years winged its way through the curling incense, I wondered if the long-remembering God of Vengeance would not, if only in pity for Mother's unselfish faithfulness, grant this last plea for the erring one of long ago.

At the temple door I made my last bow to my mother's dear body, and, with a heavy ache in my heart, stood watching the swaying *kago* with its curving roof and gilded lotus blossoms as it disappeared at a turn in the road leading to the cremation grounds. Then we returned to the lonely home, and for forty-nine days the candles burned and the incense curled its fragrant way through the carvings of the little whitewood shrine. On the last night I knelt in my mother's old place and breathed a Christian prayer to the God who understands. Then I slowly closed the gilded doors upon my prayer, believing sincerely that my mother's journey had ended in peace; and that, wherever she was or whatever she might be doing, she was faithfully taking her part in God's great plan.

My minister was sorely troubled that I should have observed these last Buddhist rites—unnecessary after my mother had passed beyond the knowledge or the hurt of their neglect. I told him that, had I died even one day after I became a Christian, my mother would have been faithful, to the minutest detail, in giving me the Christian burial that she believed would satisfy my heart; and that I was my mother's daughter. Influence? Yes. The influence of loyalty, sympathy, understanding; all of which are characteristics of Our Father—hers and mine.

CHAPTER-30

The White Cow

WHEN Hanano was fifteen, the family council brought up the subject I had been most dreading. According to Japanese custom, when there are only daughters in a family, a son is adopted, who takes the family name and marries the eldest daughter. Thus the name is perpetuated. The question of the selection of a son for me, I had dealt with in as tactful a manner as possible, but after having refused two or three offers, I saw that I was expected to give a positive decision soon.

It is never wise for a Japanese woman, if she wishes to retain a position of influence and dignity, to say much on any subject. Actions, not words, are her most successful means of expression; but the time came when I saw that I must speak. With a letter of wise suggestions from my ever-faithful American mother in my hand, I went before the council and asked to be allowed to take the children back to my former home for a few years more of study. This request caused excited discussions; but I now had friends in the council, both of Matsuo's family and of my own, and my past faithful adherence to their wishes brought a glorious reward. Again my petition was granted, and, with my heart weighted with gratitude and my soul singing with joy, I began my preparations to return to America.

With Chiyo, our going was a question of whether to be glad or sad. Leaving her little friends and her loved school, to go back to a vagueness in which only "Grandma" stood out vividly was a serious thing. But Hanano's joy was profound. She was quiet, but busy every moment, going about with light, quick steps and singing softly all the while; and I never glanced at her that I did not meet a bright smile. Many times during the weeks of preparation, as I watched her happy face, the thought came to me that if—if—such a cruel thing could happen as that she would never reach the land of her heart's love, I should always be grateful, anyway, for the quiet, overflowing joy of this season of hope. Nothing could ever take away that happy memory.

The busy weeks flew by, and at last there came a morning when the children, who had been turning down their fingers to count the days, gleefully announced that only two wide-spread hands were left. Ten days! We were almost ready, but however well one may plan, there always seem to be some unfinished things that are pushed away until the last crowded days.

The children had never been to Nagaoka. Many times I had planned to go, but life was full for us and something had always interfered. But I could not allow them to leave Japan without a visit to the place where their grandmother lay beside her husband among the graves of our ancestors; so early one spring morning we started.

How different was this trip from the one of years before which I took with my brother when on my way to school in Tokyo! Instead of a journey of several days, spent, sometimes perched upon a high wooden saddle, sometimes tucked snugly into a swinging *kago* and sometimes rolled and jolted along the rough path in a jinrikisha, this was only fourteen hours of comfortable riding on a brisk little narrow-gauge train, that wound its puffing way up the mountains, through twenty-six tunnels that represented some of the world's finest engineering. Between these dashes of darkness were welcome glimpses of sunny hillsides terraced with ricefields, and a narrow, winding road that I remembered well. Just at twilight we found ourselves on the station platform of a busy town having a background of hills bristling with the skeleton towers of multitudinous oil wells. I had been told of these changes, but my slow mind had failed to realize how entirely *my* Nagaoka was a dream of the past.

I was glad that the children's first sight of the town was in cherry-blossom time; for, even to me, the buildings looked smaller and the streets narrower than I had pictured them in my stories. Everything might have proved a disappointment to them had it not been for the glow and freshness that peeped over the plaster walls, glorified the temple yard, and showed from the tinted branches of the trees lining every street. There was a faint breeze on our first morning, and as our slow jinrikishas jogged along the strangely unfamiliar road to Chokoji the air was filled with fragrance from the pink, shell-like petals that were continually dropping, or lying in drifts on the sloping roofs of the snow-sheds which hung over the sidewalks.

"How we love these fruitless, beautiful trees—emblem of our dying knighthood!" I thought with a sigh; and then I looked toward the hill where the castle used to stand, and an amused gleam of satisfaction came to me. The old spirit of protection still dwelt amidst the ruins, for on the foundation rocks rose a huge fire-tower with its high platform and warning gong.

The old house was no more. I had hoped that Brother would decide to return, in time, and spend his old age in the home of his youth; for the gentle little wife that he had taken in late middle life had lived only long enough to bring an heir to the Inagaki family and then had drifted out of life as gently as she had lived in it during her scant score of quiet years. But all Brother's interests were in a distant city amidst the progressive whir of factories and modern life, and he would listen to no plans beyond the education of his son.

So the gods of Utility and Commerce had taken charge, and all that were left of our worthless treasures were removed to Sister's godown. Then Jiya and Ishi had gone to distant homes; and now, in place of the great rambling house with its sagging thatch and tender memories, stood the ugly foreign buildings of "The Normal School for Girls." The old chestnut tree beneath which was Shiro's grave, and the archery field, where so often I had seen Father and Mr. Toda, each with his right sleeve slipped from a bare shoulder, in a strenuous, but laughing, game of competition, was lost in a wide gravelled campus, where modern schoolgirls marched and drilled in pleated skirts and foreign shoes. Strange indeed it seemed—and full of heart-ache for me! I realized that these changes pointed toward a future of usefulness and hope, and I would not have retarded them for the world; but all the quiet pleasures and picturesque life of the past had been merged into a present that looked cheap and sordid. It was hard for me, during my few days in the old town, to keep my memories of beautiful old customs and ideals from completely overshadowing the new, progressive path that I was striving to follow.

When our duty of love and honour to the dear ones was over, we went with Sister, who had come to Nagaoka to meet us, to her home on a mountain a few hours' jinrikisha ride distant. It was an odd little village where she lived. So narrow was the ledge upon which it stretched its one-street length that, from the valley below, it looked as if a toy town of plaster walls and thatched roofs had been pinned up against the green side of the mountain.

We left the valley, each with tandem pullers and a pusher behind. It was a steep climb up a winding path from which reached out, on either side, long, even lines of scrubby trees. Occasionally the men would stop and, bracing themselves, would rest the shafts against their hips and wipe their hot faces.

"It's a breathless climb," said one, as he smiled and pointed down into the valley, "but it's worth the labour just to see yon terraces of green against the great brown rocks, and the sunny blue of the sky reflected brokenly in the rippling stream below."

"*Hai*," said another, "so it is. The city fellows see naught but level streets and dusty roofs peeping above walls or fences of wood. I pity them."

Then on they went—panting but content.

"What are all these low, twisted bushes with the gray trunks and so many little fresh buds?"' asked Hanano, in one of these pauses.

"Mulberry trees," replied Sister. "This 1s a silk-culture district, and the mountain is covered with cocoon villages. Almost every house here has wooden frames filled with trays of silkworms, and on a quiet day you can hear the rustle of their feeding as you walk along the street."

That sounded interesting indeed to the children and as we went on, they shouted questions and exclamations to each other about silkworms and their mulberry-leaf diet, until the long climb ended in a short, steep pull and an abrupt turn into a broad street of low, wide-eaved houses. At the farther end stood the large house of the village—Sister's home. Its brownish-yellow thatch rose above a wall of rounded stones topped with a wooden fence, so like the one surrounding my old home in Nagaoka that the sight brought a shadow-ache of homesickness to my heart.

With cordial country manners, the servants had come out to the big wooden gateway, and as our jinrikishas rolled between the two lines of bowing figures, I caught murmurs of the familiar, old-fashioned greeting, "*O kaeri asobase!*"—"Your return is welcome!"

The quiet house seemed very restful after our long, jolting ride, and the hot bath which is always ready in old-fashioned Japan for the expected visitor refreshed us wonderfully. The children and I had just returned to the living room, where, settling ourselves comfortably on soft cushions, we were gazing across the porch straight out into the blue sky, for the valley and the world were far below us, when two maids appeared bringing in the dainty little tables for luncheon.

"You'll have to do without meat up here," said Sister apologetically, as she came hurrying in. "We have only chickens and vegetables from my farm, and fish from the mountain streams. We cannot get meat or bread."

"That matters nothing," I replied. "The children are fond of fish and rice; and you know that I always liked everything green that grows. Don't you remember the 'white cow'?"

Sister laughed; and Hanano, always on the alert for a story, asked, "What is it about a white cow?"

So, as we ate, Sister told a story of my childhood which dated back so far that my knowledge of it was only what others told me.

"Your mother was not a very strong child," she began, "yet she was never really sick, either. At that time many of the Nagaoka people, when they were puzzled and helpless about a really serious matter, used to consult the priestess of a small Shinto shrine just outside the town; and Honourable Grandmother asked Father to send for the holy woman. For two days before she came, Etsu-bo was not allowed to eat whale-meat soup, or onion, or any food with an odour; and she was carefully instructed to be extremely good, both in behaviour and in thought.

"Early on the important morning Ishi sprinkled her with cold water. Then she dressed her in her crest dress and took her to Honourable Grandmother's room. All the family were there, and several women relatives. I remember how Etsu-bo looked as she toddled in, holding on to Mother's hand. She bowed to everyone, and Mother seated her on the mat beside Honourable Grandmother, just a little in front of the rest of us. The *tokonoma* was covered with straw matting and decorated with all the sacred Shinto emblems. Of course the priestess was in the most honoured seat of all. She was dressed in pure white, and her black hair was hanging down her back, tied behind the shoulders with a band of rice-straw, from which dangled strips of white, zigzag-cut Shinto paper. When Mother and Etsu-bo were seated, the holy priestess prostrated herself two or three times; then she lifted from the *tokonoma* a whitewood rod that had on the end a bunch of long streamers of holy paper. She waved it above Etsu-bo's head, murmuring some religious ritual. We all sat very quiet with bowed heads. After a moment of silence the priestess announced that she had just learned from the gods that Etsu-bo, in a previous existence, had been a small white cow used in drawing lumber for the building of a Shinto shrine on the top of a mountain. The message said that the little creature had toiled up the rocky path so patiently and faithfully day after day, and had lent its strength so willingly for the holy duty, that the gods had hastened the slow steps of transmigration and allowed the soul of the white cow to enter at once into the present life as a human being.

"Do you mean that my mamma was that white cow?" asked Hanano, with wide-open, astonished eyes; while Chiyo stopped eating and looked at me with alarm.

"Father didn't believe the priestess," added Sister, smiling; "nevertheless, to please Honourable Grandmother, he made a generous gift to the shrine. But he always said it was not so much a gift of gratitude to the gods as it was a token of satisfaction that he could now account for Etsu-bo's exceeding fondness for all green vegetables and her little liking for fish. Now, whether it was really true or not, doesn't matter any more than any other fairy story; but it's lucky for you children that your honourable mother is a faithful and a patient puller, for she has climbed over a rocky path of obstacles and at last is ready to pull you all the way over to America."

And she nodded merrily at the children as she served me another generous helping of bamboo shoots and greens.

A few days later one of Sister's neighbours, whose son was a successful oil merchant in Tokyo, came to see us. Meeting her recalled to both Hanano and me a very amusing incident connected with a call from the son's wife soon after we had gone to Tokyo to live. She was a lady of the new-rich aristocracy—progressive, wealthy, and altogether "*highkara*"—a recently coined word which implied the very essence of what was stylish and up-to-date. She was beautifully attired, in Japanese dress of course, for even the most progressive women had not reached the stage where European dress was worn on elegant occasions.

After a long, ceremonious bow and the usual complimentary inquiries regarding the health of family and relatives, and also a few tactful remarks in praise of the flowers arranged on the *tokonoma*, she leaned forward and unwrapped a square of beautiful crêpe exquisitely dyed and embroidered. It is an age-old Japanese custom, when calling upon a friend, to take a gift, and my guest lifted out and presented, modestly but with evident pride, a large imported paper box on which was printed in fancy English letters:

IMPORTED DAINTIES

A Foreign Delicacy Possessing the Fragrance of Flowers!
Used by Ladies and Gentlemen
in the
Cultured Society of Europe and America

It was a large, wholesale package of ordinary chewing gum. The elaborate, ceremonious manner of my guest, every movement being in accordance with the strictest etiquette, made the unexpected appearance of that plebeian package a most incongruous and amusing thing. Yet this was a perfectly natural gift for her to make. It was not easy to choose a suitable present for a person who had lived for several years in America, and who was believed to be foreign in her tastes; so my guest had gone to a store where foreign things were sold and, with considerable care, had selected this as being an especially appropriate gift for me.

Hanano and Chiyo had been in the room when the box was presented. Chiyo looked with grave interest upon the foreign lettering. Of course she could not read it, but Hanano's first careless glance, as we all bowed slightly in acknowledgment of the kindness, was followed instantly by another quick look; then, with a strange contortion of countenance, she bowed a deep "Excuse me" and slipped quickly from the room.

As soon as the caller had gone she hurried in to me.

"Oh, Mamma," she cried, gleefully, "just to think that Nakayama Sama should select that gift for *you!* What would she think if she could only know how you scolded me that time in America when I came home from school chewing a piece of gum? And how you made me wash my mouth and told me that if I were in Japan Ishi would say that I looked like the Buddhist pictures of a starving soul in the Hell of Hunger!"

Sister was very much interested in this story.

"It seems a peculiar custom," she said, "but it is not so harmful as the one from which originated our blackening the teeth."

"What did start that, Sister?" I asked. "Several people in America asked me, and I could only tell them that ridiculous old story of the homely wife who stained her teeth by mistake, and it made her so beautiful that she won devotion from her husband and envy from all other wives."

"There are many stories as absurd as that, about all our old customs," said Sister. 'When I made my first visit home with black teeth, I heard Father and Mr. Toda talking about our ancestors once having had a fashion of chewing something. But the story that Honourable Grandmother told me was this:

"Long ago, when everybody had white teeth, there lived a young wife whose jealous husband accused her of smiling to show her beautiful teeth. That day when cutting eggplant for dinner she took some thin peelings and put them over her teeth. The husband returned and, seeing how beautifully the purple colour contrasted with his wife's olive skin and scarlet lips, angrily asked why she had decorated herself. She told him she had tried to cover her teeth so that they would not show. Recognizing her modest worth, the husband was jealous no longer. Thus, more attractive than ever, she became a model to imitate, and in time, the added beauty of blackened teeth came to be the emblem of a trusted and dutiful wife. That is the story that Honourable Grandmother was told when she married."

What Sister had heard Father and Mr. Toda talking about was probably the theory which is considered the most reasonable explanation of our custom of blackening the teeth. It is an historical fact that the first conquerors of Japan, who no doubt came originally from the hot shores of Central Asia, planted betel orchards in the warm islands of South Japan where they first landed; but on account of difference in soil and climate it was almost impossible to make the trees grow. So, in a few years the habit of betel chewing became necessarily confined to those who represented wealth and rank. An ancient Imperial coach used by an Emperor who reigned more than a thousand years ago, and which is now in the Art Museum of Tokyo, was roofed with a thatch made of the husks of betel nuts. This speaks of the rarity of the betel trees at that time, for of course the Imperial cart was the most costly vehicle in the land.

When the time came that only people of the highest class had betel-stained teeth, imitations became the fashion and substitutes were found. During the Middle Ages, long after the nuts were extinct in Japan, both men and women of high rank blackened their teeth with a powder made from a wild nut from the mountains. The Imperial courtiers kept up this custom to 1868. At that time even Meiji Tenno, the Emperor of the Restoration, had blackened teeth. The samurai never stained their teeth. They took pride in scorning any fashion that spoke more of luxury and ease than of strength and power of arms. After the Restoration this emblem of vanity faded before the advancing light of Western life; but, suggestive as it was of artistic beauty and high-class leisure, it remained with the women, and all classes adopted it as the marriage emblem. From then on, they blackened their teeth on their wedding day and kept them black ever after.

The fashion is not an ugly one. When blackened every morning, the teeth look like polished ebony, and the gleam of shining black behind coral lips brings out the clear olive of the skin and looks as beautiful to Japanese eyes as did, to the eyes of a European, the dot of black courtplaster on the ivory skin of a maiden in the days of colonial America. The custom is now dying out, but it is still seen everywhere in rural districts. Even in large cities, almost all old ladies of very high rank and of very humble station still cling to the custom. The middle class of Japan always leads the way in progress.

CHAPTER-31

Worthless Treasures

WE SPENT a happy week with Sister in the little silkworm village, and our visit was almost ended when one day she took us into her big godown, where the things brought from Nagaoka had been stored. The greater part of our ancient treasures were now only worthless burdens, but there were some things that I wanted the children to see; for, in the old days, they had been both useful and beautiful, and, to me, were still full of precious memories.

We passed through the heavy door, a foot thick of fireproof plaster, and entered a large room all four sides filled with shelves, most of them crowded full to the edge. There were rows and rows of high narrow boxes containing a whole library of soft-backed books. There were rows of still larger boxes holding small eating tables, and still others filled with dishes, trays, and all the reserve belongings of a prosperous household. There were long, slender boxes of roll pictures and many ornaments—bronze vases, incense burners, and carvings of wood and ivory—all neatly tied up in squares of cotton or silk, and placed within convenient reach, ready for the frequent changes necessary in a Japanese house.

Part of the floor was taken up with chests of drawers arranged in rows, back to back; and in corners stood tall candlesticks, screens, and various large articles of household use.

"Just look!" cried Hanano, gazing about her in ashtonishment. "I never saw so many things, at once, in all my life!"

"It's like a store," said Chiyo, "only everything is put away so nicely, and yet it's all mixed up, too!"

"Don't be critical of my housekeeping," laughed Sister. "A well-filled godown is said to be the best museum of household belongings that is to be found in all Japan; and it ought to be, for it is the place where we keep everything that is not in immediate use. Things are put in and pulled out every day. I never knew of a godown that *looked* in order."

But Sister's godown really was in disorder, for in some half-filled shelves and in a wide space beyond the wooden steps leading to the floor above were gathered a lot of objects from our Nagaoka godowns, for which suitable places had not yet been found. Among some high lantern stands wrapped in oil-paper, and a pile of boxes containing war banners, I saw the big, cumbersome palanquin that Father had used on his official trips to the capital in the years before the name was changed from Yedo to Tokyo. The lacquer was dulled, the metal ornaments tarnished, and the brocade cushions faded; but Hanano thought it wondrously elegant. She crept inside, settled herself comfortably on the thick cushion, rested her elbow on the lacquer arm rest, and peeped into the toilet box in the silk pocket in front. Then she glanced at the misty reflection of her face in the metal hanging mirror and declared that Honourable Grandfather's travelling coach was convenient and comfortable enough for a trip all the way to America.

As she climbed out I pushed at the padded top, but the hinges were rusted. It used to lift and swing back. Many a time, when on a hurried trip, Father had dressed while his carriers were trotting fast and Jiya running by his side to help him now and then.

"Here's another palanquin—prettier than yours, Hanano," chirped Chiyo, from behind the stairs; "only this one hasn't any doors."

"*Maa! Maa!*" laughed Sister, going over to her. "This is not to ride in, little Chiyo. It's for a swim!" and she lifted her into an enormous bathtub of red lacquer which from my earliest recollection had stood in a corner of our godown. We used it for holding the cocoons, until the maids were ready to put them on the spindle to twist the silk threads off the poor, little, cooked inhabitants. The tub was marred on the edge, but not chipped anywhere, for the lacquer was of olden time. It still held the deep softness of velvet, and the band of braided bamboo showed beneath the polished surface like water weeds in a clear stream. It must have been very old, for it had been brought into our family as a part of the wedding dowry of my three-times-great-grandmother, the daughter of Yodo daimio, Inaba-no-kami.

"Climb out, Chiyo! Climb out and come here!" called Hanano. "I've found a wooden stove-pipe hat—only," she added, peering into it, "it has a funny inside."

She was standing in a shadowy corner where a number of miscellaneous articles were gathered on a crowded shelf, and had just lifted the tall cover from a shallow bucket of whitewood, the bottom having in its centre, rising sharp and strong, a short hardwood spike. It was Father's head-bucket that always had been kept in the closed shelf-closet above our parlour *tokonoma*.

"Let us go upstairs now," I said quickly. "Sister, won't you show the children your wedding cap of silk floss? They have never seen an old-fashioned wedding, where the bride's cap comes down to the chin."

I hurried them up the narrow stairs to the room above. I did not want to explain to the children the use of the head-bucket. Their modern, practical education held nothing that would enable them to understand the deep sentiment of honour which has inspired many an ancient samurai, who, when guilty of some unlawful act, has chosen to die an honourable death by his own hand, rather than bring upon his family the disgrace of a public execution. In such a case the head-bucket, one of which every samurai house possessed, was used to carry to court the proof that the law had been obeyed. After being identified by the authorities, the head was returned, with respectful ceremonies, to the family; and the dead samurai, his crime now fully expiated, was buried with honour.

Of course, the gruesome mission of our head-bucket had never been fulfilled. Its only duty had been the occasional holding of a coil of hemp when Honourable Grandmother or Ishi was twisting it ready to spin. It was as convenient for that purpose as a flax-box. Indeed, the two looked so much alike that no bride was ever allowed to have a flax-box, although in those days all other spinning implements were considered essential to every wedding dowry.

The upstairs room of Sister's godown was lighted by narrow, iron-barred windows set deep in the thick plaster wall. The shutters, which were really heavy plaster doors, were open, and a pleasant breeze was blowing through the room, making it cool and airy. Against the walls were chests of drawers and great wooden boxes having metal bands, on some of which I saw the Inagaki crest. I could readily guess what Sister's chests contained, for her large house was well stocked with all the requirements of a country home. There were padded-silk comforts, round pillows for men and little lacquer box-pillows for women, large mosquito nets made to swing by short cords from the corners of the ceiling, thus enclosing the entire room, and cushions of every kind—soft, thick ones of heavy silk for winter; thin ones of woven grass for summer, braided bamboo for the porch, woven rope for the kitchen, some round, some square. some plain, and some elaborately dyed in patterns—for cushions were our chairs, and every house had to have a supply always on hand.

"This holds my 'treasure dresses,'" said Sister, waving her hand toward a low chest of drawers. "The clothes that I wear I keep downstairs within easy reach; but some of these have been in the family for more than two hundred years."

She took out an elaborately embroidered trained garment with a scarlet lining and heavily padded hem—a dress of ceremony, worn, even in ancient times, only on state occasions. It looked fresh and almost new, for Japanese women are careful housekeepers, and probably this gown had been shaken out and examined on every airing-day since it was first used by the ancestor of long ago.

"It looks just like the splendid dresses we saw in that play at the Tokyo theatre, doesn't it?" said Hanano.

And indeed it did. For only on the stage were these gorgeous costumes to be seen in modern life.

The next drawer held Sister's wedding dresses—seven of them. There was the soft, white linen, emblem of death to her own home, the scarlet silk, emblem of birth into her husband's family, and the five other elaborately embroidered gowns bearing her husband's crest and the marriage emblems of pine, bamboo, and plum.

"Here is the wedding cap you asked to see," said Sister, presently, unfolding something that looked like a great satiny mushroom. It was of exquisite pressed silk floss and made to fit rather close over the head and shoulders. It looked like a thick, shining veil.

"Oh, isn't it pretty?" cried Chiyo, delighted. "Put it on, Hanano, and let's see how you look!"

I gave a half-frightened gasp, and was glad when Hanano, with a slow smile, shook her head. I don't know why the child refused. Perhaps the soft whiteness of the snowy floss suggested in some vague way the white mourning clothes we had worn at Mother's funeral. While there was no definite superstition regarding the wearing of wedding garments after the ceremony, still, it was never done. They were laid away—to wait. Both Honourable Grandmother and my mother wore the wedding dress beneath the death-robe when they were ready for the last journey.

The very next chest—just as marriage and death go hand in hand as the two most important ceremonies in Japanese life—held articles for the funeral. This chest was one of those from my home and was about half filled with a disordered array of ceremonious uniforms for the men who carried the tall lanterns, the bamboo dove cage, and the heavy death *kago*. These were all made of linen, since no silk was ever used at a funeral. There were also pleated skirts and stiff shoulder garments for retainers with no family crest, white-banded servant kimonos, boxes of knee bands, pilgrim sandals, and countless small articles essential for the various attendants in the elaborate procession. I could remember when that chest contained everything requisite for a samurai funeral except the wide straw hats that shade the sorrowing faces from the Sun goddess. Those had to be fresh and new for each occasion. The house of every high official always had these things in readiness, for death often comes without warning, and Japanese rules for ceremonious occasions were strict and unvarying.

"There!" said Sister, as she closed the lid of the chest and pushed the metal bar through the triple clasp, "the usefulness of these things belongs with their glory—to the past. Sometimes I cut up a garment to get linen binding for a worn-out mat, and occasionally, when a workman breaks his sandal cord, I present him with a pair of sandals from this chest; but the things go slowly—slowly."

"But *this*," she added, gently tapping a drawer in a fresh whitewood chest, "belongs to the future. It will be used some day."

"What is it?" I asked.

"My death-robe."

"Oh, Sister," I said earnestly, "please show it to the children. They saw Mother's, of course, but I had no chance to explain the meaning."

She opened the drawer and lifted out her shroud. We all sat very quiet, for as it was folded it looked exactly like the one we had placed on Mother. It was made of soft white linen, and instead of a sash, had a narrow band like that of a baby's first dress, for the belief was that we enter the next world as an infant. The robe was almost covered with texts from the Buddhist scriptures, which had been written by famous priests at various times. A blank strip in front showed that it was not yet finished. Beside the robe lay a small white bag intended to be placed around the neck. It would contain, when all was ready for Sister's last journey, a tiny package of her baby hair, shaved off at the christening ceremonies when she was eight days old, the dried navel cord, her cut widow-hair, a six-*rin* coin to pay the ferryman, a death rosary of white wooden beads, and a sacred tablet called "The Heavenly Pass."

While Sister was re-folding the robe she glanced up at the grave faces of the children and broke into a merry laugh.

“Why so sad, thou solemn-faced ones?” she cried. “Would it not be a disgrace should I receive a telegram to go home and have no suitable dress for the journey?”

“Yes, children,” I added, “it is as natural and commonplace for everyone in Japan to be ready for the last journey as it is in America to have a trunk in the house.”

“Come over this way,” said Sister, leading us to the other side of the room. “Here is something that belongs to you, Etsu-bo. You had better take charge of it.”

She pulled out a narrow drawer. Within, wrapped in purple crêpe on which was the Inagaki crest, lay a slender parcel about a foot long. My heart gave a bound. It was one of our three family treasures—the *saihai* used by Tokugawa Ieyasu, and presented by him to my ancestor on the battlefield of Sekigahara.

Reverently I lifted the precious thing to my forehead. Then, bidding the children sit with bowed heads, I slowly unwrapped the square of crêpe, disclosing a short, thick rod of lacquered wood, having on one end a silk cord for a wrist loop and on the other a bronze chain-clasp that held a bunch of soft, tough paper cut in strips.

We all sat very quiet while Sister told the children of the brave ancestor who, in a time of peril, saved the life of his great overlord; and how Ieyasu, in gracious remembrance, presented him with his own bloodstained coat, his wonderful Masamune sword, and this rod which he used in guiding his followers on the battlefield. “And,” concluded Sister, “all three are still kept in the Inagaki family as sacred treasures.”

“It looks like just a plain wooden stick, doesn’t it?” whispered Chiyo to Hanano.

“So it is,” said Sister. “As plain as the most simple director rod used by any ancient general; for Ieyasu lived in the age when was written, ‘An ornamental scabbard signifies a dull blade.’”

“The pieces of paper are so yellow and ragged,” said Hanano. “Did they use to be white?”

“Yes,” I answered. “They are yellow because they are so old. And the reason the papers are ragged is because so many pieces have been torn off for people to eat.”

“*To eat!*” exclaimed both children, horrified

I couldn’t help smiling as I explained that many people used to believe that because the *saihai* had been held in the hand of Ieyasu, the paper strips possessed the magic power of healing. I have heard my mother say that sick people often came from long distances just to beg for a bit of the paper to roll into a pellet and swallow as a cure. Father always laughed, but he told Mother to give the paper, saying that it was less harmful than most medicine, and that belief alone frequently cures.

We were starting to go downstairs when I stopped beside a large whitewood box having the over-lapping lid and the curved feet of a temple book chest. It stood on a platform raised a little above the floor. I had seen this box in my childhood, but never except on airing-days, and always it had the sacred Shinto rope around it. With some hesitation I called Sister to come back.

"I am very bold," I said, "but would you mind if I ask you to open the *kiri*-wood box? Our feelings have changed since the old days, and I would so like for the children——"

"Etsu-bo, you ask to gaze upon sacred things——" Sister began hastily; then, stopping abruptly, she shrugged her shoulders. "After all, women's eyes have already looked upon it," she added a little bitterly; "the new order of things has done much to take the spirit of reverence from us all."

Then we, she at one end and I at the other, lifted off the lid just as Jiya and Yoshita in their ceremonial dresses used to do, long ago. I felt a little awestruck as we leaned over and looked within. Some of the sacred relics had been removed. The coat and sword of Ieyasu were in charge of another branch of the family, and Brother had taken the books of the Inagaki genealogy; but, before us, lying shroud-like in its pressed stillness, was a garment, once white, but now yellowed by time. A pointed cap and an ancient unfolding fan of thin wood lay on top. It was the sacred robe which was used when the daimio, or his representative, officiated as high priest in the temple dedicated to his ancestors and was believed to possess heavenly power. My grandmother had told me that once, when it was worn by my great-grandfather, a miracle had been performed beneath the shadow of its wide-spread sleeve.

We gazed only a moment, then the box was silently closed. Neither Sister nor I spoke of it again, but I knew that she felt, as I did, that we had been a little daring in lifting the lid of this box, which, in ancient days, was always kept in the holy room, even the entrance hall of which was never profaned by woman's foot. I had grown away from my childhood faith in these things, but not entirely away from the influence of memory; and thoughts, beautiful and solemn, were crowding my mind when there came a sudden "bang!" from one of the heavy, swinging windows. They were always closed from the outside by a servant with a long pole, and evidently were being shut this time by someone who did not know that we were still there.

"*Maa! Maa!* It is late. Make haste, I inhospitably beg you," laughed Sister; and we all scrambled down the narrow stairs and out of the door, hearing the windows bang one after another behind us, shutting the godown, with all its treasures, into darkness.

CHAPTER-32

The Black Ships

THE night before we sailed my Tokyo uncle called, bringing with him a package of "friendship ribbons" for the children—those frail, dainty, quivery strips that bind the hands of friends between deck and dock at the moment of starting—and parting.

"I'll hold a pink one for Toshiko and a blue one for Kuni San," cried Chiyo, as the bright-coloured rolls tumbled out of the package, "and a white one for my teacher and a purple one for—for *you*, Uncle Tosa! Two of the most beautiful for you, of any colour you choose!"

"I'll hold a whole bunch of red and white ones for all Japan!" said Hanano. "Love, much love, and good-bye; for I'll never come back. I love everybody here, but I'm going to stay for ever with Grandma in 'Home, Sweet Home,'" and she softly hummed the tune as she slipped away, her face full of light. Ah, how little she dreamed that in years to come she would return—more than once—and always with a heart full of double loyalty: half for the land of her birth and half for the land of love, where were husband, children, and home.

Hanano and Chiyo had gone to bed, and I was attending to the last scattered duties of the packing when Sudzu lifted a folded shawl to lay on top of the tray before closing a trunk.

"This is rather loose," she said. "A cushion would exactly fit; but how ridiculous it would be to carry to a great country like America just an ordinary cushion that we sit on."

She did not know that in the bottom of my trunk of greatest value was something which, until I had seen it in Sister's godown, I had never dreamed could be anywhere except beside the familiar fire-box in the room of Honourable Grandmother. It was a square, flat cushion of blue brocade, old and somewhat faded.

I was alone when I wrapped it for its long journey, and, as my hands passed over the silken flowers, my mind went back—back to the day when a little black-haired girl in wooden clogs clattered through the big gateway and, hurrying her polite bows of greeting to the family, spread out before her grandmother, who was seated on this very cushion, a large, flat book.

"Honourable Grandmother," she said, pointing to a coloured map of the world, "I am much, much troubled. I have just learned that our beloved land is only a few tiny islands in the great world."

The grandmother adjusted her big horn spectacles and for a few minutes carefully studied the map. Then with slow dignity she closed the book.

"It is quite natural, little Etsu-bo, for them to make Japan look small on this map," she said. "It was made by the people of the black ships. Japan is made large on the Japanese maps of the world."

"Who are the people of the black ships?'" asked the little girl.

"They are the red barbarians who came uninvited to our sacred land. They came in big, black ships that moved without sails."

"I know. Ishi sings it to me"; and her shrill little voice chanted:

> "They came from a land of darkness,
> Giants with hooked nose like mountain imp;
> Giants with rough hair, loose and red;
> They stole a promise from our sacred master
> And danced with joy as they sailed away
> To the distant land of darkness.

"I wonder why they were called 'black ships.' Do you know, Honourable Grandmother?"

"Because far out on the waters they looked like clouds of black smoke rolling nearer and nearer, and they had long, black guns that roared. The red barbarians cared nothing for beauty. They laughed at the Japanese boats, whose sails were made of rich brocade and their oars of carved wood, inlaid with coral and mother-of-pearl. They talked like tradesmen and did not want to learn the hearts of the children of the gods."

The grandmother stopped and slowly shook her head.

"And after that?" asked the eager little voice. "And after that, Honourable Grandmother?"

"The black ships and the rude barbarians sailed away," she concluded, with a deep sigh. "But they sailed back many times. They are always sailing.

And now the people of our sacred land also talk like tradesmen and no longer are peaceful and content."

"Will they never be peaceful and content again?" asked the little girl, with anxious eyes. "The honourable teacher said that sailing ships bring lands nearer to each other."

"Listen!" said the grandmother, holding herself very straight. "Little Granddaughter, unless the red barbarians and the children of the gods learn each other's hearts, the ships may sail and sail, but the two lands will never be nearer."

Years passed, and Etsu-bo, the little girl who had listened to the story of the black ships and the red barbarians, herself went sailing on a black ship that moved without sails, to a new home in the distant land of the red barbarians. There she learned that hearts are the same on both sides of the world; but this is a secret that is hidden from the people of the East, and hidden from the people of the West. That makes another chapter to my grandmother's tale—another chapter, but not the last. The red barbarians and the children of the gods have not yet learned each other's hearts; to them the secret is still unknown, but the ships are sailing—sailing——

THE END

www.ingramcontent.com/pod-product-compliance
Ingram Content Group UK Ltd.
Pitfield, Milton Keynes, MK11 3LW, UK
UKHW041840190726
13854UKWH00002B/642

9 789390 852284